Contents

CONTENTS

LIVERPOOL POLYTECHNIC LIBRARY
3 1111 00310 3981

EDITED BY ERIC LARRABEE

Museums and Education

SMITHSONIAN INSTITUTION PRESS
Washington, D. C.
1968

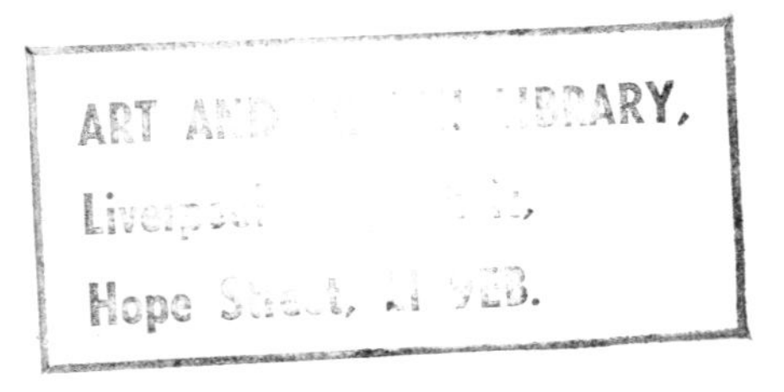

The papers herein were prepared for The Smithsonian Institution Conference on Museums and Education, held at the University of Vermont on August 21–26, 1966. They have been submitted as a report to the Office of Education of the U.S. Department of Health, Education and Welfare, which supported the conference through a grant contract.

Library of Congress Catalog Number: 68-20000
Smithsonian Publication 4721

Preface

From August 21 to 26, 1966, the Smithsonian Institution held a Conference on Museums and Education at the University of Vermont in Burlington. The three principal objectives of the conference were to: 1) survey the present relations between museums and education; 2) explore possible methods of involving museums more directly and more fruitfully in the educational process at all levels; 3) formulate proposals for research and development activities relating to museums and education. In a broad sense, the purpose of the conference was to learn, or at least to begin to learn, ways of making more effective educational use of the more than five thousand museums that exist in the United States.

In recent years, American museums have dramatically widened the range, and increased the extent, of their educational activities. Educational museum programs include guided tours for the general public, study clubs for school children, the creation of teaching exhibits geared to specific grade levels or subjects, accredited courses of instruction, and the encouragement of research at the highest levels of scholarship.

Our museums' commitment to teaching constitutes a real change in their traditional role. Until quite recently, American museums thought of themselves primarily as institutions of "open" education. This view assumed a general museum-going public desirous of self-education, for which the simple display of materials would provide the necessary basis for learning. Increasingly, however, individual museums throughout the country have become involved in more formal programs of education, either by direct cooperation with local school systems or independently. In 1962–1963, for example, the American Association of Museums found that as many as 20 percent of the 2,752 museums surveyed in a *Statistical Study of Museums in the U.S. and Canada* were conducting formally organized educational programs for children, while roughly 10 percent were engaged in educational programs geared to undergraduate college students.

Our museums' involvement in formal programs of education raises a number of problems, both practical and theoretical. It was the purpose of the Smithsonian Institution Conference on Museums and Education to bring together museum personnel, educators, and others concerned to analyze and assess these problems and the potentials for increasing educational museum commitments by considering three major areas:

1. *Present Educational Museum Programs:* The extent, variety, and success of school–museum cooperation throughout the country have not hitherto been adequately surveyed, nor is there yet any central source of information about the teaching programs in which museums are already engaged. Most museums considering educational programs must rely, therefore, on their own informal sources of information about the field and must create their own programs without benefit of the range of opinion or knowledge on the usefulness of a given approach. The Conference, it was hoped, would stimulate an exchange of information among museums about the effectiveness of their current educational programs and develop guidelines for gathering and disseminating such knowledge.

2. *Museum Educational Potentials:* The present state of knowledge about the learning process is clearly relevant to museum efforts in establishing educational programs. This is especially true in the design and construction of exhibits to stimulate inductive learning in the large range of subjects encompassed by the nation's museums. Thus, a second major purpose of the Conference was to discuss learning theory and curricular innovation with the aim of relating these to the specific needs and capabilities of museums.

3. *Research and Development:* Two implicit aims of the Conference were to identify basic problem areas, research priorities, and methodological approaches, and by so doing to develop guidelines for needed research. In a sense, the Conference could be considered the preliminary exploration for an eventual research and development program for museum education, similar to programs now under way in many other areas of education. The Smithsonian Institution would, of course, stand ready to commit its own facilities to any such program.

In pursuit of the purposes I have described, the Smithsonian Institution commissioned fifteen papers and invited some forty conference participants to discuss them. The papers form the bulk of the volume which follows. The discussions were committed to tape and a chapter summarizing them will be found at the end, together with a number of supplementary notes and bibliography which the Conference evoked.

The Smithsonian Institution is especially grateful to Mr. Richard Grove of the U.S. Office of Education, to Mr. Eric Larrabee, now Provost of the State University of New York at Buffalo, and to Mrs. Helen Bronheim for their contribution to the somewhat hectic, but always interesting, conference at Burlington.

Charles Blitzer
Director of Education and Training
The Smithsonian Institution

Washington, D.C.
January 1968

Introduction

S. DILLON RIPLEY
Secretary, The Smithsonian Institution

At times I have used the word enigma to describe a museum. It is an enigma both to those who enter as visitors and those who work within its walls. A museum is an enigma because few people ever bother to think about what it is, what goes on inside, and especially what lies behind the facade of constructions, halls, and galleries open to the public. It is an enigma to those inside who work largely out of contact with the visitor, cloistered in the shadows, buried in a multiplicity of concerns like the engine-room crew of an ocean liner—unseen, unheard, absorbed in a consuming world of their own profession.

I am sometimes struck by the juxtaposition of the words museum and education. They do not entirely relate to each other and this is too little understood. Museum visitors tend to feel, vaguely perhaps, that a museum is an educational experience if not an educational institution. Most museum workers tend to cling staunchly to the idea that a museum is an educational institution even though it does not give degrees.

To me a museum as such, a building containing collections, and with exhibits which are open to the public, is a center for exposure rather than for education. Education—that is, pedagogy, as it is largely thought of today—exists as a function of teaching. It is to a large extent a didactic process with the teacher saying, "Now hear this."

At the other end, after the courses have been attended, the exams taken and the fees paid, as the student slides down the chute, out of the tunnel into the daylight and the hot sun of life ahead, a degree is thrust into his hand—"a ticket of admission," preparing him with a neat entry for the first of the many forms that have to be filled out for jobs and careers ahead. The degree is a magic entry item, and a necessity, like the birth date, or sex, or color of hair and eyes. Without it there is a startling blank, somewhere in line six or seven of the application form. Education as such seems these days to be an inalienable appendage to life itself and jobs and careers for all.

Joseph Henry, the first Secretary of the Smithsonian Institution, was rather against the idea of the Institution's becoming a museum. He dreaded the advent of collections, and the necessity for housing and caretaking. He viewed collections and museum acquisitiveness as potential millstones around the neck of the Institution. Professor Henry was a pedagogue but of an especial type—a farsighted administrator and a philosopher as well. To him, the Smithsonian represented an opportunity to advance all of American scholarly enterprise, at home and abroad. The oracular phrase of James Smithson's instruction, "the increase and diffusion of knowledge among men," was to him a literal injunction; "increase" equaling research, "diffusion" equaling publication. The Institution's trust funds should be used to stimulate publications by America's leading scholars, and then insure that these publications are circulated abroad to get into the hands of the leading scholars and libraries overseas. Thus was the first American cultural exchange initiated; and thus too was implanted a strong impetus toward research among college professors long before the United States had a graduate school among its professional institutions of learning. Henry's plan came into operation some eighteen years before a Ph.D. was awarded in this country.

For Henry then, the Smithsonian represented the microcosmic university, for, as the *Old Century Dictionary* tells us, a university is a place for research by scholars. Students are not mentioned, or, if they are implied it is as wandering junior scholars who come to learn from senior scholars, or savants, perhaps moving from setting to setting like medieval scholar-students. By fostering research and publication, with scholars either in residence or scattered about in a loose fraternity, held together by common interests and in communication with each other, Henry created the nucleus of an institution of higher learning, but with nary a sheepskin in sight.

In this sense, however, Professor Henry was creating a museum, a sylvan grove to which scholars repaired, there to conduct research, amid discourse and with reference to books or to objects. This is the oldest definition of a museum in the Pythagorean sense and is also what many of us would hope to create today. The distillation of much of this research may be seen in the exhibits, but they are open to all, non-didactic, they can be taken or left alone. Thus, the exhibits provide a method of exposure but not of direct education.

I feel there are three levels of attention to museums and that they tend to be discrete from each other. Museums tend to have great meaning for young people up to college age. This might be termed Level One. At Level One children are taken by their parents, sometimes as a duty, sometimes to get in out of the rain, sometimes because the washroom is the nearest handy, and of course, sometimes, just like breathing, because it seems a totally natural and normal procedure. The last is the best, of course, but the effect on the child so far can be said to be incalculable. No sociologist or psychologist has yet devised a satisfactory test to tell whether a child will develop any sort of interest upon visiting a museum. Would that such a test could be prepared. Surely the process of visiting something different like a museum, and being exposed to possible foci of interest, without direction, and perhaps without the arousal of antagonism or fear or hostility, is an ideal one. There are germinal possibilities here for awakening interest. In some cases, for children who may have difficulty reading, the presentation of objects is vastly superior as a technique of arousing the interest to enter into the world of books. Certainly the images are crisper and clearer than on any television, though unfortunately they must be preserved in separate buildings to which excursions must be made. They cannot be all pervasive, enter into the home, and thereby be taken wholly for granted like a piece of furniture.

That is the signal advantage of the television set, to be all one's own, to raise no sense of antagonism, or fear-hostility on the parents' part. The museum, on the other hand, suffers from being different. It is a huge, strange building. Going into it is a different experience, reserved for different times—almost an event. This may be hard to adjust to, not like breathing at all, but rather associated with the putting on of different clothes, with different surroundings, a bus ride, or a car drive. Unfortunately for many people, this act involves crossing a threshold out of ordinary life, and this in itself is a strain which may reflect on the child.

One of the advantages of playing in the Tuileries Gardens in Paris as a child was that at one moment you could be riding a carrousel, at another eating *gaufres,* at another walking into a gallery in the Louvre Museum to examine fantastically intricate ship models, and at the end running out to watch the Punch and Judy Show. There is no essential difference. The juxtaposition was natural and easy. No threshold of tiredness and lack of concentration was reached. It was as easy as breathing in and out. For visiting children, then, museums should be infinitely easy, diverse, varied. There should be fun and games somewhere, perhaps outside, and concentration and indirect learning inside, but there should be no real distinction between the two.

Older children, up through high school, tend to feel very much at home in museums and to gain great interest and insights from them. Museums at this age are an educational tool, often badly used but still of considerable value. Schools could use museums a great deal more for extension teaching, but lack of imagination on the part of school principals, failure to coordinate curricula with museum visits, the expense of bus transportation, jealousies and smallmindedness on the part of schoolteachers, all create areas of indifference or hostility which often make the school visit to a museum a hopeless mishmash. Teachers become flustered or lose contact with docents, children gather in gaggles, giggling like so many geese, and at the end the teacher may hope that the experience need not be repeated as a "treat" the next year.

And yet, it is at this stage of my Level One that children could derive the most in an educational sense. Many museum exhibits are beautifully arranged as teaching aids with painstaking curatorial and exhibits staff care. Many museum docents are admirably qualified to present a lecture in the museum galleries associated with some course being taught in school. Too little coordination and too little extra effort on the part of the school may negate or sadly diminish the value of the enterprise.

Museums normally lack the funds to come to the classrooms. Many teachers find the only real merit in museum objects to be in bringing them into class and letting students see them, hear a lecture, and, if possible, handle the objects right on the spot. Some museums have tried this, and so long as people and funds can be found have done well. In this connection, nothing is ever quite new under the sun. Browsing through an old issue of the defunct *Museum Journal* of 1908, I came upon a fascinating account of a Reo station wagon which had been fitted up by the Field Museum of Natural History of Chicago to contain portable exhibits, mounted in framed boxes which slid easily in and out of the back of the cavernous rear end of this antique-appearing car.

I recall, too, my pleasure in seeing rubber casts of reptiles and amphibians painted in lifelike colors, which travelled with the Yale Peabody Museum docent on her trips to give natural history talks in the New Haven schools. At least these were entirely accurate and could be handled by children who had little chance of ever seeing or touching a box tortoise or a black snake.

It is true, however, that teen-age children tend to love museums and to come back to them on their own. The high school years are good ones for museum going. Hobbies are still paramount. The competitive life of college is still ahead. The open-minded, aware student of high-school age may develop an interest through museum visits which will be permanent. This interest may be suppressed only to reawaken years later. Level One then is that stage at which young and, of course, older people too come to look at the exhibits; when interest may be awakened, but where it is all open, undirected.

Level Two is the one of teaching and of college years. When docents actually teach classes of students in front of exhibits, or when college students are led in to have the illustrated lecture associated with Biology 10 or History of Art II, then there is a directed, teaching experience. It was Arnold Grobman who first made me aware of the gap in museum interest and museum visits that existed at this level. I remembered my own experience thinking back to undergraduate years at Yale. Although I was interested in natural history, I went into the Museum perhaps three times in four years.

As far as the grammar school years are concerned, I have already related my feelings of distrust of a system which is so highly dependent on individuals. When it works, it is wonderful; otherwise, it can be awful. Somehow or other, college years take students interested in science or science careers right out of the museum and many of them never get back in at all. The undergraduate life is not geared to museum work for most students in any area of science, although occasionally paid bursary jobs as museum aides lead to maintaining a thin thread of linkage with the scientific community that lives in back, behind the exhibits.

In the art field, there is more of a tangible link. History of art or classics or area study courses related to anthropology or linguistics often bring the student into touch with museum collections; but the process tends to be rarified or aseptic. Professor Smith of the art department tends to show slides of objects. This is partly because he does not get on with Curator Jones of the art gallery who once saw Smith drop a Greek vase because he stepped off the platform while reaching for the corner of the desk. It is also partly because Smith is visually, not tactually, trained. If confronted with an object or a picture of it, he will always pick up the picture. It is a more familiar dialect.

In any case, the art or anthropology student is encouraged to browse in the gallery or museum, and sometimes becomes involved in summer field trips or other forms of participation. But the number of students who really learn to feel at home in museums at this stage is very small.

My Level Three is that of advanced training, which comes during the graduate or advanced training years. This involves students who want to learn to do research and research curators who are eager to teach. This is the level which Professor Henry visualized for the

Smithsonian. It is the most keenly interesting and highest level of museum activity.

In general, then, museums do not relate closely to colleges. They experience the greatest difficulty communicating interest at this level. They are ideal for visiting by young and old, and they are ideal centers for research. There is one type of training at my Level Two which should catch on, but is almost wholly neglected at present. This is the area of technical training through museum training courses which technical, junior, or community colleges could use to great advantage. There is a whole realm of careers available in technical museum work, in exhibits especially—painting, model making, taxidermy, conservation, advanced preparation techniques—many involving the highest level of sophistication, which are unknown to technical training administrators. This is a growing field with opportunities for careers which are burgeoning in national and international directions. Many students might much rather work in such specialities in museums than in factories, but so far little has been done to relate the schools to the jobs. Museums still cling to haphazard apprentice methods, much as libraries did a generation ago.

Someone has questioned whether museum activities in microcosm represent those of a college. To some extent they do. Exhibits represent the outward show like college sports, community use of a college library, free lectures, the "Lyceum" tradition, the drama club or school, the art gallery. They affect the community in an undirected way, but unfortunately bring in all too few gate receipts. They do relate, however, to the old college tradition of "public instruction," a largely forgotten phrase, which was supposed to forge ties between town and gown, to make the town appreciate the tax-exempt burden of the gown.

The nearest thing to undergraduate instruction is, of course, the few lectures given at my Level Two. Here the big gap is in the lack of technical training which could closely resemble undergraduate instruction in many colleges. Unfortunately, student fees do not seem to be collectible by museums.

Postgraduate training is identical, whether in a museum or college. When I was a university museum director, I was at great pains to point out to the administrators that fully half of the Ph.D. recipients in at least one discipline had received their degrees through work in the university museum. Presumably they would not have come to that university if the museum had not existed. Nowadays, added to the prestige of advanced university training, there is the lure of grants. At the graduate level of instruction, university museums can bring a good measure of government-sponsored contributions to the university budget. Fortunately, the great granting agencies do not exclude private or independent museums from their largesse. The National Science Foundation, for one, clearly recognizes that museum scholarship based on collections is a valid national asset, one of our major scholarly resources.

For planning for the future, what areas of museum work and work in education overlap each other? The first is the area of exposure, difficult of analysis and not susceptible to educational rules. There should be some way to make museums a wholly natural, delightful part of all of our society, as natural, easy, and everyday as breathing in and out. There should be some way of refining and analyzing this process so that it can be understood and encouraged.

In the second place, there should be an understanding of the technical careers in museum work and the necessary training courses. Here there is a great opportunity in the international sphere, particularly in the emerging nations where education through museum exhibits could be of paramount importance.

Finally, there should be continual encouragement of original research, the quest for knowledge at the highest level, using the museum as a center for advanced studies, as indeed the "university" which Henry conceived the Smithsonian to be.

Dimensions and Approach

The Museum and Education

❧

EDGAR P. RICHARDSON
Director, Winterthur Museum

The Smithsonian Institution has rendered a service by calling a conference to discuss museums and education. It is necessary to stop, every so often, and attempt to take a broad general view of our situation. Human nature does not change but human society does change; the world in which we perform our daily duties is a different world from that of ten, twenty, or thirty years ago. It is important to make a review of our goals and the means employed to achieve them. The value of a conference is that it obliges us to pause to consider, review, and restudy our methods and our goals.

I. WHAT DO THE MUSEUMS OF OUR COUNTRY REPRESENT AS AN EDUCATIONAL RESOURCE?

In the past 150 years, the people of the United States have engaged in a vast activity of collecting. They have brought together in museums on this continent material evidence on the history of the globe we live upon, and on all aspects of life upon this globe—physical and mental, practical and imaginative.

My belief is that this is a new phenomenon historically and that the museum collections in the United States are, in sheer volume, very nearly unique in world civilization. I speak for the moment purely in quantitative terms. Some years ago, Leonard Carmichael, the seventh Secretary of the Smithsonian Institution, reported that his complex of museums contained fifty million recorded objects. The Smithsonian is an outstanding case but, nonetheless, it may symbolize the scale of American museum collecting.

We still sometimes think of the United States as a new country, yet the formation of American collections goes back to the beginning of the museum movement. In Philadelphia, for instance, there are museums of art, science, history, technology and the physical sciences, and archaeology. The Pennsylvania Academy of the Fine Arts was founded in 1805; the Academy of Natural Sciences in 1812. The Historical Society of Pennsylvania was founded in 1824; the Franklin Institute in 1824; the Philadelphia Museum of Art in 1875; the University Museum, one of the world's great archaeological museums, in 1887, only five years after Schliemann ended his pioneering excavations at Troy. Since the museum as an organized institution of human society is hardly more than 150 years old, these institutions are as old, or older, than all but a minuscule fraction of the museums on earth. In the United States there are now over five thousand museums; many new, of course, but many old, vast, rich, and of infinite variety.

I do not think we altogether realize what a remarkable phenomenon our museums are. Some great areas of the world have no museums whatsoever, while in other great areas of the world museums are merely storehouses for local antiquities. The museum as a scholarly institution, staffed by highly trained professional people, with a serious scholarly program and a serious popular program of education, is still a rather rare phenomenon in the twentieth-century world. The museums of the United States are remarkable in their number, range of interests, and seriousness of purpose. They indicate a passionate thirst for universal knowledge on the part of our people, all the more remarkable because this thirst has never been proclaimed as a goal but has arisen spontaneously and almost unconsciously in our national life.

What has been achieved? I should say that the sheer volume of collections in American museums after 150 years of accumulation constitutes a new national resource, as if a new chain of Great Lakes, or a new range of mountains like the Rockies, should appear among us. This has come about so slowly, steadily, and gradually that we are hardly aware of what has happened. Yet, when one thinks of it, this is a phenomenon to excite our curiosity and our wonder.

The immensity and range of museum materials emphasize that the subject of our discussion—the educational responsibility of museums—is vast, extremely complex, and touches every aspect of our intellectual life.

Let me state the maximum claim for the importance of museums as educational institutions. The immense story of earth through time; of the life upon earth of plants, animals, and man; the story of man's skills and imagination, of his dreaming and creative mind, are told *by original evidence* only in the collections of museums. This story is preserved and told only by objects. What was said, or written, what was sung, the record of magic and ritual, of ceremony, of drama, of dance, are preserved for only a very small portion of the earth's surface, for a fraction of the earth's inhabitants, for a minuscule portion of historic time. The massive collections of our museums represent a far longer and wider sequence of evidence than exists in any other form and they are, in consequence, of fundamental intellectual importance.

Let us admit that this maximum claim will be, and is, disputed. In some segments of the learned world, experience is divided into literary evidence, the written document, or real evidence on the one hand; and non-evidence on the other: the object without documents to support being non-evidence, which is neither observed nor read. We are all familiar with that prejudice on the part of learned people on university faculties that only the written or printed word is an intellectually respectable source for research and valid work. It is an old, sad, exasperating story which needs no retelling to a museum audience.

Since I include works of art within my sweeping claims for the significance of museum collections as documents for the story of life, I must admit that many teachers of art are not only ignorant of the history of the arts, but also resist the historian's right to have any connection with them. They hold the arts to be a preserve for what is called creativity; within creativity's precincts only the values of artistic style, form, color, and intuitive emotion are allowed. The holders of such convictions, reflecting the ideas of certain contemporary artists, flatly reject any notion of the arts as universal communication and feel that the true values of art are endangered by the rude touch of the historian—to apply knowledge to, or derive knowledge from, the arts is to do them violence.

One of my colleagues tells me of a museum somewhere which allows no labels in the gallery with the works of art; the labels are in an adjoining gallery. One may apply facts to works of art if one insists—but not in the same room. If this is not a true story, it should be.

Most of such dissenting opinions arise, I dare say, not so much from ignorance—we are not dealing with ignorant people—as from the lack of a conceptual frame for organizing knowledge about objects in museums. Let me take a case in point. We have in the past winter developed, at the Winterthur Museum, a teaching set of slides with a commentary based on the Winterthur Museum collections and illustrating the life of Philadelphia for the quarter century from 1750–1775. Philadelphia was, at that time, one of the large cities of the British Empire. Its life was, in many respects, the climax of colonial civilization in the American colonies. The most difficult problem to solve, in developing the slide set, was to develop a conceptual framework which would make the material evidences of that city usable and understandable to teachers in high school and the first years of college. Teachers of history and social studies are familiar with the written approach. They are trained to use books on political history, war, or social studies and biographies of leaders of American life. To organize in simple, comprehensible form material about a city in which there are myriad objects made during a specific period presents all kinds of problems. How does one organize this material—by categories such as the distribution of goods and services; by civic betterment or public buildings, such as churches and hospitals; by culture and art? How does one train teachers to read these material objects and draw out their significance, as one can from a book? This is the challenge presented by all museum collections, each in its own way.

II. WHAT IS THE MUSEUM'S RESPONSIBILITY IN EDUCATION?

If museums are educational institutions, they have the same basic responsibilities as all educational institutions: to train our people 1) to understand the complex and wonderful civilization they have inherited, and 2) to understand the world about them. How do we relate these responsibilities to museums? There would seem to be several large areas in which we need to do more work and more thinking.

A. *We must find out what we have in American museums.*

If one asks the question, "How accurately and fully do we know the contents of American museums?" I am afraid the answer must be, "We are very poorly informed." I can speak with some degree of acquaintance only of my own field of art history. The situation there can be summarized briefly. In the past 150 years, one of the great historical migrations has taken place, not only of peoples but also of millions of works of art from every age of history, from every continent, from every aspect of human life, from the art of Leonardo da Vinci or Rembrandt to the magic symbols of the stone age inhabitants of the Sepik River of New Guinea. These have been collected, brought to North America, then scattered into hundreds of places over the entire continent. A few museums have published catalogs of their European paintings. There are *catalogues raisonnés* of a few artists. But, for the most part, there has been no serious or consistent effort to publish comprehensive catalogs of these collections. The case of the works of art produced by our own North American civilization is still worse. Our knowledge of the American works of art in our museums is for the most part what is in our notebooks and in our own personal memories.

Our first task, obviously, is to turn the collections of American art museums into an organized field of knowledge.

I speak from experience, having attempted to write on this subject and also having attempted to attack this problem by means of the Archives of American Art. At Winterthur we have also started a Decorative Arts Reference Collection consisting of photographs of firmly documented works by American craftsmen. We have now photographs of documented works of 648 makers of furniture, 223 silversmiths, 38 ironsmiths, 72 brass founders, 48 pewterers, 86 coppersmiths, 4 tinsmiths, 134 ceramists, and 38 textile makers. It is an attempt to turn at least one small area into an organized field of knowledge.

There is an overwhelming need for inventories of existing museum material in every field, by categories, and by regions.

There is also an overwhelming need for more thorough and extensive documentation of existing collections. Every object in our museums has its own history, its special relevances, its own problems. We need knowledge in depth, as well as in breadth, if we are to do justice to the objects in our charge. One of the most admirable examples for us to heed is the corpus *"Primitifs flamands,"* published by the Belgian *Institut royal du patrimoine artistique,* which will ultimately give us an exceedingly thorough scholarly documentation, both textual and photographic, of the four thousand fifteenth-century Flemish paintings scattered throughout the world.

We must agree that until we ourselves, the staffs of museums, have familiarized ourselves thoroughly with the collections in our charge, we can hardly expect others to be familiar with them or to make use of them.

B. *Make these collections comprehensible and accessible.*

Let us suppose, however, that we have made thorough inventories, so that we may begin to be familiar with the contents of American museums. How do we make these objects comprehensible, significant, and useful to our civilization? What kind of conceptual frame of organizing knowledge about the objects in museums is it our responsibility to offer?

If I may generalize not only about the field of art, with which I am somewhat familiar, but also about museums in general, the great activities of the curators of the nineteenth century and the early part of our own century were first, collecting; and second, the identification, cataloging, classification (taxonomy, whatever the term may be for each of our specialties) of collections. When the object was properly classified and labeled, the museum's duty to the public was thought to be fulfilled.

The period of cataloging or taxonomy was a heroic one. No one can underestimate the debt we owe to the people who ordered and classified these immense numbers of classes, genera, and species of birds and animals, minerals and plants, and the vast heritage of humanity's works of art and artifacts. This period gave us the basic organization of our material and the primary tools of the scholar.

But, how much does it assist the nonspecialist to read on the label of a painting *Adoration of the Shepherds,* Carlo Bononi, Italian, 1569–1632? The answer is that, if you are taking a colleague through your museum, you instinctively give more information than is on such a label: there is a reason why you bought the picture; a story of the career of the object before acquisition; a story of the maker; a judgment of significance. As you talk with your friend, you may give him little or much of this; but you instinctively give more than is to be found on the label.

The urge to go beyond collecting and classifying objects is, I think, obvious wherever one looks in the world of museums today. I read with pleasure the journal of the University Museum, Philadelphia, called *Expedition,* edited for uninformed amateurs like myself, and I am struck by the interest of archaeologists and anthropologists in living primitive cultures. They go to places like Iran, Africa, Yucatan, or Oceania, not only to study primitive peoples in the process of rapid change, but also to learn from living men (if they can) the function and meaning of objects still in use which may be similar to artifacts in their museums, or to observe practices of life from which they can make an extrapolation to the meaning of objects left us from the shadows of time.

In my own museum I notice that the Winterthur Fellows are not content merely to study the American decorative arts between 1640 and 1840. They write their theses on how the craftsmen lived and worked, how they carried on their business, what they paid their journeymen, how they sold their wares and to whom.

Everywhere, it is my impression, there is the urge to see museum objects in their wider social, cultural, or ecological contexts. Why not? These objects were once part of life before being collected into museums. If classification is giving place to ecology, to social and cultural anthropology, to social and cultural history, it means only that we are learning to see our collections in new frames of reference. I find this stimulating and refreshing and an indication of the inexhaustible character of our collections. Nonetheless, it is important to know where we are going, for on this road, too, there are dangers within and enemies without. The enemies without I shall call the compartmentalization of academic knowledge.

C. *The compartmentalization of knowledge.*

The narrowness of vision and insularity of which learned men and women can be capable are notorious. I was recently talking with a friend who had moved from one great university to another, who said of his present place, "This is a wonderful university but I do not understand it. I do not understand why economics and sociology are in the business school, rather than in the college along with history and literature and the rest of the humanities." The explanation was that, when economics and sociology began to be taught, the faculty of that college would have nothing to do with such bastard innovations; those interested in them found a haven only in the business school. Each one of you could contribute such instances from your own experience.

Poverty, perhaps, more than conscious policy has prevented such compartmentalization in museums. Even the largest and richest art museums cannot afford to employ as many curators as there are specialists on university faculties. We do not have separate departments for English art, French art, German art, Italian art; still less a specialist for English painting from 1675 to 1715 and another from 1715 to 1775. Most museum curators must deal with a far wider range of material and a longer sweep of time than the university teacher allows himself. Perhaps this is one reason why museums, as educational institutions, are not taken so seriously as museum people might wish. We all know the fate of the university teacher who is thought of as a popularizer. Let us consider this problem of compartmentalization a little further.

When we speak of the museum as an educational institution, do we mean the departmentalized and fragmented kind of education that has prevailed so long in universities? The physical sciences made great progress in the nineteenth century by breaking their subjects down into specialized fields. The humanities followed their lead a generation or two later. It is my impression that the great scientific and technical institutions no longer wish to turn out the narrow specialists who represented the forefront of scientific and technological knowledge a half century ago. It is also my impression that the humanities are still, on the whole, fragmented into strongly entrenched separate disciplines and that attempts to establish interdisciplinary studies—the American Studies movement, for example—meet with very strong resistance.

Museums must be clear, therefore, about what they propose to do. What kinds of human beings are we trying to produce by museum education? Or, to phrase the question in another way, what is the role of the museum in education, as distinct from formal academic schooling? In this area we are confronted by confusion. There is a great deal of misunderstanding on the part of the public as well as of academic educators and, I am afraid, a great lack of clearly thought out and precisely stated goals on the part of museum people.

The public apparently thinks of museum education as something for children. We all know museums which seem to foster this notion, where the only role of the adult seems to be to keep children from wrecking the place.

On the other hand, one hears a good deal of talk about the museum's role in meeting the problem of leisure time. It is a question worth thinking hard about—to what extent is the museum responsible for filling the leisure time of our population? We often see this put forward as an argument for the existence of museums. The shortened work hours which people anticipate (although they never seem to arrive) and the lengthening of life are responsible, we are told, for leisure time which visits to museums will help to fill. Are we really responsible? Are the enthusiasm for the performing arts in museums and the creation of cultural centers all over the country a spontaneous and unconscious indication of the direction in which museums should develop? If we really believe our mission as museums is to fill the leisure-time needs of our expanding population, we should face the fact that we shall need an enormous increase of federal funds to provide staffs and physical facilities. Is this what we are in favor of?

I have already stated my position by emphasizing the importance of museum collections. I believe that the collection is the primary factor in a museum, that the interpretation of the collection is the primary function of the museum, and that this presents problems of the utmost intellectual difficulty and significance. Turning the museum into a cultural center for music theatre, ballet, and hobby classes may result in enrichment of civic life for the short term; but this is not a long-term function of the museum. The museum was once combined with the public library and with the art school. Art, history, and science were combined in a single institution. The creation of institutions with clearly defined goals has proved in the long run to be a better practice. Furthermore, the grouping of material objects into coherent collections, for convenience of study and for expert care, is imposed upon us by urgent, even brutal, practical considerations. Precious objects demand optimum conditions for their presentation and survival. The human body has limitations of attention and of physical fatigue. The movements of crowds, the movements of mass transport and the private automobile in cities, present different problems to the museum than to the school or university. And as we have a different kind of material to interpret, and a different physical organization, I believe we have a separate role to play in the life of the mind. Our role ranges from serving the awakening mind of the child to addressing minds in the forefront of human thought; this role is parallel to, but differs from, formal education.

D. *The information explosion.*

This brings me to the fourth area in which thought and action seem needed. We need new techniques of exposition to deal with the problem of the information explosion.

If Marshall McLuhan has created something of a panic in certain circles, I am afraid he is the just punishment for our sins. We all know that we are living in a population explosion and in an explosion of knowledge as well. There are more books and learned periodicals printed than any person can possibly read. We also know that the techniques of putting out information in printed form have grown to enormous size. But the instrument for taking in this knowledge remains the same, two eyes, the human brain, and a limited span of attention and time. The production of knowledge seems to be reaching toward a limitless capacity in our society. To what extent do we concern ourselves with the intake of knowledge by the consumer of this information? How are we to compress this giant flood into the tiny bottleneck of the individual human consciousness, which is so hard to focus and so easily fatigued?

We know, when we stop to think, that we are surrounded by an astonishing array of new electronic devices—devices for information retrieval, for instant reproduction and transmission of pictures; devices like computers for the manipulation of information. There are many other devices—moving picture film, microfilm and microfiche, closed-circuit television, reading machines, audio-visual training techniques. We know, or should know, that in the 1930s, industries began to use such devices in training programs with marked success. They were followed by the Army which, in the 1940s, found itself under the necessity of teaching a variety of skills quickly, from languages to the recognition of airplanes or contacts with strange and exotic peoples. We know, or should know, that new audio-visual training techniques have speeded up the process of learning and that it is now normal practice for industry, banks, and the armed forces to send their people regularly to school for training programs which will bring them up to date.

But, when we ask how much of this is carried over into the museum world, we must confess that a combination of ingrained, professional habits, on the one hand, and institutional poverty on the other, has left us far behind. Perhaps we do need Mr. McLuhan to shout "BOO" in our ears to wake us up.

Museums have relied very heavily for the past fifty years upon two techniques for the broad interpretation of their collections—the school visit for children, the loan exhibition for adults. It is my belief that both are rapidly diminishing in usefulness and need to be supplemented, or replaced, by other techniques.

The explosion of population and cities under the impact of the automobile, has entirely altered the situation for the school visit by bus.

Museums of art, archaeology, history, and to some extent of science, have relied upon the special loan exhibition to capture the attention and interest of the adult audience. This has affected our public to such a degree that the special exhibition has become the only reason to go to a museum, while the permanent collections, brought together with so much care, expense, and effort are neglected. But the loan exhibition, while in greater demand by the public than ever, shows signs of being on the decline. There will never cease to be loan exhibitions of a careful, scholarly retrospective kind since much can be accomplished by bringing together related objects scattered by time into many different museums which can be accomplished in no other way. But the loan exhibit as a major technique of education has become incredibly expensive, wasteful of the time and energy of staffs, and dangerous to the objects. I question also its success in making a serious and lasting impression upon the public; too often, it achieves little more than institutional advertising. And the profession is growing weary of its demands. This year the Royal Academy, London, which has a magnificent tradition of loan exhibitions of world significance, has given up an attempt to hold an international exhibition of Rembrandt's paintings because of the cost and reluctance of museums to lend. It is becoming easier to move people about the world than to move pictures; and this is a great deal safer and less costly.

Can we utilize the new techniques of communication—especially the camera film and moving picture film—to supplement the loan exhibition? Are there not possibilities here for the wider sorts of interpretation demanded by the new professional interests of our day? And are the new techniques of intensive, speeded up absorption of information applicable to the problem? These are questions we must answer thoughtfully.

The danger into which Mr. McLuhan falls sometimes, I fear, is that of being hypnotized by the magic of technology. The technology of electronic communication is not an end in itself any more than the printed book or the alphabet are ends in themselves. We should take a long look at the training programs developed by other fields to see what they have been able to accomplish by the new technology. Some of our techniques may still be the best ones available. Some may be obsolete.

E. *The need to raise our own training to adequate levels.*

Finally, I raise the question whether we ourselves can hope to keep up with the information explosion without regular and effective training programs. I have seen something of a highly educated industry in the past four years, during which I have lived next door to the Du Pont Company. I observe that more and more the Du Pont Company tends to send its key people back to school for a year, or even two years, at the best scientific universities. It feels the necessity to send even the ablest people, who have risen fast and high in the Company, back to school because the knowledge acquired by these men ten or twenty years ago is no longer adequate to enable them to supervise the young Ph.D.s who are entering the Company equipped with new concepts and techniques.

It is entirely possible that the knowledge, the concepts, the techniques of museum professional life need the same kind of periodic upgrading. Perhaps it will be necessary to send museum people back to school every ten years to be brought up to date in their own fields. If this holds true for naval officers or industrial chemists, is it not a possibility for museum staffs as well? The advance of knowledge in our fields may be cumulative rather than revolutionary but it can still leave us breathless.

To summarize, the educational responsibility of museums is vast, extremely complex, and touches every aspect of our intellectual life. It cannot be met only by either popular education or by children's education. It presents great challenges to museum staffs: to find out what we have; to document and publish; to give a wider conceptual frame than mere classification; to overcome the compartmentalization of knowledge; to adapt the new techniques of communication which our century has created; to overcome the explosion of information; to devote ourselves to the periodic training and retraining on which a vigorous and active profession must be based. If no single object were to be added to American museum collections for the rest of our lives, we would still have an enormous task ahead of us.

The Role and Obligations of Museums as a Scholarly Resource

❧

HENRY ALLEN MOE
Chairman of the Board and President
New York State Historical Association

A special delight of getting old, wrote Justice Holmes in one of his eightieth years, is that "there are fewer and fewer to whom I feel the need to show a youthful deference." Another delight of getting old is to remember what happened, which, though it may be in the books in the libraries, still is not adverted to. I am sorry that I am not as old as Justice Holmes was when he said these wonderfully helpful things. But there was one development, remembered by me and germane to my assigned topic, which will afford us some historical perspective on the question of the role and obligations of museums as a scholarly resource.

I refer to the development of scientific scholarship in the United States following the First World War. The National Academy of Sciences had been created by Act of Congress in 1863, during President Lincoln's administration, to be the scientific adviser to the government of the United States. When World War I was in sight for us, there clearly appeared to be the need, for purposes of national defense, of more scientific research on broader fronts than the universities then were able to cope with. Hence, in 1916, there was spun off—as the lawyers say—from the National Academy of Sciences, the National Research Council, the operating arm of the National Academy, which was to get urgent research done. By present-day standards, what the National Research Council was able to get done then was not great in terms of specific accomplishments of applied science; but its truly great accomplishment was to show that in the upcoming modern world scientific research was something we, as a nation, could not do without.

In this year you may think this so elementary as to be hardly worth saying, but this was not so in 1919. Then, the nation had to be convinced of what everybody today knows to be true—that scientific research is an indispensable ingredient for progress, even for survival, in the world as it is. I say the nation had to be convinced of this; and from that statement I except nobody: persons in government, university administrations, industrialists, even many scientists themselves had to be convinced. They were content with what we had. They pointed with pride, and justifiable pride, to our prior industrial progress, our railroads that spanned the country, our development of rust-resistant wheats, our inventions of ingenious tools, and to much besides—practically all matters of applied science.

The principal vehicle for convincing the nation was the *Bulletin* of the National Research Council started in 1919. In it, the giants of those days—Elihu Root, statesman and lawyer; George Ellery Hale, astronomer; John J. Carty, President of the Bell Telephone Laboratories—wrote both the words and the music for their gospel theme that you cannot have applied science unless you have pure science to apply. George Ellery Hale named four corporations, one of which he said then spent as much as three million dollars annually for research —which would be peanuts now—"and in all cases the resulting profits are so great that their laboratories and staffs are constantly expanding," and they continued to expand until today when corporate research expenditures annually are reckoned in the billions of dollars. Dr. Hale even thought it necessary to quote an 1873 statement by John Tyndall, distinguished English physicist, "It would be a great thing for this land of incalculable destinies to supplement its achievements in the industrial arts by those higher investigations from which our mastery over Nature and over industrial art itself has been derived."

Today it seems incredible that such things needed to be said in 1919; but those who said them in 1919 were not fools, nor were they misinformed about the necessity to say them or about the first and primordial need for the scientific progress they pleaded for. That need was for scientists trained for deeds of original discovery, in sufficient numbers to make the difference between a rushing current of scientific discovery and a trickle that would not wash the test tubes of my present-day grandson's chemistry set. So they established the National Research Council Fellowships with funds granted by the farseeing Rockefeller Foundation. The results of the ensuing studies have been incalculable for scientific development in the United States. Most of the early National Research Council Fellows studied in Europe, for there was the Pierian spring of scientific discovery from which they could drink deeply. But this is another story into which I cannot go in detail here.

What I shall submit now is that the situation of the humanistic museums of this country, insofar as they are scholarly resources, is pretty closely parallel to that of this country's universities and colleges in 1919. The term "humanistic museum" is one I had to coin during my tenure as Chairman of the National Endowment for the Humanities, to make it clear that the museums, which the Humanities Endowment proposed to assist, fell within the provisions of the Act of Congress creating the Endowment—museums of history, archaeology, anthropology, etc. (If you should ask me what I meant to include under etc., I should have to say that I do not know exactly; and I should like to be instructed.)

I said just now that the present situation of the humanistic museum is about what the situation was in respect to the scientific laboratory of 1919. It is about the same because, by and large, we do not have personnel qualified to use what is in our laboratories—our collections. We surely do not have enough trained persons. We do not pay well enough to attract and keep the best. Our humanistic museums—probably all museums—are, indeed, the neglected stepchildren of the American educational enterprise—as, indeed, are all the humanities. Moreover, the humanistic museums are, if I may put it so, the unintegrated stepchildren of our educational enterprise.

There are deep and ancient historic reasons for this state of affairs. And here I shall pause to remark that, in our line of work, as in the line of inquiry assigned to me, we must be historians, or else, assuredly, we will be nothing. Historically, the development of societies has been, in the Western World, from a "noble warrior" culture to a "scribe" culture. "Education is a collective technique which a society employs to instruct its youth in the values and accomplishments of the civilization in which it exists." Thus in Arabia at the time of the Prophet, when society was dominated by an aristocracy of warriors, education was of a predominantly military kind: as such, it aimed at training character and building physical vigor rather than developing the intelligence. But in more refined (as we would call them) civilizations, the legacy of the past embodied in written form, pressed heavily; and in such civilizations, education was dominated by the technique of writing. These were the "people of the Book," as the Koran calls the Jews and Christians, with a respect not unmixed with astonishment.

This kind of account could go on for a long time, so perhaps I had better compress a couple of millennia into a couple of paragraphs. The education of classical antiquity was by the book, and when Christianity took over, it organized education around the Book of Books, the Bible, as the source of all necessary knowledge about life. In all post-classical education, through the so-called Dark Ages, through the Renaissance, into modern times, the people of the Western World remained "people of the Book."[1] We still are. Except in the sciences, scholarship still is largely out of the book and out of manuscripts in the library. And, no matter how much a man knows about, say, the weather, the seasons, the ways of life on the frontier or in the wilds, the proper cycle of fallow fields, he is not accounted an educated man unless he has learned it from books. We still are "people of the Book."

There is still another historical sequence that must be mentioned. Derived from a Greek word meaning "temple of the muses," the ideal museum in Mediterranean antiquity was thought of as covering the whole of human knowledge, covering the fields of all the Muses. But I know of only one that attempted to do so in those days—the Museum at Alexandria, Egypt. Yet even it had not appeared out of nowhere. It was, in effect, a vaster and more inclusive form of the philosophical community—philosophy in those days referring to all knowledge, as it did even in our Benjamin Franklin's day—created by the early Pythagoreans and copied by the Academy of Plato and of Aristotle. The Museum at Alexandria was founded by the first of the Ptolemies of Egypt at the beginning of the third century B.C. It lasted—or at any rate its library did—until its pillage by decree of the Christian bishop, Theophilus. That was in 389 A.D. "The term 'museum' after the burning of the great institution at Alexandria appears to have fallen into disuse from the 4th to the 17th century; and the idea which the word represented slipped from the minds of man."[2]

But despite this fact, it is worth trying to find out what the Museum at Alexandria amounted to and what was done there. It was under royal patronage.

> "It attracted not only poets and men of letters into the city but the most eminent scholars of the day—geometers, astronomers, physicians, historians, critics and grammarians. These 'museum pensioners' . . . lived in community, close to the palace. They had no taxes to pay and no duties to perform. . . . Functionaries appointed by the king looked after the scholars' material needs so that . . . they could devote all their attention to their studies. They had wonderful facilities for their work—Botanical and Zoological Gardens and their world-famous Library. . . . The Museum was essentially a centre for scientific research, not advanced education: the scientists and scholars . . . were not obliged to give any lectures. Nevertheless, they did teach. Good is self-diffusive, and knowledge has a natural tendency to spread: this is generally recognized to be one of human nature's fundamental characteristics. . . ."[3]

This passage says several things important for us now: that the museum, a center of collections of objects and specimens, was a research center, and only peripherally a center for teaching. "We know that the scholars in the Museum did in fact attract disciples, and accepted and educated them."[4] But it was not until much later, in say the third century A.D., that it had professorial chairs in the main branches of knowledge. It was under the Roman Empire that the Museum at Alexandria became a center of higher education—at a time when there were still no universities. To a lawyer like myself, historic precedent has important meaning. It enlarges our perspective and forces us to think and "to test the validity and cogency of the reasons for our choices: it makes our decisions conscious ones."[5]

Conscious of the origins of museums, I am more than delighted to be aware that, given its collections of objects, the primordial museum was a place for research. So it should and must continue to be. Knowledge should emanate from the museum's collections and, in accordance with its natural tendency, will spread. E. McClung Fleming has truly remarked that

> "The library and the museum constitute the two halves of our memory of the past . . . but it is the rare historian who can read the museum's artifact as freely and as accurately as he can read the library's printed book or written manuscript. The artifact is a social document, but the historian has tended to ignore this primary source in his preoccupation with printed and manuscript material. He has consulted only one-half of our memory of the past."[6]

This is familiar stuff to all involved professionally with museums today. Saying it to them is like preaching to churchgoers who do not need the preaching, whereas the preaching is needed by the unconverted who do not go to church. In the present case, the unconverted are generally in the universities where, by and large, they still are "people of the Book." Many of my readers will know all this, better than I do. You also know, and you should believe, what Wilcomb E. Washburn has said: "In a great museum, as in a great university, research into the unknown must be the passion that dominates all and on which the functions of conservation and education depend."[7]

Louis C. Jones has pointed out that the historian from the ivory tower of a university finds in a good museum the same regard for scholarship, standards of research, and devotion to history as a discipline as prevail in his tower. This is as it should and must be.[8] But the sad part of the tale is that there are too few "good museums" in Louis Jones' sense, with staffs trained to such standards of knowledge and excellence of scholarship that their future in the total American educational enterprise will demand. Hence, the first need in the effort to make our humanistic museums live up to their potential as a scholarly resource is to train staffs for research—that is, to produce new knowledge.

From good research flows good teaching in the college and university; from good research flow accurate, understandable, telling museum exhibits. The museum staffer must understand the role of the artifact in its own contemporary society. It must be understood before it can be interpreted. The staff must be scholars, not just keepers of things. For, as G. Carroll Lindsay has written, "To arrive at even a general impression of a historical era, one must study not only what was written, but also what was sat upon, eaten and eaten from, ridden on, and lived in and with. This sort of thing is found most easily and in greatest quantity and variety in museums."[9]

The Reverend Ebenezer Brewer, in his *Dictionary of Phrase and Fable,* tells of a little old seventeenth-century lady who used to say to her pastor that she "had found great support in that blessed word 'Mesopotamia.'" Well, in our times the blessed word is "research" and many have found great support in *that* word. It is not as mellifluous as "Mesopotamia" but, for some, it has been accounted very blessed indeed. It has produced, for some of those who account it blessed, pots and pots of money. It has accounted, in some, for slackness in teaching. It has led many to think that they are entitled to carry on research and do nothing else to pull their freight in the educational boat. Of course, I now refer to research in the universities: "research" has not had, in the museums, anything like the support the old lady derived from the blessed word "Mesopotamia."

I plead for research as the only way for the humanistic museum to achieve its proper role as a scholarly resource. But, in so pleading, I do not forget to remember that, in these United States, the scholar—particularly the humanistic scholar—historically has had an obligation to teach and to teach well. So far as the scholar in the museum is concerned, I would not diminish that obligation. The scholar in the museum has an educational obligation—in his exhibitions, in his labeling of objects, in his advice to the little old lady who wants to know how grandmother made hominy that tasted so good, and in many other ways besides.

The museum is the only educational institution that teaches the old and the young and those in between, from the cradle to the grave. As S. Dillon Ripley has said, the museums' "exhibits must be brought into everyone's life as meaningfully as the supermarket. In our system of education, we assume that one can be educated only by learning to read. But objects are as much documents to be read as the printed page." A live cow (I once had a secretary in New York City who never had seen one), George Washington's campaign boots, a treadmill, a double-bitted ax are objects to be read. A museum requires the services of scholars and teachers as well as exhibits designers.

Dr. Ripley makes another most sensible and practical observation.

> "If then we must do more in the open education we present to the millions who throng museum halls each year, let us do so with all speed, conscious that in this way we may gain support for the inner programs of research and higher education in our laboratories. The two must go hand in hand, each program dependent on the other, deriving new meaning and understanding the one from the other."[10]

It usually is my dour fate to be obliged to address audiences a good many of whose numbers know more about my assigned subject than I do; and this subject is no exception. But, if I have been discouraged —as I have been—by what must be the relative non-originality of what I have written, perhaps I am entitled to remember what John Adams said about the Declaration of Independence—that there "is not an idea in it but what had been hackneyed in Congress two years before." And perhaps I may take comfort in Thomas Jefferson's reply that it was not his purpose "to find new principles . . . to say things that had never been said before, but to place before mankind the common sense of the subject," and to harmonize "the sentiments of the day whether expressed in conversation, in letters, in printed essays or the elementary books of public right." Not that I delude myself that I have said anything as important as Mr. Jefferson said in the Declaration of Independence, but only that I think it may be valuable enough to engage my time and yours with my setting down in one place what seems to me the enlightened common sense of the subject.

Perhaps a new day is dawning for the museum; for in 1965 the Congress of the United States, in passing the legislation that established the National Foundation for the Arts and the Humanities, declared "that democracy demands wisdom and vision in its citizens and that it must, therefore, foster and support a form of education designed to make men masters of their technology and not its unthinking servant," and "that a high civilization must not limit its efforts to science and technology alone but must give full value and support to the other great branches of man's scholarly and cultural activity." The museum must play a great part toward achieving such a purpose. Furthermore, in 1966, the Legislature of the State of New York appropriated $600,000 for all kinds of museums to be administered by the New York State Council on the Arts.

The National Endowment for the Humanities has decided to start a training program for museum personnel, and most of the monies appropriated to the New York State Council on the Arts will be used for the same purpose. I have been, and shall continue to be, associated with both of these training programs. For I believe, as did those who promoted the development of science after the First World War, that the first necessity for the development of museums in the total American educational enterprise, is to create a better trained and larger staff for research, for education, for exhibits design. That is what museums need most. Money is needed for this purpose, of course, but I confess to harboring the hope that not too much money will be earmarked for research; for it would be bad news, indeed, if "research" became the only blessed word in the museums' lexicon.

I began this paper by remarking, with Justice Holmes, that at my age it is a pleasure to think that there are fewer and fewer to whom I feel the need to show a youthful deference. Even so, there are not many whom I am minded to commit to the nether regions; but among them are those who think that research scholarship is the answer to everything. In our many-faceted line of work, it decidedly is not; whereas, in my opinion, a knowledgeable concern for the human condition matters most. In Washington, I kept telling the humanistic scholars that the first requirement of the humanities is that they be humane—that is, human and not pedantic. This is truth to me; for it is something I just cannot help believing. And what I cannot help believing *is* truth to me.

One final word: I would reserve a block of rooms in the nether regions—the most uncomfortable rooms there are in hell—for those who use the word "museology." For the use of that word would kill any hope that we are human; indeed, its use would prove that we are ignorant pedants, than whom there are none more ignorant. And I hereby offer a reward of one hundred dollars of my own cash, in United States currency, to anyone who will invent a better word, satisfactory to one who no longer feels the need to show a youthful deference.

1. In respect to the summary in this and the preceding paragraph, see Marrou, H. I., *A History of Education in Antiquity,* New York, Sheed and Ward, 1956.

2. *Encyclopaedia Britannica,* 11th ed., vol. 19, p. 65.

3. Marrou, H. I., *op. cit.,* pp. 260–261.

4. *Ibid.,* p. 261.

5. *Ibid.,* p. xiii.

6. "Early American Decorative Arts as Social Documents," *Mississippi Valley Historical Review,* 5:45, September 1958, p. 276.

7. *Museum News,* 40:2, October 1961, p. 19.

8. *Museum News,* 40:7, March 1962, p. 16.

9. *Curator,* 5:30, 1963, pp. 236–244.

10. *Museum News,* 42:2, October 1964, p. 18.

The Existing Situation

Museum Programs in Education

JOSEPH ALLEN PATTERSON
Director, American Association of Museums

American museums are currently serving an audience of much greater size and diversity than ever before. Attendance, which increased by more than one hundred million in the decade 1952–1962, is now estimated to be around the three hundred million mark. The rate of increase in museum attendance exceeds both the rate of increase of the population and the rate of establishment of new museums.

This new audience is also demanding vastly increased formal educational services from the museum, and museums are doing their best to meet this demand. The Schenectady Museum, in its 1964 Annual Report, noted a 55.8 percent increase in its educational services to the community in the three preceding years, all accomplished without expansion of budget, staff, or exhibition area, but at the expense of other areas of museum responsibility. The Museum of Science in Boston has reported that over one hundred thousand children are served under the new Massachusetts School Visits Program sponsored jointly by the Massachusetts State Department of Education and the Metropolitan District Commission. The Chicago Art Institute indicates that programs for the children of Chicago Public Schools have been limited only by the space available. At Old Sturbridge Village, the school services division handled almost fifty thousand children, and was unable to give appointments to ten thousand more who applied. The American Museum of Natural History, in its Annual

Report for 1965, reported that more than three times as many people were participating in formal classes at the Planetarium as had participated thirty years before. These are only a few examples, but they are representative of what is happening in museums all over the country.

The numerical increase in attendance at education department programs has been accompanied by increased variety in the types of programs offered, and greater diversity in the audiences for whom they are designed. Educational work in museums ranges from preschool classes to work with "Golden Age" groups, and from enrichment programs for the culturally deprived to laboratory or studio classes for the exceptionally talented. A short summary of a few of the programs offered by museums will indicate the range of demands museums are trying to meet.

The Walters Gallery, last summer, had a heavy and unexpected attendance by classes of preschoolers. These were children participating in "Operation Headstart" programs organized by the local antipoverty agency who were brought to the museum for what was hoped to be a culturally enriching experience. The Joslyn Art Museum in Omaha is running a preschool to fill local needs. There were over two hundred children in these classes, and there were many more on the waiting list.

The most extensive educational programs in museums are traditionally those aimed at grade school students, designed to introduce the child to the museum, and to acquaint him with the resources which are available to him at the museum. These programs are often sponsored jointly by the museum and the local or state education departments. One such program is the Massachusetts School Visits Program previously mentioned, another is that of the Pittsburgh Board of Education which sponsors fifth and seventh grade visiting programs at the Carnegie Institute in which each visiting class is given two forty-five-minute tours, one of the art exhibits, and one of the science exhibits. The Philadelphia Museum of Art offers ten different lecture tours, relating to the curriculum of the schools, which classroom teachers may request.

But museums have found that the guided tours offered at the

museum for elementary schools are not the complete answer to the needs of these students. Many classes are unable to come to the museum, either because they are too far away to accomplish the expedition during the school day, or because there is no transportation available, a particular problem of the urban school systems. For these schools, many museums have organized extension services. The Suffolk Museum on Long Island has kits for elementary schools containing artifacts and exhibits relating to the Long Island Indian, Long Island Shore Birds, Colonial household wares, and the cultures of Japan and Mexico. The Field Museum of Natural History, in Chicago, sends portable exhibits to more than five hundred schools and public service institutions, and serves almost five hundred thousand children through this program. The Great Plains Historical Association, in Lawton, Oklahoma, sends out history kits to grade schools, as does the Indiana Historical Society. Other institutions, such as the Dearborn Historical Museum, in Dearborn, Mich., send lecturers to the schools to present programs related to the school curricula and the subject area of the museum.

In addition to programs oriented toward the school, museums also present classes and courses for individual elementary age children, designed to supplement the work of the school. These courses, at this age level, are usually in some phase of studio art work, or in natural history subjects, neither of which can be adequately presented in the limited time available during the school year. The Everson Museum of Art in Syracuse conducts art classes to supplement the program of art education in the schools or, in some cases, to provide the major source of art training for the student. The Detroit Institute of Arts has been cooperating with the local Neighborhood Service Organization to provide art classes for children in an inner-city housing project. In 1963, 10,857 children attended art classes at the Wadsworth Atheneum. In 1964, attendance at museum school classes for children, aged six to twelve, at the Fort Worth Children's Museum was 13,333, including many enrollments in natural history subjects.

Museum educational work with junior and senior high school students is ordinarily directed toward the individual student and is intended to provide him with additional work and encouragement in a subject in which he has already developed an interest. In the academic year 1964–1965, the City Art Museum of St. Louis presented two series of four Saturday morning auditorium events which were designed to bring to the museum students with more developed interests in the various cultures that have produced significant art forms. Nearly two thousand students were present at these programs. The Seattle Art Museum conducts special classes in the history of art for students in the high school age group. The Museum of Natural Science in Cleveland conducts a science seminar for approximately five hundred honor students from more than forty high schools in the greater Cleveland area, designed to give the students a better insight into the natural sciences. The Charlotte Children's Nature Museum has sponsored a seminar on oceanography to acquaint interested students with opportunities in this field. The Field Museum of Natural History arranges holiday science lectures for outstanding high school students to hear firsthand reports of work being done by eminent scientists. The Museum of Science and Industry, in St. Louis, runs a Science Career Program in which unusually talented high school students, each with his own advisor, undertake a year of original research. The Los Angeles County Museum has been running Natural Science Workshops since 1944. Since then some three thousand young people have spent many weekend hours attending lectures and participating in field trips under the direction of the museum curators. As a result of this program, 84 percent of the former students are now working in one of the sciences. During the summer, the Brooklyn Children's Museum offers an intensive work–study program in cultural anthropology and archaeology for students who have completed the tenth, eleventh, or twelfth grade. The New York State Historical Association sponsors clubs for students who are interested in local and state history.

Museums are also working with young people from low-income families, assisting with stay-in-school programs for junior and senior high school students. The Franklin Institute has held a special space symposium for Explorer Scouts to encourage and motivate the boys to continue their education and explore various careers in the space field. The boys were told of instances where a high school education had qualified young men to work in this field, and it was hoped that the potential high school dropout might thus be influenced to continue his studies. The New York Botanical Garden, through the Municipal Cooperative Education Program, has been training selected high school juniors and seniors to be gardeners, through a program in which they attend lectures and do related work. The Old Dartmouth Historical Society in New Bedford, Mass., has been a cooperating agency in the employment program of the Neighborhood Youth Corps.

At the college level, many museums have formal or informal arrangements with local educational institutions in which members of the museum staff teach in their speciality, either at the school or at the museum. Often the special facilities of the museum make it possible to expand the offerings of the educational institution. For instance, the astronomy course of the University of South Carolina is given at the planetarium of the Columbia Museum of Art. The Connecticut Valley Historical Museum in Springfield, Mass., has a cooperative program with Springfield College in which students have the opportunity to take a course on research in local history at the museum. The cooperative arrangements between Columbia University and the Metropolitan Museum of Art are well known.

A number of museums also provide opportunities for college students to get additional training in their speciality in the summer. The Nantucket Maria Mitchell Association has a National Science Foundation supported summer training program in astronomy for college women. The Field Museum is employing college students interested in the natural sciences in the museum's scientific departments during the summer, and offering them a unique opportunity both to increase their knowledge of a scientific field and to discover what a large research institution is like.

Another important service performed by museum education departments is providing instruction for teachers. The Fels Planetarium offers a course entitled "Introduction to Astronomy" which is approved by the Philadelphia Board of Education. The Dallas Independent School District gives credit for a summer art history course given by the Dallas Museum of Fine Arts. Among other courses provided for teachers are: an in-service course in horticulture given by the New York Botanical Garden; a course on "Utilization of the Bronx Zoo in the Science Program of Elementary and Secondary Schools" offered by the New York Zoological Society; and teachers' seminars covering various theoretical and applied aspects of physics, chemistry and biology given by the Charlotte Children's Nature Museum. Michigan State University, Cranbrook Institute, and the Henry Ford Museum and Greenfield Village cooperate in a workshop on using museum resources in teaching. The Walker Art Center and the Minneapolis Institute of Arts co-sponsor a cultural reference course for junior and senior high school teachers, a series of four classes to acquaint teachers with these art collections as a rich teaching source. Through these courses and others like them, museums are helping to improve the quality of instruction in the public schools.

While attention has largely been focused on the role of museums as adjuncts to the formal educational systems, the museum also plays an important part in providing informal educational experiences for those who have completed their formal schooling. Museum education department programs for adults can be divided roughly into two groups, those designed to introduce and explain recent developments in the field of interest of the institution, and those dealing with traditional subject matter in which there is sufficient interest to warrant a course of lectures or demonstrations.

In the first category would come such programs as the Santa Barbara Museum of Art's six-meeting series on "Contemporary European Trends; The Past Decade," or the Corcoran Gallery of Art's slide lecture on the proposed Pennsylvania Avenue and Mall plans for Washington. The Franklin Institute has presented a series of lecture–demonstrations explaining computers and computer-theory, and a program on number theory and the new math. Lectures at the Oriental Institute in Chicago have informed the public of new discoveries made during excavations, such as additional evidence of early contact between Nubia and Mesopotamia. The outdoor museums of history such as Old Sturbridge Village and Colonial Williamsburg have introduced the concept of social history to many of those for whom Charles Beard and the economic interpretation were once the latest word.

In the second group are such programs as the Wadsworth Atheneum's "Meet and Eat" Sandwich Lunch and Gallery Talk Program, in which lectures are given on such topics as a loan collection of miniatures, or works by Connecticut painters in the museum's collection. Adult education courses, offered by the Staten Island Institute of Arts and Sciences for the spring of 1965, also come under this class, and include "Foundations of Modern Painting," "Bacteriology in Everyday Living," "Bird Study," and "Field Course in Natural History."

Additionally, museums may initiate special educational programs to meet the needs of a particular group in the community or to use the unique facilities of the institution to best advantage. Among these programs are the North Carolina Museum of Art's project to teach the blind to appreciate art through their sense of touch, and the Museum of the City of New York's Spanish-language walking tours of the city. The American Museum of Natural History, in cooperation with the Department of Welfare of the City of New York, has conducted a program of gallery talks and exhibition hall tours for elderly persons. Plimoth Plantation has produced a series of pilot lessons on life in the early Plymouth Colony, and has joined in a cooperative effort with the Society of Visual Education to produce film strips on Pilgrim history for classroom use.

The examples cited above provide only a partial documentation of the work which American museums are doing in the field of education. However, they are useful in indicating the wide variety of demands which museums are attempting to meet. As the least formally structured of all our educational institutions, museums are being asked to assume responsibility for all those programs which do not fit into the formal educational systems and, at the same time, to provide closely correlated programs for use by these formal systems. A number of museums already have reached the saturation point in terms of space and staff available for education programs, and others are rapidly reaching this point. These institutions will either have to find new financing and staff members, build new buildings and exhibits, or become increasingly selective in the types of programs offered. However, since each of these programs appears to meet a real community need, museums should be extremely reluctant to limit them without first exploring every means of continuing.

In discussing museum education programs, it should not be forgotten that all of these activities are predicated upon the existence and exhibition of collections in art, history, or science, and upon the availability of museum professionals to service these collections. The tremendous increase in museum attendance and in the rate of establishment of new museums since World War II has not been accompanied by a comparable development of professional museum personnel. Irving G. Reimann, Director of the Exhibits Museum at the University of Michigan, stated in an article for *Curator* in 1960, "It is probably conservative to estimate that seventy-five percent of the present employees of ninety percent of our museums have no previous museum training or experience."[1] At the present time, training opportunities for these people are almost nonexistent.

The shortage of trained museum professionals is aggravated by the lack of authoritative reference works and handbooks on various aspects of museum work. The untrained museum worker is often unable to obtain the necessary guidance to enable him to perform in a professional manner.

Museums are also having difficulty in obtaining adequate financing. In many cases, the expansion of education programs has been accomplished by diverting funds from other areas of the museum budget, and these areas have suffered. Museums must find new sources of income if they are to perform properly all the tasks assigned to them.

The American Association of Museums is very much aware of the problems facing its member institutions in museum education, staffing, financing, conservation and restoration work, and general museum administration. For this reason, on 25 May 1965, the Council of the American Association of Museums went on record as unanimously endorsing the proposed National Museum Act, which would bring needed public recognition of museums as representing one of the nation's most important national resources. In the fall of 1965, all of the Association's regional conferences also went on record in support of the Act.

The proposed National Museum Act will inaugurate a continuing study and consultation program for the development and strengthening of museums throughout the United States. The Act specifically calls for training programs, publication of a wide range of museum handbooks and technical works, and a continuing survey and documentation of museum resources and needs. These services and the assistance envisaged in the Act will enable museums to improve and enhance the quality and content of the programs they provide for millions of Americans.

The Association views the National Museum Act as a call for its member museums, other public and private institutions, and governmental agencies to join together in an effort to solve some of the pressing problems facing the museum field. The National Museum Act will enable the museum profession, with the assistance of other interested organizations and agencies, to take stock and determine the most effective means of providing professional solutions for museum problems. This will in no way detract from the museum tradition of decisions being made at the local level, or the equally long-standing tradition of private and local government financial support of the museum.

While we very much hope the National Museum Act will soon become law, the Association has not been inactive while awaiting this eventuality. Under our Joint Publication Program with the Smithsonian Institution, we have issued the second edition of *The Museums Directory of the United States and Canada,* and with the cooperation of the U.S. Office of Education, *A Statistical Survey of Museums in the United States and Canada.* A revised edition of *Museum Registration Methods,* which is now out of print, is ready for the presses and will be published as soon as funds are available.

The Association has long recognized the need for additional professional training for museum workers. In the past we have sponsored museum training programs in anthropology, astronomy, biology, and geology under grants from the National Science Foundation. We have recently submitted proposals to the National Endowment for the Humanities for museum training grants in the humanities. One proposal is designed to provide training opportunities for museum technicians and junior curators working in isolated situations in small communities throughout the country. It would provide cost-of-living stipends for museum staff members to study advanced museum techniques in formal training programs or in organized on-the-job, in-service training programs at well-equipped sponsoring museums. A second program is intended to produce well-educated graduates with a demonstrated interest in and training for museum careers, and calls for fellowships for students of the humanities pursuing programs for the M.A. and Ph.D. with strong museum electives at universities having cooperative programs with museums.

The Association continues to provide seminar programs abroad for American museum professionals and—in conjunction with Colonial Williamsburg, the American Association for State and Local History, and the National Trust for Historic Preservation—an annual seminar for historical administrators.

The Association is also interested in documenting and investigating the relationship of museum exhibitions to education. Working with the U.S. Office of Education and the Smithsonian Institution, we arranged for Mr. Bartlett Hayes to undertake the study of the relation of museum art exhibitions to education, which follows next in this volume. We hope in the future to arrange similar studies of history and science exhibits.

We feel a strong sense of urgency about these programs because we believe that the museum will play an even more important part in public education in the future than it has in the past. The museum exhibit may well be the only point of visual contact between the individual and the problems of our increasingly urbanized and technically complex civilization. Exhibitions such as those in the Water Resources Hall at the California Museum of Science, in which an extensive explanation of California's water problem is presented, or the model of Philadelphia's urban renewal area at the museum of the Philadelphia Civic Center, explain much more clearly than a thousand lines of newsprint what the problems are and what is proposed.

Finally, the rapid advances in science and technology which have been made in the last decade, and which are expected to continue, have resulted and will result in great lacunae in the knowledge of those not actively involved in the sciences. The museum exhibit will be increasingly important in helping to bring new discoveries and new techniques into the general knowledge of the adult American.

1. Reimann, Irving G., "Preparation for Professional Museum Careers," *Curator*, 3:3, 1960, pp. 279–285.

A Study of the Relation of Museum Art Exhibitions to Education

❧

BARTLETT H. HAYES, JR.
Director, the Addison Gallery
Phillips Academy, Andover

Lest the scope of this report[1] be misconstrued, I feel bound to explain that, due to certain unfortunate timing, I consented to perform this study when I was at liberty to do so, but I could not commence then for lack of a contract. When, eventually, this commitment was negotiated, my "leisure" was encumbered by other obligations. Despite such impositions, I visited some fifty-seven museums in forty-nine cities of the United States within eleven months. Knowing of many more museums which, for lack of sufficient time, I could not reexamine at first hand, I feel that my observations here are possibly representative of a nationwide phenomenon, but are by no means exhaustive. Furthermore, in the interest of immediacy, I have made the present analysis on the basis of only a few of the visits—several made at the outset, several just before the contract closed, two or three midway through the survey, which were chosen at random. A final report must await the generosity of additional time.

At the beginning, I decided that a survey is most usefully made subjectively; not that facts are irrelevant but that, examined out of context, they may not reveal an accurate view of a situation. Consequently, I chose to proceed without a formal set of questions, and to ask the kinds of questions and to elicit the kinds of responses which might be suggested by each conversation in its own way. Any similarity between one interview and the next might, therefore, be all the more meaningful. If this may suffice to account for what follows, let me proceed.

When the survey was first proposed, I was advised to focus my attention primarily on those art exhibitions designed for educational purposes. I have not only found that there are relatively few of these, but also that the many museum staff members with whom I raised the issue invariably queried, "What exhibition is not educational, including the permanent collection?" Moreover, I learned that temporary exhibitions are not always central to the educational activities of art museums and that whatever long-range impact museums may have on elementary and secondary education is generally through their permanent collections. This is not to discount certain vivid experiences which temporary exhibitions may provide, especially in museums where the permanent collection is limited; rather it is my contention that permanent collections play a more important educational role than is commonly understood, and that the need for travelling exhibits is greatest in communities where there are no permanent collections.

Although there exists no statistical evidence as to the purpose of total visits per capita per annum, my impression is that over 75 percent of the visits are for the sake of "exposure," that 20 percent are related to topical concerns of the classroom (largely history), and that 5 percent are for the sake of heightening artistic understanding and taste, or learning about art history. The evidence for this is the preponderance of visits at the fifth, or more commonly the sixth, grade level. Visits at this age are accounted for by two considerations:

1. *The convenience of the school schedule.* Below the seventh grade, the classroom teacher has control of the work of the day and, if a morning is occupied by a field trip, she can make it up in other subjects by her own ingenuity later on.

2. *The relative maturity of the pupils.* Sixth graders, I was told whenever the question arose, are less self-conscious than older children and pay better attention when escorted into a museum environment. They are also noticeably more mature than younger children and, therefore, benefit in a more marked degree from the visit.

So it is that in certain communities there is an attempt to achieve an exposure for every child at the sixth grade level and, for most of the children, this is the sole formal visit of their entire school career. One wonders if the little knowledge gained is worth the museum's effort. It is relatively easy for the individual teacher to shepherd the annual trip and the child suffers at most a relaxing change of pace. On the other hand, the museum staff exert themselves with these swarms day after day. Does the staff, or does society as a whole, benefit from the experience?

There is some evidence that certain children and their parents, too, do benefit. In many museums, staff members have spoken of the return of certain children (accompanied by their parents) on a week-end or two following a visit. Indeed, in a few cases, museum memberships have resulted, producing a continuing response. And there are always, of course, personal exposures which may justify the entire museum educational program, such as the solitary child from an impoverished area of Cincinnati who brought his kitten to the Taft Museum so that the pet might "see how pretty it is." Nature sows abundantly that one seed may sprout and the reward of museum educators is to see the sprout strengthen, blossom, and seed again.

If one chooses to be pessimistic about the small percentage of pupils who derive benefit from an art museum experience, one may wonder about the rising flood of interest in art museum programs during the past two decades. Here again, however, accurate statistics are not available, especially as to the kind of reaction on the part of those who attend in such numbers. "Much as a crowd at a dog fight gives no indication of the pedigrees of the animals involved," museum attendance is difficult to analyze. There is much in the public notices with which museums seek to announce their services that tends to attract visitors without gratifying them with anything more than the privilege of having savored culture. This savoring seems to provide a certain status in society and is a relatively recent phenomenon. Not only may it indicate a widespread change in social attitudes, but it also may require museum trustees and administrators to reappraise their community roles.

At the center of most museum activities are the ladies who serve on various committees formed to promote the simultaneous welfare of the community and the museum. The hard-working, serious, devoted women who serve as docents are indispensable to much art museum educational work. To some extent, they are the bond between whatever is exhibited and the local school system whether they are professional or amateur, salaried or volunteer. Their duties vary widely according to the nature of the museum, the character of the community, the concern of the museum administration and the interest or diffidence of the school authorities and parents.

The latter play a more important part in determining the strength of educational ties with museums than one might suppose and, in communities where parental interest in cultural matters is strong, there is apt to be a fairly active school museum program. Conversely, for lack of parental interest, a school may have very little traffic with museum activities. It is in such cases that the women connected with educational programs, who possess the time and energy to penetrate the school, can do so in ways that the regular educational staff of an art museum (usually too few in number and with little money) cannot manage. To be sure, the directives of the museum director and the head of the educational department (if there is one) are all important, but, no more than the coach and the captain could play the entire game could numerous educational programs currently flourishing in many parts of the country operate without a "team" to execute the plays. The quality of an orchestra, to alter the image, depends on the sensitivity of a conductor, but his baton is silent before an empty stage.

Although professional opinion differs strongly as to the educational utility and validity of non-professional assistance, as well as to the degree and kind of training such people should undergo, the strength and effectiveness of many an art museum educational program depend importantly on the community interest which these many volunteers represent.

Because many art museums have been established by art groups or associations, those groups or clubs help with local relations and educational efforts. Nevertheless, the influential and educationally significant effort in city after city has been the local chapter of the Junior

League; not only with its financial support (by no means insignificant in many cases), but also by supplying interested and willing personnel, the League has done much to encourage museum–school relationships and to actively operate certain programs. Most League programs have sprung up since World War II; some are only three or four years old. Over a period of twelve to fifteen years, however, the personnel rotates, after serving three or four years, so that the museum influence spreads through the community as younger members come along. Moreover, many of the young women involved possess the means to buy works of art from the series of changing exhibitions, thereby not only fostering a constructive local respect for the arts, but also enhancing the esteem with which local artists are held whose works are so recognized. Through such a process, the museum collections themselves may ultimately be enriched by gift or bequest. This possibility, in turn, challenges the museum administrator to be as scrupulous in the choice of works exhibited as his discrimination will admit. Museum education is not for children alone.

The art education of the teacher is usually a case of small exposure with little knowledge resulting. At the elementary level, the classroom teacher possesses a minimum of art experience if, indeed, any at all. At the secondary level, the subject matter method of instruction makes it impossible to teach art unless the school employs a professional art teacher. Of all the high school pupils graduating yearly throughout the nation, nearly 93 percent have had no contact with the arts at the high school level. Despite increasing museum attendance, general public indifference toward art is a characteristic of modern American society. Certainly, some of this apathy must be attributed to the lack of an effective contact with the arts during the years of developing maturity. An art experience at the elementary level does not commonly grow into an understanding of art, nor does it form habits that become part of adult life. Imagine what might happen to American society if all the instruction in the English language, all reading, all writing were dropped from the school curriculum after the seventh grade. Would libraries be expected to carry the responsibility for continuing and developing the articulation of concepts and the clarity of analysis which are currently the tasks of the English classroom? Yet, this is the role in which museums appear to be cast by the society they seek to serve. Moreover, museums are asked to serve not only as schoolrooms, but also as teacher-training institutes, in many cases with nothing but private money to carry on the work, not even with the help of teacher or pupil tuition fees. Money for art education is scarce. One may buy a work of art but, except by attending professional schools or art courses in the universities, one cannot be expected to buy knowledge about it—or so it would seem from prevailing practice.

What should a teacher who takes a class to an art museum know? The answer seems so obvious as barely to need asking, yet opinions differ widely as to an answer. As I moved from city to city, I found myself confronted with differences and attitudes that I had not anticipated. Not a few staff members believe that the museum itself should do its own explaining and that whether a teacher has an art background or not is immaterial as far as the museum visit is concerned. Others believe strongly in the importance of having teachers who are trained in art serve as leaders of the museum visit. As well as I could determine, the former point of view was held largely by staff members of institutions owning important historical collections and whose experience had convinced them that, even though a few teachers might be competent to explain the collection, the majority could not, and that it was simpler for the museum staff to assume the full responsibility. The latter point of view was expressed more frequently by staffs of museums owning limited collections, and having small operating budgets and small staffs. In such museums, the temporary exhibit is a relatively important educational facility. The brief presence of the temporary exhibition, combined with a certain detachment on the part of the staff (arising from a lack of responsibility for the ownership of the works in the exhibit) tend to make the staff more ready to welcome aid.

Despite such basic differences of opinion as to who can and who cannot make use of an art museum for educational benefit, there is common agreement as to the teacher's need for knowledge of the history of art. This, in fact, runs counter to the training of many professional art teachers, for whom the major emphasis has been on techniques for developing the children's expressive opportunities rather than on the intellectual aspects of art history. Consequently, a dichotomy exists, especially insofar as art class visits are concerned, between the interests of the art teacher and the museum educator. The docent has been taught to relate the museum object to its place in time and geography; the teacher may see it as no more than a technical specimen. All is not evil, however; there are efforts in some communities to provide teacher seminars, as well as to learn what teachers are teaching for the sake of better museum–school coordination. There are teachers who study museum announcements in order to alert their pupils to cultural opportunities. Such people are not numerous, unfortunately. The average school point of view is that lessons come first and even though a teacher who is knowledgeable in the arts may wish to expand the horizons of her class, it is often very difficult to do so because her superior may be adverse to such "indulgences." Equally handicapped is the teacher who is ignorant of art and serves under a principal who may wish to encourage art education. American education is in the midst of many reappraisals, and the difficulty of adjusting teachers to new experiments is no less than that of adjusting the attitudes of administrators and school boards and taxpayers to the need for a fresh look.

In common practice, the school lesson does come first and some of the more successful programs shared by school and museum are those related directly to class work. The opportunity occurs most fruitfully at grade levels where the broad historical, or cultural, studies occur. These vary slightly from one part of the country to the other; however, geography at fifth or sixth grade and world history at the seventh (and again at the eleventh) are areas where museum objects provide evidence of the character of the subject under study. These subjects also provide a ready focus for panel exhibits assembled by the museum and displayed in corridors, libraries, classrooms, or the auditorium lobby. In some communities such exhibits are never harmed; in others, teachers claim that, unless they are locked in cases, vandalism is inevitable and that even the cases do not guarantee protection. Certain museum officials assert that such exhibits are worthless, that the original object is all important; others believe that, without preliminary exposure to artistic ideas in the school, a visit to the museum is too fleeting to be of substantial value. Still others look askance at such efforts, whether in school or in a museum, feeling that the experience is too shallow to be worth bothering with. Art, they feel, cannot be experienced casually. Still others believe that continued exposure will be artistically rewarding. In one case—the Allentown Art Museum—this kind of continued exposure has resulted in a considerable volume of voluntary student attendance and the Director has learned that whenever a downtown event is to be held (such as a parade) extra guards must be engaged because of the influx of children as soon as the event is concluded.

Except for a few municipalities, television and the motion picture have not played a particularly important role in cementing school–museum relations. In many interviews, the hope was expressed that more use might be made of such media. The Kansas City Art Museum has produced motion picture films of certain aspects of its collection which it sends to the various schools in the city; the Museum of Art in Portland, Oreg., distributes slide–tape lectures to the high schools; the Museum of Fine Arts, Boston, broadcasts television programs from the Museum through the local educational channel; theater and motion picture programs—such as at Richmond, Va., and the Museum of Modern Art, New York City—broaden the educational base of museum activities, though not always from a strictly fine arts point of view.

Television, probably the most important medium for dispensing information the world has known, possesses the potential of penetrating remote areas in a way the average travelling exhibition cannot, and there are some who advocate its use rather than panel exhibits consisting of photographs, reproductions, or fourth-rate works of art.

The experience of the Virginia Museum of Fine Arts, the Art Center at Little Rock, and the Detroit Museum (to name three) with the Artmobile, whereby with reasonable precaution valuable works of art can be widely displayed, suggests that the use of this method of museum education is likely to grow. Nevertheless, there is doubt in the minds of some as to whether or not the expense is justified if only a very few objects can be displayed for a short amount of time for the sake of an experience that may be once in a lifetime. If, on the other hand, they argue, the justification of the Artmobile is to stimulate visits to the museum itself, may not television be equally effective?

In the minds of most museum officials, the function of a museum is to assemble, care for, and display the works of art which document the cultural interests of man. Like the library it is an institution, whether private or public, to which people may turn for enlightenment and satisfaction. Its educational efforts are intended to inform people who are ignorant of the nature of its contents. The questions arise, however, as to the limits of the museum's ability to carry on this process of informing and how much beyond mere informing should the museum educational staff be required to go.

It may not be out of place, by way of illuminating the importance of these questions, to cite a passage from the introductory essay of the October 1946 issue of *Art in America* magazine:

> "From the standpoint of service to the individual, the spread of museums may be compared to the mushroom-like appearance of libraries a half century earlier. Due perhaps to a considerable difference in time, they function, however, in nonparallel ways. Were the librarian, in addition to his present curatorial, reading, accessioning, lending, and supervisory duties, to write, edit and publish a discursive bulletin on literary affairs, dictate articles for newspapers and magazines as a normal routine, give frequent readings from the works of Shakespeare or Joyce and conduct interpretive seminars in conjunction with them, institute and carry out research into the letters and biography of obscure or deceased authors, conduct competitive programs to stimulate the creative effort of contemporary writers and concern himself with their livelihood and literary welfare, take occasional part in the advising and formulation of commercial copy, lend a friendly hand to the frustrated aspirations of local would-be novelists, devote himself to the constant appraisal and connoisseurship of old and ofttimes spurious manuscripts brought to him by hopeful citizens, advise on the design and decoration of private libraries, plan and post notices of concerts, lectures, movies and exhibits to replace signs reading SILENCE, conduct classes in writing and public speaking, shepherd swarms of school children through the library while training them to compose and recite their own poetry, journey about the countryside talking to civic groups, women's clubs and church gatherings which open-mouthed await his pill of literary uplift, address radio audiences on the merits and demerits of the latest banned book, play host at a tea or a cocktail

party every time a book of the month appears on his shelf and finance it all from private instead of tax-raised money, he would be performing in the service of literature what is expected of the average museum director."

One may well ask if art education is not properly the obligation of the schools.

HIGHLIGHTS OF INTERVIEWS AT SEVERAL MUSEUMS

Dallas Museum of Fine Arts, Dallas, Texas, 26 April 1965

The Education Department used two to three exhibits annually for docent-guided teaching. Tours of the small permanent collection take place any time upon request.

No special exhibits are arranged exclusively for the schools, but an effort is made to make all exhibits understandable.

Groups usually visit once, sometimes twice, annually—especially with seasonal emphasis, e.g., the Baroque show in the autumn, followed by a Biedermeyer show in the spring sponsored by Neiman-Marcus Company.

Museum visits, principally children between fifth and eighth grades, number 5000 to 6000 a year out of 150,000 in school. Visits last about forty minutes.

The museum staff sees a need to know what teachers are teaching and to integrate the museum program with school work. The school–museum coordinator on the staff of the Board of Education helps by sending notes to teachers alerting them to special exhibits.

The use of the museum depends essentially on the interest of the teacher, but also on that of the principal.

Although there is a need for exhibits in the schools, there is a problem of scheduling them in 170 different schools. Where to display the exhibits—the halls, auditorium, library—is also a problem. "The personality of a speaker with slides may be more effective than in-school exhibits."

A program of auditorium talks and Saturday seminars are proposals of the museum staff to involve teachers.

A high school senior program of occasional visits to the museum is followed by a two-page test to inspire attention during the visit.

The PTA can be useful; children's visits are an influence on the parents.

The school–museum coordinator believes arbitrary assignments do not promote natural interest and that there is a need, therefore, for a coordinated program to involve both teachers and pupils.

The museum arranges extra programs, assembly talks and exhibit tours, especially Saturdays, for high school children.

Fort Worth Art Center, Fort Worth, Texas, 27 April 1965

There were no special exhibits for solely educational purposes. "Exhibits which interest adults are also good for children."

The Junior League manages docents collaborating with the museum administration. They seek to involve 9000 city sixth graders in one visit per year; emphasis is on looking and becoming sensitive. The Preview Gallery, designed for adult education, is used for high school art classes. The emphasis is on analysis. (This gallery is a small stage seating approximately one hundred people in the auditorium which is, in fact, a storeroom. It was designed for local clubs to study forthcoming exhibits on racks and to discuss them prior to actual installation.)

League docents serve three to five years. The effect of this experience is to develop art patrons with the possibility that some works of art, purchased from exhibits through such patronage, may eventually return as gifts to the museum. The museum director is concerned that proposed withdrawal of League support may destroy this community interest and participation.

The Junior League has stimulated classroom teachers to give follow-up factual tests following visits.

The League also conducts a program for eighth grade junior high students whereby objects from the museum are brought into the classrooms.

Very often children return to the museum with parents on weekends following a museum visit.

The vitality of the art supervisors and individual art teachers, and the interest of principals influence the way the museum is used.

McLean High School has own small purchase fund for art. These works are hung in a gallery which was created by converting a broom closet.

Fort Worth Children's Museum, Fort Worth, Texas, 27 April 1965

Attendance amounts to over 200,000 children per year.

"Smithsonian exhibits are not sophisticated enough."

A need was expressed for the services of a laboratory under the aegis of the American Association of Museums.

One third of the lessons within the museum are concerned with art. Most children are younger than sixth grade and are predominantly not involved with art classes in school, in contrast to the children who visit the Fort Worth Art Center. The emphasis at the Children's Museum is on personal involvement through exhibits and demonstrations.

Museum of Fine Arts of Houston, Texas, 28 April 1965

There is no school specialist in art at the elementary level.

Ninety percent of the candidates for high school art teacher positions have had no professional art school experience.

The museum is making an effort to improve art appreciation and art history education. "Don't separate art history from history."

"Elementary teachers are key people, usually with limited attitudes." A need was expressed for a good, required course in teacher education for the arts.

It was confessed that there was a weakness in the fact that a visit was made to the museum by a given child no more than once a year; often no more than once in an entire school career.

The museum has arranged an exhibition in conjunction with a half-day seminar for principals during the summer season. Attendance has been modest.

A parent-guided program, "Art in American Life," was illustrated with specified exhibits.

Art exhibits in schools have been arranged similar to a science fair initiated by the schools themselves.

An exchange of art room work between elementary schools and high schools has proved effective. Each age group is more impressed with the work of other age groups than with their own.

With 210 schools in the city, of which 20 are senior high and 28 junior high (a total of 225,000 children), there is not much opportunity for the museum to serve more than the sixth grade level once a year, although individual teachers in high schools do send pupils independently.

A summer program for ages nine to thirteen reaches two thousand pupils.

The museum conducts a program of visits for parents from underprivileged areas.

The Junior Museum exhibits are designed to attract teachers and children, but they are adult oriented. The Tinguely exhibition installed for adults seemed to excite the children as much as the display of their own work in the Junior Gallery.

Marion Koogler McNay Art Institute, San Antonio, Texas, 29 April 1965

The community was becoming acquainted with the museum by means of several experimental processes.

Fifth and sixth grade pupils were being brought to the museum on a tentative basis.

The museum staff makes a special issue of how to behave in a museum and describes beforehand what the children may expect to see.

Although the McNay Art Institute makes available colored reproductions as well as film strips and tape recordings for in-school use, there is a strong staff conviction that the museum must be visited, otherwise these visual aids are invalid.

The museum conducts a program for the culturally deprived, grades three to seven, paying one half of the bussing cost.

Witte Memorial Museum, San Antonio, Texas, 29 April 1965

There is no art supervisor in San Antonio because the school administration is not especially interested in art. "Can't afford an art teacher."

Because of the nature of Witte Memorial Museum exhibits, the emphasis of school visits is chiefly on natural history and history.

The transportation of children is difficult because of the administrative attitude. "We don't want our children to go off on picnic junkets." The Director of the museum expressed an interest in Smithsonian Institution exhibits. He proposes to arrange an exhibit, "The Head in Art," with an ethnological orientation.

The Junior League conducts its own program of slide lectures in the schools using material from the museum independent of the museum staff.

A museum volunteer program brings art history talks to the junior and senior high schools. Museum art slides are available to all teachers at all grade levels without fee.

The Women's Art League arranges occasional general art exhibits.

Brooks Memorial Art Gallery, Memphis, Tenn., 5 May 1965

Children's Gallery exhibit, a display arranged by the Art League for the sixth grade level to demonstrate basic design principles. The exhibit remains all year to allow the entire sixth grade pupil population to visit once during the year.

The museum is operated by the Municipal Park Commission. Various ladies' groups are active in different aspects of the operation.

The Director is interested in a special program, "an alphabet of design," for grades two to five and intends to enlist the cooperation of the teachers to establish the program in the schools. The program is intended to demonstrate basic design principles through colored reproductions of paintings with emphasis on the emotional content. In certain cases, details of originals would be enlarged for purposes of illustrating such elements as line, shape, and value.

The Director would prefer animated television to demonstrations in the school.

The Director feels a need for closer cooperation with schools. "Children are helped more by piping art programs into schools than by museum visits."

Small staff and a lack of money inhibit museum–school relations.

A craft show, designed by the museum, was used little in the schools except by a handful of interested teachers.

Birmingham Museum of Art, Birmingham, Ala., 6 May 1965

The museum exhibit policy consists of four parts:

I. Two or three exhibitions assembled each year by the staff for the general public interest, but which schools can use, e.g., Mexican exhibit; a group of modern paintings and crafts along with pre-Colombian examples.

II. Local shows sponsored by the Arts Association: one, a juried show, the other open. Also the Alabama Watercolor Society, a national invitational show.

III. Cooperating exhibits, e.g., State Fair Grounds exhibit.

IV. An intermittent series of local one-man shows to exhibit the work of professionals teaching locally.

Despite this emphasis on professional teachers, schools are still apathetic. Each principal is largely autonomous and the art supervisor can be effective only if the principal is interested.

The Director of the museum feels that efforts so far have had only a slight influence on the total attitude toward art education in the schools.

City transportation is privately owned. Union drivers cannot easily transfer to charter buses; therefore, municipal visits depend on car pools, walking, or other means. Some county schools have transportation, but there is apathy toward museum visits during school hours. Forty volunteers are taught by the staff to make package lectures using thirty to forty slides selected from the Carnegie 5000-slide set owned by the museum. These lectures generally are given in art, home economics, and American history. Exhibits to serve as a follow-up in schools and also at museum are highly desirable, but money and staff are needed to implement such a program. Saturday programs for sixth graders cannot reach all the children in a year—from 150 to 300 children attend each Saturday. Seniors from Birmingham Southern College serve as docents. Children are shown films on art theory and are then given a tour of the museum. A minute and a half orientation precedes these visits on "The Nature of the Museum—The Value of Man-made Fragile Objects with Caution as to Behavior."

The effect of these visits is observed in increased Sunday attendance by children, often with parents. The museum opens Thursday evenings. The Director would like to include other evenings, but staff and money are not adequate presently.

There is difficulty in borrowing good originals for a sufficiently long period to be educationally effective; however, the Director feels that original work is of prime importance and does not book panel exhibits.

Alabama artists act as circuit riders to rural schools using slides relating to the museum. There is a need for simple exhibits to accompany them, such as "Crayon Etching" or "Style Contrasts Between a Pre-Colombian Pot, a Tanagra Figure, and an American Indian Pot."

The Educational Council at Auburn distributes suitcase exhibits (folding exhibits mounted on six-foot stands). These deal with design principles illustrated with one or two original objects. The response of the children depends on the quality of their guide rather than on the subject matter of the exhibit.

Museum volunteers take a six-week course, three lectures per week, to work with eleventh-grade American history classes. Teacher certificates require very little art experience and teacher understanding is weak. Some volunteers carry into the schools original examples from their own homes—i.e., early American pewter and fabrics.

There is a need for good films on basic principles. Television programs concentrate too much on "how to do it."

Highlights of Recent Developments in Birmingham Since My Interview

A new Superintendent of the city schools seems interested in improving the art experience.

Twelve schools have established summer schools on the largest scale ever through Title I of the Elementary and Secondary Education Act of 1965, including music and art instruction.

A cooperative proposal between city schools, the museum, the museum Art Education Council and Auburn University has been filed under Title III of the ESE Act of 1965.

Active participation of the Negro PTA in Saturday tours and a widening interest on the part of this group in the museum.

The apathy of the schools is gradually being overcome by the constant dissemination of information given on tours and by slide program given at the schools. Evidence for this is that forty volunteers spoke to more than 12,000 children in American history and art classes, 1965–1966, upon request.

During the past year, of 15,000 school children invited to the museum, 10,000 actually came.

Two teacher workshops were oversubscribed.

Arkansas Arts Center, Little Rock, Ark., 7 May 1965

There are no special exhibits designed for school education except for an annual juried show of children's work.

Children's field trips to the museum are preceded in the auditorium with orientation talks and films. Teachers are urged to move slowly through the galleries to allow time for looking. On departure, children are given a souvenir, usually a colored postcard.

The Center attempts to relate, where possible, family participation in the museum exhibits, concerts and theatre, children's theatre, especially the dance.

State colleges and universities have good art departments, but graduates tend to leave the state for lack of opportunity and good teachers are scarce.

The State Department of Education provides no leadership and legislators are generally not interested in art.

There is no art supervisor below the junior high school level. Elementary school teachers cannot teach art and only in Little Rock are there art teachers in the junior and senior high schools. Hence there is practically no art program in the schools with which the museum can cooperate.

A three-credit course at the University of Little Rock has recently been established to provide art training for teachers. Also, working with the University of Little Rock, the museum is helped by fifteen BFA candidates working with Saturday classes for children.

An experimental children's theatre program is coordinated with two- and three-dimensional experiences—painting and sculpture. This, then, is integrated with kinesthetic and intellectual analysis of relationships between movement, sound, and writing in order to broaden perception in all these areas.

Strong support of the Junior League, beginning in 1958, has now been withdrawn, but members of the Art Center Committee and the Fine Arts Club provide volunteers who serve as docents and in other capacities. They buy from various exhibits and are becoming influential collectors.

Based on the Commonwealth of Virginia precedent, thirty rural chapters have been organized throughout the state. Ten art center members in a given community constitute a chapter. A regional craft exhibit is in the planning stage.

A workshop program has been organized in a dozen towns to teach basic design and pottery. Sixteen teachers circulate to these workshops in their spare time at thirty dollars a day.

Exhibits are sent to monthly chapter meetings consisting of fifteen to thirty objects, e.g., nineteenth-century American paintings, twentieth-century American paintings, films, and a bibliography. Chapters are urged to relate the exhibits to local school programs.

An Artmobile tours the entire state. Exhibits are programmed two years in advance and include Barbizon painting, Impressionism, and Folk Art from the Rockefeller Collection in Williamsburg. Reaction to the latter: "What do you send us this stuff for? We can do it ourselves." Chapter members serve as hostesses when the Artmobile arrives. Film strips, printed material, and radio and press releases precede the Artmobile arrival by four weeks. Community reaction varies: one principal, seeing a modest nude in a landscape said: "Cover up that picture or the children won't go."

Des Moines Art Center, Des Moines, Iowa, 9 September 1965

The permanent collection and special exhibits are designed for adults but schools make use of them.

The major educational effort is centered around the Junior Gallery under the supervision of the museum's Department of Education which operates with seventy-five volunteers.

Over the past four years, thematic exhibitions directly related to the curricula of several grade levels have been installed in the Junior Gallery. Primitive culture was symbolized by a reproduction of the Lascaux caves scaled to the size of children; the House of the Pharaohs was constructed for children to go into; the Greek Temple was built to correlate with ancient history.

High school pupils helped with the construction of these Junior Museum exhibits. Younger children brought their parents to "watch Greece grow."

The Junior League pays for much of this work. Special committees work on different aspects. They also help to plan and design panel exhibits which are sent to the schools. These exhibits deal mostly with basic design topics and are shown in halls or classrooms. Pupils respect these exhibits. There is no problem of vandalism, although packaging and transportation are still problems.

The Greek Temple was constructed in connection with Greek Week with various programs appealing to different levels. Similar to previous intensive programs, this week consisted of five afternoons for grades five to seven. Activities consisted of designing pottery, discussing mythology and/or the functions of the temple, theatre masks, and the life of a Greek boy and girl. A theatre performance, "Perseus," was given by children. As a consequence of these activities, the culture of the age "was put into the children's heads through their involvement."

In connection with these general topics, the Junior Museum staff suggests to the city libraries books which can be featured while the activity is in progress.

The Junior Museum activity (in no way related to the museum's permanent collections and only occasionally amplified by loan exhibitions) is paralleled by parent–child workshops on Sunday afternoons. These are open to anyone up to the limit of the space available. Children who come to such programs for the first time adapt themselves readily to the new situation; not so their parents who take time to overcome awkwardness.

Creative activities often start with stories such as *Alice in Wonderland,* or *The Wizard of Oz.* Toward the end of the story, a staff member unexpectedly appears in some costume, such as the Mad Hatter, whereupon there is a scramble to make impromptu costumes out of paper or fabrics which are available. Children are encouraged to take the lead in such activities.

Nearly 11,000 children are offered guided tours through the Art Center each year. The Educational Department of the Center sends monthly bulletins to the school teachers. ("The teachers are learning.") The Board of Education would like Artmobiles to supplement the school Bookmobile. Plans are being laid to teach art history and give this course the same credit as history, but the project still needs state accreditation.

A summer program of six weeks brings more than one hundred underprivileged high school children to the Center. These children are selected by city welfare agencies. The Art Center pays the bussing cost—twenty-five dollars each trip. Parents will not take the responsibility of driving students. Visits are twice a week for an hour and a quarter each time. Drawing, painting, print making and crafts are the activities.

The Center's educational staff trains guides. There is an art survey course with assigned reading for them, given from October to May.

The Center serves as the source for a television social studies program which could use Smithsonian Institution help.

Slater Memorial Museum, New London, Conn., 8 October 1965

The Slater Memorial Museum is a department of Norwich Free Academy which, since its founding in the mid-nineteenth century has maintained its independent status. All Norwich High School pupils who elect art receive instruction from the museum staff of ten teachers. Fees are paid by the School Board. Pupils from other neighborhoods pay individually.

The emphasis of all special exhibits is on aesthetic quality which "suffers if exhibitions are oriented too closely with academic subjects. The worst art exhibitions are those attempting to correlate with academic subjects."

"Too often teachers bring their pupils before a work of art, such as a Dutch seventeenth-century still life, and have nothing better to say about it than 'What kinds of vegetables do you see in the painting?' "

The permanent collections (examples of Western European art, Medieval, Renaissance and some later, as well as an Oriental collection, and full-scale reproductions of Classical sculpture) work well for teaching.

"Pupil visits, whether in art, history, English, or science classes, depend on the interest of the individual teacher." Notices of special exhibits are sent to all teachers in the high school. Many who bring their classes have a follow-up when back in the classroom.

"The da Vinci exhibit was aesthetically good and appealed to many. More exhibits of like quality are needed." The cost of travelling exhibits is a deterrent to frequent borrowing. The annual exhibition budget is $2,500. "Inexpensive art exhibits with a broader outlook than local artists' shows are needed."

Docents link examples of the permanent collection by using historical references, but the emphasis is principally on the work of art itself.

Boise Art Gallery, Boise, Idaho, 3 November 1965

The Junior League has helped develop the Art Center by gifts of money both for exhibitions and purchases. Originally the amount was $300; this coming year $2,500.

With a population of 63,000, Boise has twenty-nine District Schools—seven junior high, three senior high.

The Junior League is important in all aspects of the Art Center. In 1966–1967, the Secretary of the Board of the Center will also be President of the League.

The most important recent exhibition for educational purposes has been "History of Idaho Art."

Art Center work with the schools is intensive yet opportune; e.g., an annual junior high school award; a certain amount of work is carried on with the audio–visual department of the school system; small exhibits are taken to the schools. Without bus facilities, transportation costs to the museum are prohibitive.

If exhibits of original art were to be put in classrooms, supervision would be a problem. A slide series of objects to be seen in the Art Center which could be circulated to the schools would be useful.

There is still a question whether it is more important to take museum exhibits to the school under museum supervision, or the children to the museum. It depends on teacher attitudes. "Do you bring art to the teacher and hope the teacher will give the children an art experience?"

It has been proposed to have interested students become docents at the Center.

The involvement of local educational television is important for the Center's work, especially programs on weekend mornings from 7:00 to 8:00 a.m. The problem with television is who will "bell the cat in a small community?" This question was raised with reference to commercials, cartoons, etc., which are relayed over the air from distant sources.

Toledo Museum of Art, Toledo, Ohio, 1 March 1966

All money derived from museum memberships is devoted to educational activities. It is felt that in this way the museum is identified as a community enterprise.

The educational effort has been farsighted for a quarter of a century and, despite the floating population characteristic of Toledo, there has been an increased awareness of the museum's civic importance, in the opinion of the Director. The evidence for this is a 300-percent increase in membership during the past decade.

The museum has relied largely on its own permanent collection for public school education. Nevertheless, it has found the Smithsonian Institution's and similar teaching exhibits useful in the school lobby; e.g., Twelve Churches, Craftsmen of the City, and Pre-history of the Great Lakes. These exhibits were selected as being of interest to pupils of all ages, and the variety of topics was not necessarily didactic.

The museum is an affiliate of the University of Toledo. Special high school pupils, recommended by teachers, can register for a university course. Teachers can also get university credit through museum work.

Television teaching has not been found effective to date. The medium has been used chiefly to announce timely programs. Museum slides serve better in the schools.

A general policy should be to take the child to the museum because objects which can be sent to the school are not aesthetically good and, therefore, not effective enough.

From a very complex program which has been operating for over a quarter of a century, conducted in collaboration with the public schools, certain significant statistics emerge. There are fourteen full time instructors weekdays and three part time. These are supplemented by five more Saturday instructors. These people take care of one child every twenty-two seconds during the time the museum is officially open.

City schools, grades one to three, pay approximately six visits a year to the museum. Each teacher knows in advance the nature of the visit and correlates her work so as to anticipate it. Upon arrival at the museum, the essential experience revolves around answering the question, "What is a Museum?"

Grades four, five, and six visit the museum eight times a year—four times for an art program and four times for music. The museum's yearly schedule in some forty schools reaches almost 80 percent of the student body.

In every case, visits are focused on a specific topic—e.g., how a painter works. A general art survey program is provided for grades six, seven, and eight which visit the museum twice a year to study such topics as ancient art and European painting.

Although all programmed visits are studied in advance with an outline, the curatorial staff seeks to change the subjects from year to year.

Distant schools come on all day trips in the spring. There are so many schools that the museum instructors meet a week in advance of a visit to plan their routes and avoid conflict when walking through the exhibits.

The school district art supervisor and assistant supervisor have previously served on the museum staff, thereby providing personnel coordination.

The museum staff would like to see more art history and appreciation taught in the schools as preparation for visits.

A heavy Saturday program gives certain children more depth.

The two small children of the museum's Director of Education said to him at home, "You must come to the museum and let us show you what we saw yesterday."

Cincinnati Art Museum, Cincinnati, Ohio, 2 March 1966

Although the Cincinnati Art Museum was one of the pioneers in special exhibits to instruct adults as well as children in basic design principles, the present emphasis is on the use of the collections themselves with interpretation appropriate to each grade level. Although third graders frequently ask their teachers, "When can we go again?" fifth and sixth graders prove to be the best age for general visits. These children have a reasonable background and have not acquired the inhibitions which the seventh and eighth graders display. Also, the museum can work with one class teacher at this elementary level; from the seventh grade on studies are compartmented and too many teachers are involved to make visits readily feasible. The Junior League works with the sixth-grade social study classes, using the museum collections to illustrate the topic, "Background of American Freedom."

Docents with a B.A. degree have intensive training under the Director of the museum, along with school art supervisors. This includes required reading in art theory and history. Their performance is evaluated at the end of the second year. The Board of Education has provided a coordinator between school, museum, the library, and other cultural organizations.

Recently the docents organized a charter flight to Europe, coordinated with the museum collections, in order to understand them better.

Seventh, eighth, and nineth graders have been brought in buses from as far away as Louisville. They were briefed beforehand well enough so that they could identify style, such as a painting by Corot.

Taft Museum, Cincinnati, Ohio, 2 March 1966

A teaching exhibition on the nature of color at the Taft Museum brought science teachers into an art environment. In connection with the exhibit, a special teacher's meeting led to student visits relating science to art.

Buses from Covington (a distress area across the Ohio River) normally cost forty-eight dollars a trip, but underprivileged students are brought free. "Everyone who can leaves Covington."

Usually outlying communities without an art supervisor (few have one) do not respond to the museum announcements.

"Not all classes can go to the museum and the schools need exhibits."

The teachers "would like to see special galleries in the museum devoted to educating all ages. Painting and sculpture should be installed low. Objects should be touchable and a child motivated to return by feeling the area belongs to him."

"A museum environment provides a flow of culture which is not sensed in the classroom."

The Taft Museum is in a slum area and children have been encouraged to drop in at will. A great many do so. However, urban clearance is beginning and the museum may lose one of its most effective opportunities, namely, to aid poor children informally on their own volition. "One small boy came with his battlescarred cat. When asked why he was coming to the Taft, he replied, 'I want him to see how nice it is.'"

"Art is limited only by teachers who don't know what to do."

Dayton Art Institute, Dayton, Ohio, 3 March 1966

"No exhibits are sent to the schools because works of art of requisite quality to provide proper seeing are too precious to circulate."

On the other hand, the Board of Education has purchased travelling exhibits related to social studies which are circulated at the request of the teachers. These consist of topics such as masks, fabrics, and varieties of ornament.

"There needs to be a coordination between art and art seen as social studies. The latter is merely a function which explains the cultural relevance of a style rather than its aesthetic quality."

"Adults assume children can't see. The museum brings all ages, from kindergarten through high school, describing the total range of its collections."

Most school visits are "once in a lifetime"; however, requests for a second visit on the part of the teachers are growing.

"The museum would like to prepare 'canned' presentations for the schools. Title III might help."

Dayton school officials are rethinking their own program. "Does every class have to meet every day? There is a current move to open the high school schedule to take advantage of cultural resources such as the Art Institute."

"We hope that Title I may help to provide buses for children who come from destitute families and hire a staff that will work with the museum."

"From the museum's point of view, there is not enough time to orient new teachers. The children come with open eyes, but teachers don't."

"School administrators are afraid to make commitments to the museum because of their own lack of experience and ignorance."

The numbers of pupils from grades four, five, and six throughout the city cannot be accommodated by the museum staff. Pupils are selected by their teachers for visits and are asked to report in class to those who did not attend.

The reports of the children provide evidence of their initial interest and this could be importantly enlarged by means of television. Although in practice an art museum is an upperclass institution, school visits can open doors. The evidence is that Sunday attendance reveals no class distinctions.

The teacher load is always too heavy. Teacher seminars conducted by the museum once a month are sparsely attended. There is a question as to whether the Board of Education might increase participation by offering credit.

Recently, pupil drawing and painting in the galleries have been transferred to the art school. This includes three hundred to four hundred Saturday morning students. The school provides one half day of training, five days a week, for recommended, talented high school students. This group numbers between ten and twelve.

The museum tours are provided by docents who have had two years of intensive briefing in art history and in various visual experiences.

Montclair Art Museum, Montclair, N. J., 9 March 1966

No exhibit is ever labelled *educational*. With changing techniques, all exhibits contribute to an interpretation of art in life. There are no pressures and the term art appreciation is avoided.

In general, the museum serves northern New Jersey, but Newark classes visit because of the American Indian and Japanese Doll collections which tie into social studies classes.

A given school child normally visits the museum as a member of a school tour no more than twice in his entire school career.

The Junior League supplies docents, but has little to do with the program otherwise. On the average, there are fifteen League members serving, whose term of service lasts between five and ten years. They then become Trustees and candidates for museum committee work.

Outlying schools visit the museum on schedule, but because there are no local school buses and the distance generally is too far to walk, city pupils visit infrequently during school hours. However, on occasion the Junior League helps with local bus service.

Friday afternoon visits are discouraged. The children are tired and the teacher comes only because she is at a loss as to what else to do.

Docents take a four-month course meeting once a week for two hours, plus outside reading. They become involved with art theory and research, are taught to analyze objects of art and learn from observing experienced docents at work. Docent staff meetings are held twice a month. Special emphasis is laid on the need to guide each visiting group according to its own needs and interests. With aid from the Sears Roebuck Foundation, Junior League volunteers take slides to the schools which focus chiefly on social studies. The Junior League also has it own extension service to the schools with two docents working from the museum.

A small number of "mini-shows" custom designed in response to school requests provide contact with pupils and teachers to stimulate visits to the museum. These shows are largely from the American Indian collection made ready for installation by the classroom teacher, who follows diagrams which accompany each exhibit. Other locked-case exhibits are for installation in corridors and libraries. Announcements of the availability of such exhibits are sent two months in advance. Original quality, as opposed to reproductions, is stressed throughout.

Brooklyn Museum, Brooklyn, N. Y., 10 March 1966

The museum represents itself as a "tool for teachers" and, in order to supplement the small staff of the education department, has offered in-service courses for school teachers, thirty hours during a fifteen-week period for two credits for a master's degree. The content of the course is related to the nature of the various collections and also involves workshop experience in painting, sculpture, block printing, etc. Classes are held after school and limited to twenty-five. Participants are chiefly elementary school classroom teachers who have had no art experience in their teacher training. Occasionally, high school teachers register. There has been little opportunity to study how effective the program is.

Formerly, there was a guided tour of museum collections for larger teacher groups, but currently, because of lack of time and staff, the tours are not being given.

Three paid professional docents are kept busy with 14,000 children per month who come by appointment. Volunteers have not been found reliable. Bus transportation is free. Fourth, fifth, and sixth graders comprise the majority of visitors. High schools are difficult to schedule because of the subject matter arrangement of the high school curriculum, but high school students visit the museum independently.

Individual children may apply for junior membership. The activities of this group include treasure hunts and studio demonstrations. Each member must sign a pledge to respect the museum. There are no dues and membership is in no way connected with adult membership. A junior member may visit the museum unaccompanied by an adult. Older students are given junior aide jobs, such as helping with art classes and the lending library service.

Summer trips provide an effective means of enlisting junior interest.

About one thousand children visitors each day cannot be taken care of by docents. Teachers are given tape recorders to wear which describe certain exhibits as they walk through with their classes.

Albright–Knox Art Gallery, Buffalo, N. Y., 23 March 1966

Proximity of an elementary school allows classes to visit at the will of teachers.

The well-to-do residential area in which the school and museum are situated presupposes parental interest in the cultural environment which influences their children.

Elsewhere, very little bus money is available and regular buses are busy except during mid-morning. Accordingly, most visits occur during the 10:00 a.m. period. The small staff makes appointments difficult. Visiting classes are predominately sixth grade using the museum exhibits to amplify social studies. They come at this grade level "because the fifth grade goes to the philharmonic."

When high school classes come to the museum, it is rather with an emphasis on the humanities. Often these children ask their teachers to meet them at the museum on Saturdays.

A new, ungraded school for low IQ (50–75) children, who were previously kept at home, plans to bring small groups to museum exhibits to stimulate responses because "children feel secure when drawing."

Encouraged by borrowing colored reproductions (Chagall, Renoir, etc.) from the museum education collection, an independent school (Nichols) has begun its own collection of Western New York artists by purchase and gift.

A need was seen by the head of the English Department of Nichols School to organize museum classes for English and history teachers from public, as well as private, schools so that they might teach art appreciation. In his own experience, Albright Gallery has been an important influence.

Although the museum's education department has been called on to give talks in schools (principally seventh grade), formal follow-up visits are rare for want of bus transportation.

"Art and the museum are not identified with school study in the minds of many parents. Children become aware of this and when challenged as to museum visits say, 'We've already been to the art gallery.' "

Teachers do not like the rigid pattern demanded by docents who often do not take advantage of pupil interest and are annoyed because "they didn't get upstairs." Contrarily, docents object to teacher attitudes, "Now, will you explain why this junk is here?" Or, again, "You can't talk about that, we haven't studied it yet." One combined teacher–docent feels the need to look in depth at a few objects rather than to survey casually.

Saturday and summer museum classes, including parents, are effective, but reach a small proportion of the students. "Could Albright provide a program for artist-speakers in schools?"

Church groups ask to be taken to the museum on Sundays. "One minister is still trying to figure out Mark Rothko."

1. This paper is a preliminary version of what will ultimately be a final report to the U.S. Office of Education.

Reasons for Concern

Some Problems in Museum Education

RICHARD GROVE
Arts and Humanities Program
Office of Education

Anyone who sets out to talk about museums is instantly faced with the task of trying to figure out just what sort of creature this is. It is a nearly unique peculiarity. A hospital is a hospital. A library is a library. A rose is a rose. But a museum is Colonial Williamsburg, Mrs. Wilkerson's Figure Bottle Museum, the Museum of Modern Art, the Sea Lion Caves, the American Museum of Natural History, the Barton Museum of Whiskey History, The Cloisters, and Noell's Ark Chimpanzee Farm and Gorilla Show.

This diversity is, in a sense, a strength. No stultifying standardization here. All things to all men. But it is also a handicap, because museums suffer from a case of blurred identity. What is fat, thin, large, small, good, bad, young, old, has many heads, eats money, is fuzzy, gives itself with joyous abandon, and is loved by absolutely everyone?

Museum men conduct fund-raising campaigns and order guards to turn off the gallery lights as soon as the visitor has moved on. That evening, they bid fiercely against each other for a 2.4 million-dollar Rembrandt. They plead for tax money, and their cries ring out from vast, old, temple-like structures, aristocratic and intimidating, or perhaps from one of those cool, elegant, vaguely disdainful buildings by Philip Johnson. You and I know the reasons for these apparent contradictions. Does anyone else—the public, foundation executives, congressmen?

If we persist in pursuing museum identity, we are led into a land of mirrors where nothing is what it seems and the inhabitants call themselves "the museum profession." I am myself accustomed to the use of this term because it makes me feel important and substantial and it impresses the uninitiated, but there are some matters which have been disturbing me and I think I shall say them right out, because this should be a place for questioning as well as celebration.

Is this not a soft profession, fearful of establishing standards, curiously reluctant to discuss underlying issues? By selection and training polite, diplomatic, and conciliatory, museum men too rarely encourage dissent or arrange occasions for the open exchange of views about bothersome issues. They say "don't rock the boat," forgetting that one of the characteristics of a moving boat is that it rocks occasionally. A case in point was the debate about museum accreditation which crackled ever so briefly a few years ago. Suddenly, there came a silence, which continues to this day, broken only by a tiny sound . . . like a bomb ticking.

An essential determinant of personality is development through time. Few professions made up of such literate people with such a stake in the past have shown so little interest in their own past. No one has written a full-scale, irreverent, probing history of museums in the United States, tying in social, economic, cultural, and political factors. Until this happens, an extraordinarily revealing and meaningful chapter in our educational and intellectual history will be missing.

As a matter of fact, debilitating bibliophobia is pandemic. An outsider might expect to find on the museum director's shelf such books as the following: *Handbook for Museum Trustees, The Museum Education Department, Training the Museum Volunteer, Museums and Taxes,* or *Fund Raising and Museums.* Do not bother to look. They have not been written; articles, yes, books, no. And Laurence Vail Coleman's *Museum Buildings, College and University Museums,* and *Manual for Small Museums,* have been allowed to become outmoded and out of print.

At national and regional meetings, museum people talk tirelessly about what they are doing. Only infrequently do they discuss publicly *why* they do what they do, what principles guide, what theories inform. Meetings are not organized around issues and the shadows are filled with problems waiting for someone to speak their names.

What about museums and the federal government, what stance, what welcome, what defense? State government? What will the museum of 1981 be like? How do museum personnel get trained? Is the present training situation satisfactory? What about that aging Code of Ethics for Museum Workers? Does it require updating? Why has the Office of Education's Cooperative Research Program received only a handful of proposals from museums? Does museum education evade rational inquiry? What is the role of museums in implementing the new education legislation, with its uncompromising goal of equal educational opportunity for all? What is our present duty toward disadvantaged populations? Is it enough to merely have the doors open to all? And, by the way, how is it that we remain a substantially unintegrated profession? And what should we do about it?

Any one of these questions might do for a starter.

Museums receive dangerously automatic acceptance. An Anti-museum League is an absurd thought, but if it formed, it would surely be hissed and stoned. You can go a long way with such an advantage, maybe far enough to get laws passed and to gain massive support—maybe. On the other hand, would it hurt to face issues and fix standards?

So much for this little essay in museopathology, but perhaps these matters help explain some recent and somewhat puzzling phenomena. Within the past eight months or so, the new education legislation began to have a considerable impact on the museum world. In effect, it urges a closer rapprochement of museums and schools. Both are experiencing a slight discomfort.

Museum men feel that this legislation fails to recognize them properly. They are surprised by what seems to them the lawmakers' lack of perspicacity. Are museums not an unparalleled and mighty educational resource? Have they not developed their own enormously effective ways of teaching? Why are they not directly eligible for federal aid? Why should they have to go, hat in hand, to the schools, perhaps only to suffer an uncomprehending and chilly rebuff?

School administrators are suspicious and ask what kind of educational institutions are museums, anyhow? They are quite outside the establishment. They award few grades or certificates. And, worst of all, they tend to prefer silent, mutely questioning artifacts to golden words. How wrongheaded can you get?

There is a good deal of quiet humor in this situation, for, in a certain way, U.S. museums are the creation of—along with the Internal Revenue Service—the schools. If the schools were suddenly to attend to certain neglected areas, the educational function of museums would alter drastically, diminish, and become something of an anachronism—each man his own docent. "Go away," says the school. "I'd rather like to, but I can't," the museum replies. "We are bound together. You see, I am your conscience."

It is a bittersweet moment. Proud, aware of accomplishment and genius, jilted, museum directors sulk among their books and specimens and pictures. But now the school administrators cast covert and curious glances from behind the tassels on their mortarboards. How do museums accomplish so much learning, accompanied by so much joy? How do they maintain so much flexibility? Could there be some secret? And so suspicion is paradoxically mixed with suppressed admiration. Indeed, many educators pay strange tribute to the museum mystique. They think it beneficial to children to simply march them through a museum at top speed and in as straight a line as possible, considering that those exhibits keep blocking the way.

The main cause of this drama is the Elementary and Secondary Education Act of 1965—more specifically, Titles I and III. Both make direct funds available only to schools. Both call for activities pioneered by museums: special education programs for the disadvantaged and supplementary educational services.

Title I is, it seems to me, the most deeply problematical. Museums have a long and honorable history of responding sensitively and imaginatively to the needs of the underprivileged. But Title I asks for more. Much more. It tugs at the conscience like a responsibility. It is part of that body of recent legislation which includes the war on poverty and the large-scale effort to provide equal educational opportunity. This legislation is creative and just and it adds up to a national movement, revolutionary in its implications.

I am, of course, aware of the fact that many museums are presently engaged in Title I projects, benefiting multitudes. Are there museums which might be involved, but are not? The pressures, the demands for attention and services that come to bear on the museum tend to be from one direction. The museum is in tune with these voices. Many of the owners of these voices are the museum's donors. The disadvantaged send no spokesmen, no emissaries. And they are not represented on the museum board.

Once there was a museum. Maybe it was an art museum. It was built in what once was an attractive and open location, and it served an earlier aristocracy of wealth and connoisseurship. Now the entire pattern has changed. It is surrounded by an urban morass. It knows only middle-class values, so it tailors its entire program to the requirements of the white, middle-class suburbs. "Our doors are open to all," it says, "but slum kids and their parents do not come to us. Buses arrive in a steady stream from the suburbs, but our neighbors, oddly, avoid us." End of short, preposterous fable.

Skill has to be employed if the museum is not to seem in and of another world, remote and meaningless; but museums are peculiarly equipped to reach educationally deprived people. Museums are full of the finest things made by men, dramatically presented in a total environment removed from the ordinary, aesthetically ordered, and subtly demanding. Indeed, few more stimulating educational environments have ever been created.

It is easy to say that Title I is the problem of the schools. They are the eligible applicants, so let them take care of the whole mess. Or let them come to us and ask for cooperation and we will decide how much to give and on what terms. We have our own troubles. Yet, museum professionals have a profound responsibility to rise to this challenge. It is worthy of their best effort.

But if Title I is problematical, Title III is, so far, a triumph only very slightly tinged with comedy from the museum viewpoint. Across the land, schools and museums are working together in a productive partnership. Only here and there is there a trouble spot. Encouraged by the Office of Education's brisk and bracing call for the innovative and the exemplary, planning groups set to work, their imaginations on fire. True, there is a museum across town, but why involve them? Museums are open and public. You just walk in. People work there, but they seem—mysteriously—very busy.

What if we were to create a new kind of supplementary educational center, a sort of super materials center? What if we represent the various arts? Let us hire highly qualified specialists. What if we stock the place with all kinds of pictures and books and scientific and historical realia? Send for an architect. Flushed with the pleasure of discovery, they apply to the government for funds. Are we cruel enough to tell them? They have invented the museum.

Although I have made some critical observations about my colleagues trying to act as a group, there are other things they do superbly. They know how to run a museum. They invented discovery learning a long time ago. They think of education as something beyond a torrent of words. And they know the value to everyone concerned of their independence.

But changed national conditions now call on the museums not only for more of what they have been doing, but also for new emphases, new reflexes, new abilities. I submit: 1) that the crisis in education is, willy-nilly, a crisis in museums; 2) that passivity is not an appropriate response; and 3) that initiative and multi-level action are called for. Individual museums may assess local conditions to determine what role they can play and discuss it with educators. The concerned independence of museums is a vantage point. But museums need a realistic understanding of the actual, daily problems of the schools and a sense of educational priorities. Then, if government-financed programs are not taking advantage of museum resources, or if those resources are being duplicated, the museum has an obligation to say so publicly. Compelling arguments will be heard.

Regional and state museum associations can perform a similar function for entire sections of the country. Educational priorities are determined by educational leaders. Are these leaders informed about museum resources in their region? Are they sufficiently alert to the values which museums stand for? What do these leaders have to say about regional educational problems?

The state arts council movement, spurred by the National Foundation on the Arts and Humanities, has now created, or is about to create, an arts council in every state. These councils are charged, among other things, with overall state planning. How may museums cooperate with them for mutual benefit?

At the national level, museum representatives may view the scene in the entire country, determine national policies, and communicate them to the field. They may discuss museum educational problems and strengths with the top officials responsible for the administration of federal educational legislation.

It would be unwise to wait much longer.

Some Thoughts About Secondary Schools and Museums

RUTH ZUELKE
Art Coordinator
Birmingham Public Schools,
Birmingham, Michigan

It has been enlightening to read of the keen interest extended to the arts and the exposure to the arts of students in our schools. As I have read the numerous papers, I have felt a mounting concern on the part of the museums as to how they can serve this interest best. I can only speak from a limited viewpoint, but I feel it imperative to record several thoughts for discussion. To the question, "Should we not leave the education of children in the arts to the art educators in the schools?" my reply would be: "Please—you must help us and show us your ways." The following are some of my reasons.

Museums as we know them have really existed for only a half century. Art educators, too, until just around the turn of this century, have had little or no means for relating objects of art to actual classroom goals and procedures. Library shelves still house textbooks on art appreciation containing biographies of individual artists with six or seven poorly printed black-and-white reproductions and the writer's interpretation of the works. Can you imagine Raphael's "Abraham and the Three Angels" enjoyed in its carbon print, size four by six inches? Art education, in other words, has had few art object resources, or quality reproductions of art objects, and even less academic preparation.

A fairly recent nationwide study reveals that the usual art history requirement for undergraduate art educators is no more than six semester hours. With no nationally accepted curriculum requirements in teacher education, the content or quality of this so fleeting exposure is impossible even to guess at. Moreover, art educators are usually matriculated from their teacher training institutions as equipped to teach in *any* grade of our elementary and secondary schools. I smile when I realize how naive all of us in art education and in secondary administration are when we so readily accept the idea that any art teacher can teach any art technique or facet of appreciation to any youngster. In contrast, it is interesting to note that other areas of the school curriculum are becoming so highly specialized that teachers teach only certain levels of a subject and usually no more than one or two areas of the discipline.

Hugo Munsterberg, professor of psychology at Harvard University, took a broader view of art education than may have existed in 1904 when he wrote the following in his book, *The Principles of Art Education:* "Their entire school knowledge and surroundings train them for practical needs, for skill and achievement; that must be so, and it is well. Let them fight and run and pull and push, but let them never forget that the fight is not merely for fighting: we must aim for an end in which we can find satisfaction, repose, and happiness."[1]

We have changed the wording, but this is still one of the basic justifications for a program of art education in our schools. Undoubtedly teachers, in their school programs, attempt to create an atmosphere where students can create art, discuss art technique, and learn something of art's historical aspect. Unfortunately, the methods used often suffer in the transition from a laboratory for creating experiences to the study of art objects for their own sake. The straight lecture technique, which may emulate a revered art history professor, often does no more than transmit authoritative opinion and impose the teacher's values upon the students. Discovery–learning is often not related to this traditional component and teachers remain unaware that it is as relevant here as in the creative, productive experience which the field of art education has long been justifiably proud to provide.

When art curriculum materials are displayed at conferences, it is possible to find as many different art curriculum guides as there are conference participants. My personal reaction is one of determination to affirm one's freedom to gear a curriculum to the needs of the individual. This idea of meeting the needs of all students through guides has also created its own inherent obstacles.

The first problem arises when we have to decide who shall be the writers of these guidelines for teachers and the teaching of our students. The educational journals frequently state that the teachers must write the curriculum. One reason given is that it will be more easily accepted if they construct it to fit their needs. I wish all educators would question this reasoning in the area of the arts. This method of operation has brought about a vast wasteland in art education—not because of the quality of the effort expended, but because so much expertise has thus been placed in a situation of starting from scratch, when we have had so many resources in personnel and materials which could have saved so much time as well as set directions more clearly.

An unofficial curriculum has been widely adopted throughout the United States in the areas of math, science, and foreign languages. There have currently been wide reforms in the language arts and social studies. Acceptance has been widespread and steady even though it required an extensive retraining of teacher personnel. Improvisations gear the materials to meet situational needs. The writers of these materials have been selected for their outstanding proficiency in the subject itself, or their outstanding ability to teach it in the classroom.

I would like to see curriculum experts from the field of art education working with the experts in the museums. I would also like to see the artists of our society become resources as well. I think it is here where educational television and the film makers could help us. Not all our children will necessarily get to the museum—in spite of the fact one writer has discovered that there is no place in the United States mainland more than twenty-seven miles from a road.

Another need of prime importance is to discover the best means for schools and museums to work together in making their resource materials mutually available. The computer is as yet an untapped resource in art education, and its implications can be overwhelming.

In the area of catalog indexing it is easy to conceive of a project of collaboration to collect data—sources of knowledge about specific museums, artists, materials, techniques, terms, books, films, etc. Printed-out titles and codes, cross references, and accurately annotated bibliographies could direct any museum staff member or any art teacher to the troves of knowledge available through electronic searching. A centrally located film and visual rental storehouse could be "impulsed" and any teacher would have the working materials available in less than forty-eight hours, with the cost accounting handled on a deposit basis.

Whatever success we have known in the field of "art appreciation" can be attributed, I think, to the job the museum has done in evoking interest in students and teachers. Another rich source has been the commercial film. I might add it is not unusual to find John Canaday highly revered by secondary school art students. Unfortunately art education's film budget does not always get budget preference in our secondary schools. During the past three years, another film form has been made available, and this is the single concept cartridge film, a device which has the merit of being equally usable in museums or classrooms, by teacher or student, by an entire class or a single person.

Personal involvement is the key to success in any of these projects. If teachers of art are stimulated by in-service training, grants for travel and study (possibly a traveling seminar), and the ready availability of materials, then better teaching and learning will stand a much greater chance of being the result. Thanks to Title II of the National Elementary and Secondary School Education Act, we will probably see an almost immediate heightening of interest on the part of that small number of art educators who were fortunate enough to find school librarians who knew of the relevant books and visual materials which could be purchased with these funds. The 700's are too often a sparsely occupied space on the shelves.

These to me are the cold facts of life in the schools. In the light of them, I believe we should begin to extend toward art appreciation the same amount of time and money as we have toward other areas of the curriculum. We should begin to use the technological and human resources available, the experts in the museums combined with the educators—needs and know-how—to bring the appreciation and interpretation of art into more than casual acquaintanceship with students. It is heartening to think that action in this neglected area of education may be close at hand. My dream is of the day when it will be an accomplished objective.

1. Munsterberg, Hugo, *The Principles of Art Education,* New York, The Prang Educational Company, 1904, p. 113.

Methods of Presentation and Analysis

Exhibits: Interpretive, Under-Interpretive, Misinterpretive

*ABSOLUTES AND RELATIVE ABSOLUTES IN EXHIBIT TECHNIQUES**

ALMA S. WITTLIN
Radcliffe Institute for Independent Studies

The term "techniques" denotes manners of expert performance or procedures in any art or science. In everyday language the term is often degraded to a "bag of tricks"; to avoid any such connotation, I prefer to speak of *Exhibits as Means of Communication*—communication being the focal purpose I have in mind and procedures being the means to achieve it.

The "absolutes" in using exhibits as media of communication hinge on the fact that human beings are both the source and target of the process: of a chain reaction of output–input–output of knowledge that may be generated by an effective exhibit. Human senses and man's capacity for the processing of knowledge in his mind have both potentialities and limitations.

The qualification "relative absolutes" refers to the perception of people of the environment through the lenses of the culture in which they were born and reared, as well as of the subculture they represent. They interact with the environment in accordance with their perceptions.

Effective communication, by whatever medium, rests on principles allied to that particular medium and yet in many ways basic to all media alike. A poet may take greater liberties with grammar and syntax than the writer of a technical report, but the difference is only a matter of degree in the observance of generally accepted laws. Within this framework, individual styles have ample scope for expression. Communication in any style, however, is bound to suffer from breakdowns if it lacks a set of rules. Responses of viewers of experimental exhibits I have conducted over the years indicate that the potential of an exhibit for establishing an intended communication depends on the application of certain principles in the selection and presentation of materials, to a considerable degree irrespective of the subject matter dealt with. I am referring mainly to topics of science and technology, of archaeology and anthropology, although in some respects art exhibits could be included.

In order to understand and to appreciate a language, linguists study its origins and its characteristics at different times of development. There is also an *etymology of exhibits*. To provide a perspective for a few of the experimental exhibits of which I shall give an account, I propose first to consider briefly processes of communication by means of exhibits during past periods of history in which today's public museums have their roots, and secondly to sum up the main types of current exhibits as I see them. "The only use of a knowledge of the past is to equip us for the present."[1]

A GLIMPSE OF EXHIBITS FROM THE PAST AND THEIR FUNCTIONS

A woodcut of the year 1515 by the artist Altdorfer represents what was probably a typical medieval Treasure Chamber of a prince, in this particular case that of the Hapsburg princes of Austria.[2] Works of art and craftsmanship shaped in precious metals and studded with gems were periodically transferred from this storeroom to places of their actual use—reliquaries and vessels to churches, imperial insignia for ceremonial appearances of the potentate, and sumptuous plates for the master's table. The coined money in the open chest in the foreground of the picture emphasizes the function of the entire contents of the treasure chamber as a hoard of surplus wealth, which in an emergency could be sent to the mint and serve as means of exchange and of barter. The ancient Athenians used votive offerings and vessels from the treasuries in their temples to build ships for the battle at Salamis against the invading Persians and to fight the Peloponnesian War. Before standardized currency was widely accepted, in periods of primitive economy and of limited trade, hoards fulfilled the function of our contemporary banks.

To the individuals who were admitted to such hoards in private treasure chambers or in temples, or who viewed single objects on ceremonial occasions, each object was highly meaningful and relevant to their own lives. It exemplified their heroic ancestors and the might of the nation that sheltered them. It acted as an intellectual and emotional stimulant. The aesthetic qualities of many of the objects heightened the impact of the displays on viewers.

The well-known picture of the seventeenth century by the Flemish artist Teniers the son, now the property of the National Museum of Art in Vienna, shows Archduke Leopold Wilhelm of Hapsburg viewing paintings in his palace in Brussels, at the time the capital of a province of the Austrian empire.[3] Again we are seeing a storeroom from which works of art are taken periodically to the apartments of the owner. Selected artists who submitted sketches for future commissions were permitted to view their patrons' collections. Everybody admitted to this storeroom was a connoisseur of art, had the opportunity to become familiar with each single picture, and was, therefore, immune to the "visual noise" resulting from the crowding of the pictures. It was a favorable setting for an interaction of the paintings and the feedback of viewers.

Consider, on the other hand, a view of a gallery of paintings of the kings of France in their residence in the Louvre Palace.[4] The engraving of 1699 by an anonymous artist is kept at the Bibliothèque Nationale in Paris. Again, the arrangement is that of a storeroom where all space is used and where the viewers are a select company, courtiers and guests of the king. There is little impedance to the flow of communication between display and viewers, and among the viewers. The pictures represent topics familiar and important to them —portraits of French celebrities, scenes from the Bible, from history and mythology, with each painting contributing an informational detail or an emotional tone to the store of similar images in the viewers' minds. Being members of a homogeneous culture and subculture, they exchange observations which add to the impressions in the gallery. The margin of possible misunderstandings is small and the experience is likely to strengthen the feeling of identity and of stability of each individual and of the group. It reinforces directives toward an established pattern of life.

Let us now consider a few collections of scholars, of the late sixteenth and seventeenth centuries. Illustrations served as frontispieces of catalogs of the collections, sometimes lengthy works written by the owners.[5]

In one of them the Neapolitan naturalist Ferrante Imperato may be among the four men in his private museum, discussing some topic of natural history. The arrangement looks like a compromise between a storeroom and a reference library of objects. Another picture shows Signor Cospi of Bologna, one of the numerous amateur scientists of the seventeenth century, in his private museum. Still another illustration represents the collection of Olaf Worm, who is often referred to as a Dutchman but supposedly was a Dane. The catalog of his famous private museum was a popular textbook of the period.

In these and similar collections, the purpose was clearly defined. They were to serve as study materials for scholars. The function was reflected by both the selection of the specimens and their presentation. To persons whose minds were tuned to the messages, the communication issuing from each single specimen was intensely meaningful, and few other people are likely to have approached these exhibits. Indeed, according to the standards of present-day communication theory, every object on those crowded shelves is likely to have fulfilled a function of highest merit—to have contributed to the reduction of uncertainty in the minds of the beholders.

We have so far considered two lines of origin of the Public Museum —the Hoard and Storeroom collection and the collection in the style of a Reference Library of objects. Let us look at a third line of origin and decide on a term for it later. In the early eighteenth century the art treasures of the imperial house of Hapsburg were housed in a palace in Vienna known as the *Stallburg*. A preserved, illustrated catalog shows individual paintings by famous masters demoted to pieces of flamboyant covering for a great sweep of walls.[6] In keeping with the baroque style of art and architecture, the display proclaimed the might and wealth of the emperor; it dazzled the beholder and sapped his powers of rational thinking. Indeed, a paragraph in the catalog above this particular illustration warned people not to indulge in hasty judgments in matters beyond their knowledge and insight. Baroque style was largely a style of the Counter-Reformation; it was one of the means of the ancient catholic church in its struggle against Protestantism, and it became adopted by secular rulers opposed to the common man's questioning of established authority. In this sense the message issued by the imperial collections in the *Stallburg* was a facet of sophisticated propaganda in another Cold War.

The Cabinet of Frederick Ruysch of Amsterdam, a professor of anatomy and botany at the turn of the seventeenth to the eighteenth century, conveys a similarly propagandistic message. Note the double communication emitted by this Cabinet as represented in the frontispiece of the owner's scientific treatise *Opera Omnia*.[7] There is the voice of scholarship, but there is also the pitch of a clever salesman who uses sumptuous decoration and images taken from mythology as silent seducers of prospective buyers. Among the clients for whom the professor built up collections was Czar Peter the Great and the Polish king Jan Sobieski, who paid tens of thousands of guilders for a Cabinet. The goddess with the Horn of Plenty, to all appearances advertising the benefits to be derived from specimens of science, the Key to Knowledge and the Dove of Peace somehow remind one of the scientific jargon used out of context in modern advertising. In a like fashion, a group of Ruysch's anatomical preparations challenges exploration but does so with a facetious and yet threatening reminder of death.[8] A pleasing grouping of objects welds the two incongruous messages together.

What should one call displays of such kind? They are attractive, but the term *misinterpretive* would seem to be more pertinent. They declare one message to be their only intent but in fact they issue two discrepant communications.

The legacy of public museums is by no means limited to these three different types of exhibits of the past. There is a chorus of communications in this heritage, but in this paper we shall focus on a few major strains and watch how they emerged under changed circumstances, as some of the great private collections became accessible to the public, or underwent a metamorphosis into public institutions in the later eighteenth and early nineteenth centuries.

It was the so-called Era of Enlightenment; a period of socio-economic ferment and political upheaval. The French Revolution and the events that culminated in the founding of an independent United States reverberated in many parts of Europe, even though their effects remained contained for some time to come. In the calendar of cultural human evolution the stretch of years between those days and the outbreak of the First World War is very brief indeed; it has characteristics of a single big pulse toward a deeper recognition of the responsibilities and the rights of man. The admission of the public to museums was but one aspect of a process which still continues: one of extending educational privileges ever more widely—at times a dilatory process, revealing ambiguous attitudes on the part of those who have the power to grant favors to others.

To be admitted to the Czar's art treasures in the Hermitage, early in the nineteenth century, visitors were required to present themselves in outfits worn at court functions; men had to wear dress suits. Since few owned such attire, the majority of the population remained excluded from these sights—which the contemporary French traveler Viardot described as a disordered labyrinth. In spite of the high quality of many of the works of art the entire experience of the visit was dazzling rather than enlightening. It was an affirmation of the sovereign's superhuman status and, by implication, the low station of others.

The British Museum in London, founded in 1759, grew out of the collection of Sir Hans Sloane, a noted physician, who in his will expressed the wish that his natural and artificial curiosities be of benefit to mankind.[9] He hoped that they would be of most use in London owing to the "great confluence of people in that city." Yet in 1785 the German historian Wendeborn wrote on his return from England that persons desiring to visit the British Museum had to deposit their credentials in the office and wait weeks or months for a decision by the pertinent authorities. Those who were found "not exceptionable" were permitted to join a company of fifteen persons under the supervision of an attendant who hurriedly led his flock through crowded exhibition halls and who discouraged questions. The first, rather scanty, printed catalog appeared in 1808.

Even after being admitted physically, the majority of the European public remained mentally debarred from the offerings which were under-interpreted, and there existed incomplete communication for anybody but experts who could fit single items of the displays into contexts available in their own memory banks. For the majority of visitors at that time of very limited education, the collections were as cryptic as a foreign language, with a few striking objects having the appeal of curios and titillating short-lived, unproductive curiosity. A guide book of the British Museum of 1838 described the grand palatial staircase and the entrance hall with its statue of Shakespeare, Indian idols, the skeleton of a hippopotamus, and paintings illustrating the Roman poet Ovid's verses.

Another strain in exhibit communication which we have inherited goes back to the World Fairs of the early age of industrialization. There is a close resemblance between some museum halls of the nineteenth century and the huge exhibition halls of the international trade fairs, the first of which was staged in the Crystal Palace in London, soon to be followed by even larger fairs in the U.S.

In the course of years, some European museums became pioneers in the diffusion of knowledge, for example, the German Museum in Munich, the Scandinavian outdoor museums, the *Palais des Inventions* in Paris, and some others; but most European museums were slow to assume new methods. The legacy of the past also affected the style of American museums.

THE MAIN TYPES OF CURRENT EXHIBITS—AS I SEE THEM

I shall sum up current types of museum exhibits under three headings: *Under-interpretive, Misinterpretive,* and *Interpretive.*

We would have no difficulty in locating the *Under-interpretive Exhibit* in the United States, but in the context of this paper and of the account of my experiments I shall refer first to a display of this kind which I used during an earlier phase of my work. It happened to be a small gallery in one of the university museums in Cambridge in England and it was an outstanding collection of archaeological and ethnological currencies. Its main purpose was to serve as a reference library of objects for university students, but the general public was admitted, and it was the "general public" I interviewed in the course of my experiment. Among the ninety-six persons who saw either this display or a comparative one I set up on the same topic, were adults with a college education, undergraduates who were neither archaeologists nor anthropologists, and pupils of a private high school. Here are some of their statements with regard to the Study Collection:

> "For pure curiosity value it was quite good."
> "We were given plenty of facts but no information. . . ."
> "I would have left normally . . . there is so little explanation. . . ."
> "It needs patience to sort out the jumble . . . one should ruthlessly throw out all repetitions."
> "A cluster."

As these statements show, the offered ample information remained largely unconsumed. Here is the lingering tradition of the Reference-Library of scholars, which has its place in a study collection for modern students but must be newly appraised as part of a museum for the general public. Yet in spite of its power of survival, the *Under-interpreted Exhibit* appears to me to be a challenge rather than a danger; there is a mounting awareness of its incongruity with mass education. In fact, I would advocate retaining it as a part of museums where visitors may browse, meet puzzling probems, and be stimulated to ask questions of themselves and of others. It should, however, not be the only kind of display offered to the general public.

An area of no challenge and of acute danger is in my opinion the *Misinterpretive Exhibit*—in the sense of not attending sufficiently to a professed purpose, or of not having any purpose that could be validly pursued in an "embodiment to teach"[10] known as a museum.

Let us consider a few museums where earlier in this century exaggerated decorations of the interior architecture distracted attention from the actual specimens. Emperors had disappeared by that time but citizens were still supposed to be overwhelmed rather than helped to perceive meaning; and many were inclined to blame the breakdown of communication on themselves rather than on what was presented to them.[11]

Currently we have our own brand of *Misinterpretive Exhibits.* My first encounter with this technique was a few years after the war, in Europe, when the science museums endeavored to meet demands for popular education. A noted designer was called in to plan an exhibition on the subject of "Making Fire–Making Light." The result was a delightfully designed number of small rooms in dim light where the actual specimens were parts of a decorative ensemble. With small tables and chairs added, the setting could have served as an elegant restaurant or as a stage decoration. Indeed, the artist was a brilliant theatrical designer. You have probably seen comparable exhibits, for they are conspicuous in this country. They may be summed up as "over-designed," and they are probably a reaction to the under-interpreted exhibit. Vague demands for "color" and for "drama" were among the motives that prompted them and brought about a situation in which the artist, who first entered the museum scene as a helpmate of experts, frequently takes top command. He deserves no blame; being a designer, his primary interest lies in designing. It is the function of museums to prevent the blurring of educational opportunities.

We have had some warnings in recent years when surveys revealed the difficulties of visitors in understanding science exhibits at the Brussels Fair and at the Seattle World's Fair. Were these exhibits really "above the heads of laymen" and under-interpreting, or were many of them simply misinterpretive? We may be underestimating the public. In an article"Communication of Mental Health Information" in *Behavioral Science* (2, 1957), Jim Nunnally reported that the views of the general public on mental health were closer to those of experts than the views represented by mass media.

An exhibit contains two simultaneous messages: the intellectual content and the communication arising from shapes, spaces, lines, colors, and light, and of course from the interrelationships among all those aspects. The two have to be synchronized and have to support each other. If they are in conflict, a breakdown in communication is likely to result. If exhibit designers would read and reflect on what Gyorgy Kepes, professor of design at MIT, has written eloquently in *Language of Vision,* we might experience fewer breakdowns in communication as we enter a time of information explosion. Yet the unbridled *Misinterpretive Exhibition,* which has gained such prominence in recent years, is a phenomenon which requires explanation.

As I see it, one of the circumstances favoring this type of exhibit is the preponderance of a subculture of our culture, which developed from the marketing of goods and has spread almost unwittingly beyond its original confines. What may be a vital, energizing force in a particular situation, may have a warping and debilitating effect in another. We are all familiar with an approach to education, in the style of books and courses advertised as "Fun with Calculus" or "French with Giggles," which is akin to the adroitly lopsided world of competitive advertising. In a comparable manner, communication by exhibits may become contaminated by the pervasive custom of prettily packaged goods: with intellectual contents shrouded in attractive mobiles or wallpaper-like murals so stunning in themselves that they drain attention from the visually less strident messages. If one translated this trend into language, one might find oneself close to the singing style of an operetta or of vocalists in television advertisements.

If the *Misinterpretive Exhibit* may be considered as a reflection of a facet of American culture and, one may hope, a passing fad, the *Interpretive Exhibit* is a much more significant phenomenon of the United States: a symbol of the emphasis placed on the flow of communication among the greatest number of people; of the diffusion of knowledge represented by the vast network of the public school system in this country, in contrast to many other areas where even secondary education to this day remains the privilege of a minority.

We are all sufficiently familiar with the *Interpretive Exhibit.* It presents a context or an entity of items rather than a series of single items. It formulates ideas illustrated by specimens, instead of objects that illustrate ideas only in the minds of viewers possessing an appropriate background of knowledge. At its best, the *Interpretive Exhibit* transmutes inert information into viable communication to laymen; at its worst, it gets lost in gimmickry. There are great and as yet unused opportunities for a coexistence of interpretive and under-interpretive exhibits, and for reinforcing formulated ideas with materials which in turn would stimulate further formulation by the public.

The *Interpretive Exhibit* fascinates me as a projection of the school of contemporary thought which assumes man to be a pattern-seeking creature. This assumption is at the basis of the *Gestalt* school in psychology, and more recently and in a somewhat wider sense, of cybernetics and of general systems theory, all of which study the relationships among facts rather than facts in isolation. Museums have great potentialities for such a presentation of knowledge; their resources are frequently interdisciplinary and their main endeavor lies in the field of general or liberal education. Indeed, *Interpretive Exhibits* transcending rigid disciplinary boundaries may contribute to the realization of the second phase in the study of science, as the seventeenth-century English scientist Robert Hooke conceived it: an assembly of the various parts of knowledge into systems, after the preceding phase of systematic collection of single facts which had begun with Galileo. Descartes, Leibnitz, and other great natural philosophers of the time were aware of the need for the second phase and of the danger that heaps of fractured, specialized knowledge might veil their view of the world.

AN ACCOUNT OF SOME EXPERIMENTAL EXHIBITS

May I now make a comparison between different types of exhibits, as seen through the magnifying lens of experiments in which their features were considered and evaluated on the basis of viewers' reactions. They were mainly under-interpretive and interpretive exhibits.

The experimental exhibits I planned and evaluated were for both adults and children. There was a wide range of topics, from archaeology and anthropology to history, to the natural and physical sciences. There was a variety of approaches, from static to participative exhibits set up in cooperation with visitors (the "make-as-you-go exhibit");

from a self-contained experience to the exhibit as a focal, activating agent in a school situation, which would lead beyond the subject matter represented by specimens (the "Framework Exhibition"). Five of the exhibits were statistically evaluated; in other cases interviews with participants provided material for a qualitative assessment of advantages and disadvantages; work done in cooperation with some of the schools was recorded both by the experimenter and by a teacher. Topics were presented in several different ways to serve as mutual controls.

My main criteria in setting up experimental exhibits were developed in the course of the work; they were not cut-and-dried when I started out. I found little guidance in museum literature but a good deal of help, of stimulation and support for my own theories, in the writings of psychologists dealing with learning, visual perception, and language, and of those concerned with communication—a motley crew of intellects, from mathematicians and engineers to people concerned with the human mind, psychologists and psychiatrists.

Any evaluation of results has to begin with a statement of purpose. My purpose was obviously related to learning, and I was endeavoring to find techniques of exhibition which would fulfill this purpose in two ways: by putting information across to people and by stimulating certain mental attitudes and processes in them—paying attention, observing, making a choice among alternatives, making decisions, being curious beyond what was immediately presented, processing skills in organizing an experience, recording it in memory and retrieving relevant features when recall was asked for. Certain stimuli or features in the exhibit were provided to generate such results. Some attempts in this respect were rewarded by success, repeated, and further developed; others led to no results.

ATTENTION AND COMMUNICATION BY EXHIBITS

In a museum, or wherever people view exhibits, attention is not enforced, or reinforced, by extraneous rewards in the form of grades or credits, or by potential success in a competitive game. The reward can only be an intrinsic part of the experience itself. Considering the stress laid in our society on school marks, paper credits and competition, museums are seemingly at a disadvantage. Since human beings are members of a much larger community than their contemporary civilization, however, they are highly responsive to stimuli alerting and holding their attention—a congenital part of their biological makeup. Without response to the environment no organism could survive; without attention to signals from the environment man could not have achieved the measure of control over it he possesses. If we responded to all signals bombarding us, however, we could not survive. Hence, the need for selective responses and for an inhibition of responses to irrelevant stimuli.

In experimental exhibits, I endeavored to begin with an input—mostly by means of specimens, sometimes by words—which would strike people as being relevant to them—to human beings, in general, to members of our culture, to nonspecialists. In an exhibit of archaeological and ethnological currency ("Money—What is it?") I started with modern money familiar to everybody. Novelty was offered in the form of large illustrations of some of the functions of currency in our culture, but strident stimuli were avoided. There is evidence that too much novelty militates against concentrated attention.

In other exhibits a bid for attention was made in the form of a challenge to find answers to questions or to seek order in a miscellany of objects. The number of such challenges had to be limited to promise a solution in the existing situation. Furthermore, there had to be something of a primordial quality; like the aesthetic appeal of some selected fifteen insects differing in shapes, sizes, and colors; or the menacing sight of animals skulls with an imposing and varied dentition.

I found that attention can be captured and held by opportunities for people to *identify* themselves with a topic—however remote the topic may have seemed at first. There was also from the beginning, and at many following "relay points," an *appeal to different senses*: to seeing, touching, and hearing. Occasionally labels can be replaced by brief tape recordings.

LIMITATIONS ON THE QUANTITY OF INPUT

There must be a sufficient number of items to create a measure of complexity, illustrating a problem from several points of view, but the quantity must remain controllable lest it create discouragement or confusion. There is ample literature on the human limitations to record and to remember stimuli, from W. Hamilton and his *Lectures on Metaphysics and Logic,* of 1859, to our contemporary George A. Miller of Harvard and his Magic Number 7, plus or minus two.[12]

THE STRUCTURE OF INPUT

Quantity cannot be considered strictly by itself. A greater quantity of items presented in a structured way is a lesser information load than fewer items unstructured. One has only to think of the learning of nonsense syllables as compared with the learning of words or sentences.

Structure in an exhibit, or in any form of communication, implies a variety of aspects. There is the combination of "bits" to "chunks," the lessening of the input load by combining single objects into meaningful groups which become perceivable as single items. There is the need for an *integrity of segments,* which must not eclipse each other in the manner of words spoken very fast. There is the need to eliminate as much as possible all interfering *visual noise,* anything that is irrelevant or leads too far off the main line of argument; visual noise is not merely a dead load of communication but also a deadening one.

There is the need in an *Interpretive Exhibit* for *context.* Psychologists and communication experts are supplying us with a choice of terms for it: set, plan, program, field, system, organization, and of course *Gestalt.* According to Norbert Wiener and other representatives of communication theory, the degree of the organization or structure of a communication is an index of the amount of information it supplies.

Another point to be kept in mind in the light of my experience is the need of the viewer for a *reduction* of his *uncertainty* as he proceeds in his inspection of an exhibit, and this again is a central theorem of communication experts. In our perception of the environment—and an exhibit is a small, planned environment—we make an effort to sort out our impressions and to divide the field of inquiry into smaller regions of uncertainty. Hence, communication with too many fences and pitfalls has limited chances of being received and recorded by human minds, and of remaining retrievable. A grading of the uncertainty reduction is necessary, however, to prevent a slackening of attention.

Another aspect is the need of the receiver of communication for a certain measure of *redundancy,* to prevent misunderstanding and to fill voids created by lapses in attention. The degree of redundancy in languages is very high, but we are hardly aware of it. (There is, of course, planned and unplanned redundancy.)

Any kind of teaching may be approached from two points of view—from that of a person who knows the topic or from that of a person who begins to learn about it. In the course of emergency training programs, during the last world war for example, it was found that training in basic knowledge was effective and accelerated if it was taught from the point of view of the raw beginner. In many ways all people are raw beginners. Teaching films took off from where their audiences were and went from there to the subject matter.

Abstraction has to follow experience, and not the other way around. Experience has to have dimensions of width and of depth—it is advisable to deal with each of a few variables in a number of ways, instead of reaching out for numerous variables and showing them in a single state. There is a wealth of experimental evidence to support this proposition.

Colin Cherry, one of the foremost students of communication has stated that a message is an orderly selection of signs. Any communication suffers from shrinkage when grammar and syntax are violated. Transferring these statements into the realm of exhibits, one may suggest that exhibits are in peril of becoming outlaws among media of communication if those using this particular medium do not agree on some *code for exhibit makers.* Without aiming at the precision and strictness of grammar and of syntax, such a code or codes would serve as equivalents of linguistic rules. Alphabets have approximately thirty letters, but the segments constituting an exhibit are far more numerous; hence the need for and the validity of a more flexible code of rules. Experimentation is gathering momentum in several places, but we would make our task very laborious if we neglected to take notice of experiments done in psychological laboratories where the very word museum is rarely if ever heard. If we consider museums largely as a self-contained enterprise, we shall, in my opinion, find it difficult, nay impossible, to identify our tasks in education.

Alfred North Whitehead believed that there was one main goal of study and one main curriculum, and that it could be summed up by the single word "Life." Personally, I prefer to think of the ultimate goal of education as that of aiding human evolution. To be effective, therefore, learning situations have to facilitate biological tendencies. As Karl S. Lashley and other eminent neurophysiologists have remarked, it is a characteristic of human cerebral activity to apply to perceptions a serial ordering and a hierarchically organized plan. We counteract this tendency when we provide atomized or confusing environments. Associative faculties are characteristics of the most recent and most advanced parts of the human brain and learning situations ought to contribute to the increase in the number of associative neurons, as Thorndike suggested. *Misinterpretive Exhibits* encourage a disintegration of associations and represent the opposite of intellectual maturity. *Under-interpretive Exhibits* may be either a challenge to associations or a hindrance to the associative process, depending on their place within the framework of a museum, or of a single, large exhibit.

The perennial appeal of museums arises from the concrete, tactile, immediate qualities of the specimens which are their stock-in-trade. Our word-bound civilization has only short roots. Alphabets which developed from pictures of things span mere thousands of years. There is only speculation with regard to the origins of spoken language, especially beyond the reference to objects of immediate use. It may well be that for some nine tenths of our one million years plus on earth all business of human living was transacted in a *First Signal Environment* of things and events, here and now. Survival depended on the alert distinction between edible and poisonous plants, on swift reactions to prey or predator, on an orientation to mountains, streams, and stars. All this is programmed into our senses and our nervous system, even though the symbolic *Second Signal Environment* of language has since assumed overriding status and—together with the even more abstract and skeletonized *Third Signal Environment* of numbers, charts, and graphs—has spurred the development of our higher mental faculties: the perception of universals behind incidental particulars, memory of the past, imagination of the future, and imagery of things and events at a distance.

Officially, only children and artists continue to live in a *First Signal Environment,* but in fact most people—if not all, on occasion—claim admission to the primordial world. Sightseeing seems to satisfy a genuine craving; the kaleidoscopic changes in fashion reveal the human satisfaction derived from a stimulation of the senses. And the lack of judiciousness shown by museum visitors toward the sights they are sometimes offered may result from the impact made by objects on people. If one inquires in a social situation how good or bad the new exhibition in a museum is, the answers are, as a rule, both laudatory and vague; probing does not always lead to a validation of the original judgment, and sometimes reverses it.

If and when museum workers arrive at a code for exhibits, they ought to share their insights with the public—the consumers of their offerings—as well as with the as yet hardly existing profession of museum and exhibit critics. There are well qualified drama, book, music, and even sports critics, but reviews of museum exhibits are all too often written by persons without special qualifications for the job, if they are written at all; sometimes they are written as though they were part of the social news. Yet to derive full benefit from the offerings of museums, the public will have to be served by appropriate guides; and the feedback of public opinion on museums might greatly contribute to their further development. At present museums are somewhat exempt from the pressures to which other public institutions are exposed. Apart from rare experimental situations, no tests exist that would evaluate how much visitors gained or lost in the course of a museum visit—in terms of knowledge, stimulation, and self-confidence. Few people consider a dull hour in a museum a wasted investment; they rarely pay directly for it. The very fact that museum services are not publicly evaluated may add to a feeling of noninvolvement on the part of taxpayers; and to a lack of confidence of many people in their own ability to assess, even in a subjective manner, what is presented in the aloof halls of a museum, set apart from the stream of life. Museum membership is open to all comers who are prepared to pay a contribution; it seems to confer status and may militate against an analytical frame of mind.

It would be a fascinating undertaking to offer a workshop in exhibit making—not on paper only but with actual specimens, screens, and cases—in which a variety of people would come together—designers and curators, representatives of trustees and of museum members as well as of the general public—to discuss and formulate communications by exhibits. If museums established a regular flow of communication with the public and became more visible in this respect, they might receive more attention in future government publications referring to educational agencies eligible for special funds. (There is no reference to museums in the Higher Education Act of 1965.)

Museums are exceptionally well equipped to contribute to continuous education on a great variety of topics in an infinite variety of ways. Incidental learning from a small exhibit in the waiting room of a medical clinic, in a restaurant, on a train, or even in a supermarket should not be underestimated and need not be frowned upon. It is surprising how much can be achieved within ten minutes. I observed this when I had to comply with the time allotted to high school students for the viewing of an exhibit.

To what extent do museums interact with their culture? To what extent do they reflect and mold it? "To what extent are they mirror or beam of light?"—to adopt a phrase coined by Robert M. Hutchins in reference to universities.

The major educational function of museums lies within the somewhat indefinite margins of general or liberal education, as distinguished from professional and vocational training. Museums have the potentialities to help individuals obtain a perception of order in the "buzzing, blooming" confusion of the environment, natural and man-made, by identifying themselves as a part of the web of life, from the immediate family and community to the galaxies, including the energies emanating from atoms and the achievements of human genius across distances of space and time.

To what extent do museums present and interpret all such events and ideas of the past which can be represented by displays? To what extent do they occupy themselves with current challenges on the "Cultural Shockfront," to borrow a term from John Rader Platt's *The Step to Man* (New York, John Wiley and Sons, 1965, p. 195)?

While we frequently refer to geographically displaced persons in search of new roots, we do not altogether open our awareness to the phenomenon of displaced persons with regard to time, who include the majority of human beings around the globe: they, or we, are *dis-timed persons*. Major technological, political and socioeconomic changes within the lifetime of a single individual have made us all, to some degree, aliens in our environment.

Over two generations ago, the philosopher Whitehead wrote of "The middle class pessimism over the future of the world," which he explained as a confusion between civilization and security,[13] but we have as yet not recognized that on the whole "great ages have been unstable ages," and we would seem to need a variety of learning situations to develop a matching inner stability. In these circumstances the great task of continuous liberal education, from child to senior citizen, would appear to be the creation of an informed open-mindedness and a reduction in traumatic experiences at a time of a radical shift in emphases: from a man-made, goods-producing culture to a man-making culture; from a culture striving foremost for man-power to a culture striving foremost for manhood. For better or for worse, new technologies desired and designed by man are setting the scene for a new phase of human evolution. It is the mission of museums, as it is of other educational institutions, to contribute as fully as they can to mankind's fitness to occupy this scene, and to do so in the full sense, as Norbert Wiener meant it, of the human use of human beings.

* The experimental work on Exhibits as Means of Communication to which reference is made in this paper was funded consecutively by the International Federation

of University Women, the National Foundation for Educational Research in England and Wales, and the American Association of University Women.

The following institutions lent facilities for the work: the University Museum of Archaeology and Anthropology in Cambridge, England; the Horniman Museum of Anthropology, the Victoria and Albert Museum, and the Science Museum, all three in London. The University of California, and the Museum of Natural History, both in Santa Barbara, Calif., and the County Museum of History and Science in Los Angeles, Calif., lent specimens for experimental exhibits and cooperated in other ways.

1. Whitehead, Alfred North, *The Aims of Education,* London, 1950, Williams and Norgate, Ltd., p. 3.

2. Wittlin, Alma S., *The Museum, Its History and Its Tasks in Education,* London, 1949, Routledge and Kegan Paul, International Library of Sociology and Social Reconstruction, fig. 1. A revised edition will be published by the M.I.T. Press.

3. *Ibid.,* fig. XI.

4. *Ibid.,* fig. XX.

5. *Ibid.,* figs. VI, VIIA and B.

6. *Ibid.,* fig. XXIIIA.

7. *Ibid.,* fig. XVA.

8. *Ibid.,* fig. XVB.

9. *Ibid.,* figs. XVIIA and XVIIIA.

10. Committee on the Role of Education in American History, *Education and American History,* New York, The Fund for the Advancement of Education, 1965, p. 9.

11. Wittlin, *op. cit.,* fig. 9e-h.

12. *The Psychological Review,* vol. 63, 1956.

13. Whitehead, Alfred North, *Science and the Modern World,* New York, Mentor Books, 1956, p. 208. The book was based on lectures held in 1925.

Noseprints on the Glass

OR HOW DO WE EVALUATE MUSEUM PROGRAMS?

SCARVIA B. ANDERSON
Educational Testing Service

Unfortunately, there has been a tendency in this country to equate the term "education" with what happens in the schools or, at most, with what happens in schools, colleges, and universities. This leaves out other agencies and influences which, for better or for worse and to greater and lesser degrees, may have a great impact on the knowledge, skill, understanding, appreciation, and judgment of our people: television, radio, motion pictures, the non-textbook press, the family, the back-alley gang, the teacher of "private" lessons, fairs and expositions, industry (through its greatly expanded training programs), the military, and the *museum*.

Let us look for a moment at the area of art alone. In working on a project to assess the progress of American education in a number of fields, we at Educational Testing Service have been most hard pressed to find assessment tasks in art which would seem appropriate for any sizable fraction of the population.[1] Our dilemma was stimulated by national public school statistics which show that:

1. a very small percentage of elementary school class time is allotted to art (medians: 60 minutes per week for grades 1 to 3, 70 minutes for grades 4 to 5, and 72.5 minutes for grade 6);
2. little in the way of supplies and equipment is available for art instruction (e.g., only 42 percent of elementary schools have any kind of picture or slide collection); and
3. the secondary school art program is even more limited than

that of the elementary school (e.g., in grades 10 to 12, only about 15 percent of students in medium size and large schools are enrolled in art courses).[2]

We were further depressed by the statement of the Commission on the Humanities that "At the present time our schools are woefully lacking in teachers with the capacity to approach the visual arts . . . in a way to help their pupils develop discrimination, judgment, and taste."[3]

Now, unless the schools can accomplish miracles in preparing teachers and revising student programs in art in the next few years, who is going to take the responsibility for meeting "the need for increased understanding to match the increase in attention to the arts in American life?"[4] A study of folders from all over the country indicates that art museums are already trying to help fill the gap. How much they *can* do to stimulate understanding of art is, of course, a function of their personnel, time, and objectives.

Sir Frank Francis has asked, "Is it possible for museums and galleries to be all things to all men?" and has gone on to warn against letting the interests of "the ordinary man on the street" (and he included the child from the school) impinge increasingly on the time of the scholar.[5]

Even those of us who are more emotionally involved with schools than with museums, and who would like to see every school child in the country allowed frequent access to the great galleries, must grant Sir Frank his point. There will be nothing for the school child and "the ordinary man on the street" to see unless museums give primary attention to "the acquisition and preservation of works of art and craftsmanship or antiquity" and the research that is a necessary concomitant.

Of course, this is not supposed to be an essay on the functions of museums; if that had been the case, a psychologist from ETS would not have been given this place on the program. However, recognition that most museums can give only a portion of their time, space, and imagination to educational programs, as well as recognition of the size of the population a museum has to serve, is important to the basic proposition of this paper, which is:

If, of necessity, an educational program has to be brief, it had better be good.

How can we begin to find out whether a museum has a good educational program? And, if its sponsors are willing to admit that a program may not be as good as it might be, how do we get information to help them improve it?

DEFINITION OF PURPOSE

Alvin Toffler has said that "Much of the difficulty troubling arts institutions today stems directly from a failure to define their own purposes precisely, cleanly, and concretely . . . . Until we learn to get specific, until we come to regard arts institutions quite unsentimentally as instruments for accomplishing well-defined ends, we are going to wallow about futilely."[6] It is probably true that Mr. Toffler's criticism could be leveled at almost any institution; certainly it would apply to most schools and colleges. For the present purposes, however, let us think of his comment as advice rather than as criticism, and extend it to include art and other museums (e.g., of science and health), and narrow it to include only the educational ends which these institutions have accepted as within their province.

Any institutional educational program probably should have two sets of objectives, big ones and little ones. The big ones apply across the board—to the reasons why the Metropolitan or the Smithsonian or the Cleveland Health Museum open their doors to the public in the first place (and throughout this paper I will be referring especially to the opening of the doors to school children). The big objectives may be stated less explicitly than the little ones, but they should be explicit enough to permit decisions about whether any proposed instructional series or tour is an appropriate one for the institution. In other words, the goodness of the general objectives can be determined pragmatically, on the basis of the guidance the list offers with respect to selection of specific programs and activities.

By general objectives, I have in mind such items as the following, assumed for the Metropolitan Junior Museum program for elementary and junior high school classes:

> to provide children with greater understanding of American, European, Ancient World, and Far Eastern history through enrichment experiences;
>
> to make children aware of techniques and provide them with experiences which will contribute to art appreciation;
>
> to provide information and experiences which will help children understand the meaning of the museum and its importance in the community;
>
> to stimulate personal interest in the museum and a desire to visit it independently.[7]

Specific programs relevant to these objectives include gallery tours and films on Life in Colonial America 1640–1750, China's Ancient Arts, and How to Look at Paintings. (The earlier point about limited availability of museum educational programs is supported here by the fact that any given class may book no more than *one tour a year.*)

Some examples of specific programs in other museums include the following:

> the "Human Growth" program of the Cleveland Health Museum, designed to acquaint fifth to seventh graders with "the simple facts of reproduction, birth, and growth";[8]
>
> the advanced astronomy workshop of the Brooklyn Children's museum;[9]
>
> the Franklin Institute summer course on probability, for junior high school students;[10]
>
> the Chicago Museum of Science and Industry tours focusing on such topics as metals, space, communications, and biology;[11]
>
> "The World We Live In" series of the American Museum of Natural History in New York, offering for grades three to nine choices of topics from "The Rise of Mammals" to "Indian Life in the Upper Amazon Region."[12]

Putting ourselves in the role of director of one of these specific programs, we have two hours to achieve some effects on third, fifth, or tenth graders and we want to determine what these effects, if any, will be.

The first step is to state explicitly what we hope to accomplish with these students. Without such explicit statements made in advance, we may find ourselves in the remarkable position of a counselor in a large New Jersey school system who was patting himself on the back over the outcome of a weekend field trip to Williamsburg for "culturally deprived" teenagers. The evidence cited? The boys' statements about how wonderful it was to have something to do over the weekend besides just sit at home.

If the main objective of the field trip was to provide kids with something to do over the weekend, one cannot help asking, "Why Williamsburg?" Certainly the objective could have been accomplished less expensively and more easily at a nearby beach or campsite without taking the group all the way to Williamsburg. There they used up valuable "spectator space" which might better have been allotted to groups concerned with some of the lessons Williamsburg can uniquely offer.

I am assuming that trips to museums do not properly belong in the category of "larks," at least not in the same category of larks as ball games or picnics. Certainly we want children to enjoy their museum visits, but we must have more in mind than enjoyment. What? Information, new interests, enhancement of other experiences?

(Let me add here, parenthetically and probably to the dismay of some of my scientific colleagues, that, if the director of an educational program goes *only* so far as to state his objectives in specific terms and then review his program in the light of those objectives, the program may benefit. A careful "armchair" analysis of a program in terms of clearly defined objectives may point to redundancies, gaps in coverage, and other program faults which can be corrected. However, none of us will deny that it is probably better to try to collect information about the effects of the program.)

EVALUATION OF THE PROGRAM

The most satisfactory approach to finding out about the effects of an educational program is the experimental approach. For example, we randomly assign one group of pupils to the "treatment" or program and we deliberately withhold treatment from the remaining pupils—who we can safely assume are comparable because of the random assignment. Then we measure outcomes in each of the groups and are in the strongest position to make causal inferences; i.e., that the program was responsible for the differences we observe between the experimental and control groups. Unfortunately, to quote Webb *et al.*, "It is a sad truth that randomized experimental design is possible for only a portion of the settings in which social scientists make measurements and seek interpretable comparisons."[13]

In cases where we cannot exercise experimental control, we are thrown back on collecting what data we can and then trying to rule out plausible rival hypotheses which might account for our findings just as well as the educational program which we hope is the cause. (For example, an upswing in teenagers' summer museum attendance might be attributable to the "interest teenagers" program put on by the museum in the spring *or* to the fact that this summer brings unusually hot weather and the museum is air-conditioned.)

Whether we can set up a good experimental design or whether we are forced to collect the best data we can, the next step after definition of objectives is to turn these objectives into measurements. What kinds of measurements are most likely to fit some of the objectives of museum programs?

Tests

Assuming that a program is designed to foster some increase in knowledge and understanding, it is reasonable to consider development of a school-like test to cover these cognitive objectives. It is unlikely that time can be found at the museum for administration of such a measure; so, in cases where the school and museum are working closely together, the test might be administered in the classroom after pupils have visited the museum.

The objectives may go further than the content of the particular museum presentation, or facts about the museum itself, and include relationships between the museum content and materials encountered earlier in the classroom. In such cases, questions covering such relationships should be prepared for the test. For example, in American history, children might be asked why certain early American household objects displayed at the museum were made of the materials they were made of, in order to see if they related the practical crafts of the period to the resources available to the Colonists.

Questionnaires

In spite of special problems with questionnaire data, it may sometimes be useful to get teacher and pupil reactions to the museum program by having them answer questions about it or rate aspects of it. In general, the more specific one can make the questions the more likely one is to obtain meaningful responses. For example, instead of asking simply, "Did this exhibit relate to what you have been studying (or teaching) in Course X?" it is probably better to add, "If *yes*, name one related topic you have been studying (teaching)."

Other questionnaire focuses might include: a) teachers' ratings or responses to questions about the effects of the program on subsequent behavior of pupils (pupil references to "the trip," voluntary reading on the subject, etc.), or b) pupil responses (if they are old enough to respond for themselves) to such questions as these:

Since you visited the X Museum in (month), have you been back on your own?
No
Yes, once
Yes, more than once

Since you visited the X Museum in (month), have your read any books about (topic)?
No
Yes, one — What? ____________
Yes, more than one — What? ____________
____

Interviews

Interviews with samples of teachers or pupils (or maybe even parents) may be used to obtain some of the same kinds of information as the questionnaires, and interviews may have the added advantage of allowing intensive questioning on some topics and opportunities for clarification of questions and responses. As in the case of the questionnaire, the more structured the interview is in advance, the more likely you are to obtain interpretable results.

Webb *et al.,* have estimated that "some 90 percent of social science research is based upon interviews and questionnaires" and they "lament this overdependence on a single, fallible method."[14]

One of the several arguments against exclusive use of tests, questionnaires, and interviews is summed up by Selltiz *et al.*:

> "The measurement process used in the experiment may itself affect the outcome. If people feel that they are 'guinea pigs' being experimented with, or if they feel that they are being 'tested' and must make a good impression, or if the method of data collection suggests responses or stimulates an interest the subject did not previously feel, the measuring process may distort the experimental results."[15]

Available to researchers are sources of information not suffering from these particular deficiences, and Webb *et al.,* have done the social sciences a great favor by reviewing some of the physical trace, archival, and observation measures which have been used in studies.

Some of these would seem to be particularly relevant to museum directors concerned, first, with whether certain exhibits or displays attract attention and, second, with reactions to exhibits or programs.

Physical Trace Measures

To introduce the notion of physical trace measurement, the authors of *Unobtrusive Measures* use a Sherlock Holmes example:

> "The fog had probably just cleared. The singular Sherlock Holmes had been reunited with his old friend, Dr. Watson (after one of Watson's marriages), and both walked to Watson's newly acquired office. The practice was located in a duplex of two physician's suites, both of which had been for sale. No doubt sucking on his calabash, Holmes summarily told Watson that he had made a wise choice in purchasing the practice that he did rather than the one on the other side of the duplex. The data? The steps were more worn on Watson's side than on his competitor's."[16]

Two examples cited in the same chapter illustrate applications of erosion and accretion measures to museum exhibits:

"A committee was formed to set up a psychological exhibit at Chicago's Museum of Science and Industry. The committee learned that the vinyl tiles around the exhibit containing live, hatching chicks had to be replaced every six weeks or so; tiles in other areas of the museum went for years without replacement. A comparative study of the rate of tile replacement around the various museum exhibits could give a rough ordering of the popularity of the exhibits. Note that although erosion is the measure, the knowledge of the erosion rate comes from a check of the records of the museum's maintenance department."[17]

"The relative popularity of exhibits with glass fronts could be compared by examining the number of noseprints deposited on the glass each day (or on some sample of time, day, month, and so forth). This requires that the glass be dusted for noseprints each night and then wiped clean for the next day's viewers to smudge. The noseprint measure has fewer content restrictions than most of the trace techniques, for the age of the viewers can be estimated as well as the total number of prints on each exhibit. Age is determined by plotting a frequency distribution of the heights of the smudges from the floor, and relating these data to normative heights by age (minus, of course, the nose-to-top-of-head correction)."[18]

Archives

When the word "archives" is mentioned, tombstones and artifacts may come readily to mind. However, the kinds of archives or records that would be of interest to the director of an educational program may be illustrated by the following examples:

records of books checked out of the school library (as the titles related to a particular program to which students are exposed, and in relation to such an objective as "show interest in topic X"); and

records of museum attendance (by students exposed to the museum through one of its programs, and in relation to such an objective as "visit the museum on their own").

Observations

Observations of reactions to an exhibit or program may be recorded simply by an unobtrusive observer or in more complicated fashion by mechanical or electronic devices.

In the first instance, the observer should have a clear idea of what he is looking for (laughter at the "wrong" places, signs of drowsiness, expressions of enthusiasm, touching the exhibit after a "don't touch" instruction, etc.). If possible, some check should be made on the reliability of the observations, perhaps by having more than one observer make records of the same event and then having them compare their notes. Another consideration, of course, is the possible influence the presence of an observer may have on the behavior being observed. Various effects of observers have been noted, from "lending assurance" to nursery school children to "threatening" boys in a summer camp.[19] It seems safe to propose for program evaluation purposes that the less obtrusive the observer the better.

In recent years social scientists have taken advantage of hardware developments which facilitate recording human behavior; e.g., tape recorders (to get actual conversations or, in some cases, simply noise level), still cameras, television and movie cameras (to record fine movements such as eye behavior or grosser behavior; infrared techniques have been used in darkened movie theaters to record audience reactions), electrical or mechanical devices to record body movement (e.g., audience fidgeting), "electric eyes" (to collect data on the number of people attending an event), and devices to measure physiological phenomena such as perspiration or heart beat.

The practicality of a museum's investing in such devices for studying its programs and exhibits would depend on the amount of use the devices would get and alternative ways of collecting the same kinds of information.

The choice of any measuring technique (test, questionnaire, interview, physical trace measure, record, or observation) is, of course, dependent on what one wants to measure, why one wants to measure it, and how much data one wishes to collect. Especially in situations where experimental controls are missing or inadequate, the program director may want to obtain a number of different measures, the results of which may be used to reinforce one another. Several different weak measurements (weak, in terms of causal inference) of the same phenomenon may not substitute for one strong measurement but are certainly to be preferred to only one weak measurement.

SUMMARY

In summary, let us review the content of this paper and the steps a museum goes through in assessing the quality of an educational program:

1. The museum decides whether it wants to develop and offer special educational services. This decision is a complex one and not the subject of this paper, although some suggestion has been made that the decision can be made only in light of the total mission which the institution sees for itself.

2. If the museum has decided to offer an educational program, further decisions must be made about the resources it can allot to the overall program and what the general objectives should be.

3. Any proposal for a specific program (say, in Oriental art for high school students) is accepted or rejected on the basis of its "fit" with the general objectives.

4. The specific objectives of the accepted program are outlined. What knowledge, skill, understanding, appreciation, etc., is it hoped the program will foster?

5. Attempts are made to find out whether the program really encourages these behaviors—to measure the outcomes by whatever techniques seem most appropriate (test, questionnaire, interview, or an "unobtrusive" measure such as noseprints). The more carefully controlled the situation in which the measurements take place, the better the position one is in to infer that the program "caused" the results. In the absence of good experimental controls, a multifaceted approach to measurement and analysis is probably desirable in order to accumulate enough evidence to rule out as many alternative explanations of the outcome as possible.

6. On the basis of the results of the evaluation, the program is continued " as is," modified, or discarded. The greater the pressures on the museum, the less room there is for an ineffective program and the more need there is for careful evaluation and selection.

1. For a general discussion of the National Assessment Project, see the *Carnegie Quarterly*, 14:2, 1966, pp. 1–4

2. "Art Instruction in the Public Schools," *NEA Research Bulletin*, October 1963, pp. 90–93.

3. *Report of the Commission on the Humanities* (American Council of Learned Societies, Council of Graduate Schools in the United States, United Chapters of Phi Beta Kappa), 1964, pp. 23–24.

4. Supplement to the *Report of the Commission on the Humanities* (American Society for Aesthetics, introductory comment), 1964, p. 52.

5. Kramer, Hilton, "Art: Fete at Cleveland," *The New York Times,* June 14, 1966.

6. "Symposium: The Institutions of Art," *Arts in Society,* 3, 1965, p. 317.

7. See the pamphlet, "Making the Most of Your Museum Visit . . .," The Metropolitan Museum of Art Junior Museum, distributed by the Board of Education of the City of New York.

8. See the booklet, "Field Trips with a Difference," Cleveland Health Museum.

9. *Annual Report 1964–65,* Brooklyn Institute of Arts and Sciences.

10. See the brochure, "Summer 1966 Science Workshops," Philadelphia, The Franklin Institute.

11. "Handbook for Self-guided Tours," Chicago, The Museum of Science and Industry.

12. See the information sheet, "1966/1967 The World We Live In," a Program for the City of New York Schools, New York, Department of Education, The American Museum of Natural History.

13. Webb, E. J., Campbell, D. T., Schwartz, R. D., and Sechrest, Lee, *Unobtrusive Measures: Nonreactive Research in the Social Sciences,* Chicago, Rand McNally, 1966, p. 6.

14. *Ibid.,* p. 1.

15. Selltiz, Claire, Jahoda, Marie, Deutsch, Martin, and Cook, S. W., *Research Methods in Social Relations,* New York, Holt, Rinehart, and Winston, 1959, p. 97.

16. Webb *et al., op. cit.,* p. 35.

17. *Ibid.,* pp. 36–37.

18. *Ibid.,* pp. 45–46.

19. *Ibid.,* p. 113.

Kinds of Museums:
Youth. Art. History. Science

The Great Incorporation:
The Youth Museum and Education

HELMUTH J. NAUMER
Executive Director, Fort Worth Children's Museum

What is this institution called a "Children's, Junior, or Youth Museum"? Is it educational or is it merely a playhouse? Does it really have anything to offer? One consensus sometimes voiced is that a youth museum has no business entering the field of education. Against this charge, we in the profession must defend ourselves. We know the museum's educational production and potential. A youth museum does not fit the popular concept of a museum as a dark, dusty, vaulted edifice displaying curiosities. The concept of a youth museum is comparatively new; the first was established in Brooklyn in 1899. Today, there are approximately 490 youth museums and youth departments of larger museums in the U.S. that have been organized specifically to teach children through phyisical contact with collections and exhibits. All attempt to be programmed and designed around the child's attention span, his interests, and his rate of understanding.

Confronted with this large number of museums devoted to youth, one might well wonder why they have come into being. Of course, there had to be a need, either for individuals or groups to increase their social prominence, or possibly to find a place to store their children for a few hours. However, in most instances, a community will also have a definite need for more educational facilities, as well as for a storehouse for its collections of art or artifacts. The youth museum concept has good community appeal, not only financially, but educationally, and is an ideal kind of museum for a smaller community to start.

Youth museums are as varied as the needs of their communities, and what makes them unique is their adaptability to these needs. They range from small, one-room museums with part-time or volunteer staff—such as the Children's Museum in Bowie, Texas—to the country's most extensive, the Fort Worth Children's Museum, which has a physical plant of nearly one hundred thousand square feet, plus an observatory, on a ten-acre site and a four-hundred-acre nature center.

What the youth museum has to offer is usually misunderstood, not only by the museum profession but also by the public. A perusal of the programs and activities of some youth museums around the country is the only proper way to evaluate what they are doing. One unique feature of youth museums is the type of collections they maintain, which are both inert and alive, used not just as exhibits behind glass but as three-dimensional aids to introduce the world to children. All youth museums make valiant efforts to interpret their collections not just in exhibits but in the classroom. It is felt to be of the utmost importance that an artifact not merely be listed for its historical or cultural significance, but that it answer such different questions as: How was it made? How was it used? What was it used with? To whom did it belong? Does it relate to other artifacts? *ad infinitum*. A good example would be a tomahawk that can be used to show a part of Indian culture, or placed in an exhibit of world axes, or displayed with war implements, or used to explicate the evolution of the ax. Fortunately, having this attitude, youth museums are not inhibited by their lack of collections, though many of them suffer that lack because of their newness to the field. Sometimes, a whole story can be told with a single artifact or exhibit case. Another advantage to this type of museum is that, if the original artifact is not available, an exact replica may be used in its place. Other museums are usually not afforded this leniency. Youth museums have an independence to experiment on exhibits and activities in order to see what exhibit or pattern works best. A good example of this experimentation is a birds' egg exhibit at the Fort Worth Children's Museum. Here a small exhibit of birds' eggs in their nests was put together with a concise description of the birds, their nests and habits, but no mention of eggs.

A study showed that the eggs were what was remembered best in the exhibit simply because the youngsters had discovered the eggs for themselves. The exhibit would have been useless without the interpretive labels, but using this method of presentation made the impact that much greater. Through this method of interpretation and experimentation, youth museums have become leaders in interpreting collections to visitors.

There are several basic categories which museum exhibits fall into: the permanent exhibit, or halls telling complete sequential stories; the comparative exhibit, where a youngster may do his own identifying of a fossil, bird, or shell; the push button quiz boards where the challenge is to learn; the changing exhibit that alters the pace of the museum and keeps visitors coming back; experimental exhibits that do not always succeed; exhibits outside the museum that reach the non-museum visitor; the live animals that are every child's favorite; and the exhibits borrowed from others that help to acquaint the youngster with the world outside his own milieu.

The most important part of a youth museum, however, is not the exhibits but the programs planned around the collections, exhibits, and facilities. Most museums have a school; it varies in scope and size, but it is the real justification for the museum's existence. Unfortunately, although museums start with good intentions, usually, at first, this program leaves much to be desired because of the lack of trained personnel or proper direction or even adequate collections. These schools often become baby-sitting sections of a museum, but after growth, development, and higher standards are demanded of it, the museum school becomes the backbone of the rest of the museum program. Museum schools are designed to teach children, as well as adults, extracurricular subjects under ideal conditions of proper equipment and expert supervision with students learning at their own rate of speed. In this type of atmosphere, students learn from each other in nearly every subject imaginable, though of course mostly in subjects that relate to the museum's scope and interest.

Many youth museums have a preschool program, a relatively new area, but one that has so far been very successful. At the Fort Worth Children's Museum, where over six hundred children are enrolled for a nine-month period, a definite curriculum and faculty of child guidance experts have been set up to teach three-, four-, and five-year-olds art and science through exposure to artifacts and special equipment, such as the planetarium, the transparent woman, or the live animal room. As yet, this program is too young to be tested for real, concrete, long-term results, but an early study has already shown that the preschool program makes the later learning process easier and more fruitful.[1] Comments collected during this study from teachers in the Fort Worth Public School System show that museum preschoolers really want to learn and that their subsequent social adaptability to the first grade is far above the non-museum preschooler.

Every museum, on the other hand, is likely to concentrate attention on the older students, from age six up. A six-year-old can learn basic chemistry or physics, or have an opportunity to learn proper shading and perspective for the first time, as in the Experimental Art Program of the Fort Worth Children's Museum, where for years the graduates have won every state or local art contest they have entered. These interest courses last from six to fourteen weeks in most museums and are designed around participation and interest stimulation, so that a child will want to become more proficient in the subject. There is a decided effort to make these classes both educational and fun. Most children do not really know that education can be fun, and some museums find they must spend the first class period simply describing the excitement involved in a subject like physics. Many classes let the children select their own subject within a given field. Most museum schools rely on field trips as a stimulus to active participation. These range from a short farm visit to a full day's study of a nuclear reactor or a two-week scientific safari to study conchology or collect mammals for the museum's collections. Getting students out into the field with professionals not only speeds the learning process but also gives a more vivid picture of a possible, future profession. Museum school education is an exceptional success because students are not treated as children but as participants, and the instructor seems to, and usually does, learn with them. Museum schools exist to inspire in children an awareness of their surroundings and thus teach them to teach themselves. These schools vary from an attic of an old house to a school wing with sixteen fully equipped laboratory-classrooms, where every six-year-old interested in microscopy has his own microscope.

It is likely that the largest program, sometimes the first one started within a museum school, will be the group tours, where classes from surrounding schools take field trips to the museum to supplement their classroom work or just make a general walk through of the exhibits. The Fort Worth Children's Museum offers some eighteen different coordinated tours to classes in the social studies and sciences. Some museums have school coordinators assigned by the school system to put this program together; others try to do the job with existing personnel. Either way, this is one of the museum's most valuable programs since it offers hundreds of thousands of school children every year, throughout the country, a living view of their classroom subjects. When properly planned by the teacher and the museum, the school tour produces superb, lasting results and has become so popular with schools that many museums find it difficult to schedule every group that wants to participate.

Within the youth museum, there is nearly always a hard core of youngsters for whom the regular classes of the museum school do not offer enough of a challenge. These youngsters can become members of clubs under the direction of a curator or specialist. Here an intense interest is taken in the student, who has a chance to work behind the scenes with the professionals and truly become a part of running the museum. These organizations produce unbelievable results, such as in Fort Worth, where students do variable star research for the American Association of Variable Star Observers or where they have secured 35 percent of the type mammal specimens in the state of Texas. Some of these youngsters have found "firsts" and, after proper scientific work and publication, have had their discoveries named after them. Other museums, such as the Brooklyn Children's Museum, use these young people to assist in running summer archaeological field excavations. The Dayton Museum of Natural History uses these productive youngsters to actually run the museum. The most important part of this program is the introduction to legitimate research that is provided. Other museums—such as the Charlotte Children's

Nature Museum or the Rensselaer County Youth Museum, to mention just two—sponsor similar programs in archaeology, natural history, paleontology, and geology. Some museums, such as Fort Worth, again, have profitable arrangements with universities, such as the University of Oklahoma summer field school at Lake Texoma, where junior curators sometimes do better work than their university counterparts and are constantly welcomed back. A fruitful by-product of these club activities is seen in the science fair entries. Because the entire museum facilities and personnel are made available to the students, their entries for science fairs are much more scientific and intensive than the average. These students are not only learning and making a real contribution to science, but more important to the student is the fact that he has opened his own door to the scientific community.

Youth museums could not accomplish these programs without special facilities like planetariums, observatories, nature centers, live animal rooms, or special equipment like a mechanical, transparent woman. One of the most impressive and costly pieces of equipment is the planetarium and its theater. With this very effective tool, museums have not only been able to teach astronomy and astronautics to classes and the public, but also have adapted it to the earth sciences and history. With certain modifications, it can now be developed into an atmospherium, which explains meteorology more easily and simply than any other method yet devised, by filling a domed ceiling with stop-motion photography of the daytime sky. To the three-year-old or adult, a trip through space or seeing a thunderstorm develop is a thrilling, unforgettable experience. Several youth museums are fortunate in having observatories and telescope programs that extend astronomy to the public, as well as permitting research of the type already described with the club activities. Some have moon-watch programs like Fort Worth's where satellite observations have been made and turned in directly to the Smithsonian Astrophysical Observatory.

The vastness and beauty of the universe which a child sees through a telescope can also be demonstrated through nature centers, as is done so effectively at the Sacramento Junior Museum or the Stanford Museum. Many children's museums concentrate much of their activity on the outside environment. The more a child or adult becomes actively involved with the wonders around him, the greater his interest, and a true nature center or wild-life refuge—with interpretive labels along the trails, and/or a naturalist to describe the surroundings from grub worms to a darting fox—can be the catalyst that causes this to happen. A carry-over of the nature center will be the live animal room, the hallmark of every youth museum, where children can learn not to fear, but to respect and appreciate the animals that share their world. The live animals are used to their greatest advantage as teaching tools of conservation and nature, and their display in cages is only secondary.

The newest piece of equipment that is currently receiving much consideration by youth museums is the mechanical, transparent woman. One of the real deficiencies in this country's education program has been in health and medicine. The Fort Worth Children's Museum is the first youth museum to develop a program on health and medical science for youth. Not only will children learn the history of medicine from the rheumatoid arthritis of pithecanthropus erectus, 500,000 years ago, to the mechanical heart of today, but they also will be able to see a scientific presentation of how a baby is conceived, developed, and born. The transparent woman will help make this process much more understandable as she explains how the body functions and introduces an extensive exhibit hall on the physiology of man. This program is continued in the classrooms of the museum school, as well as in the clubs of the natural science department. The schools, colleges, universities, and hospitals of the area also have found it an excellent adjunct to their curriculum.

Youth museums have other programs that do not necessarily rely on the physical facilities. Among them are extension programs, round-table discussions, careers programs, in-service teacher training courses, lecture series, outside staff lecturers, and marionette programs, to name but a few. One of the most valuable types of assistance that any youth museum can provide for a school system is an extension program of loan material, which enables school systems to get many artifacts and three-dimensional materials for classroom use that could not be found elsewhere, thus increasing the educational productivity of the classroom. Most of these visual-aid materials take the form of mounted animals, fossils, shells, plants, and historic relics that either come singly or as small, interpretive "suitcase" exhibits. An excellent example of this program is the Boston Children's Museum's MATCHBOX project, sponsored by the Elementary and Secondary School Education Act, Title III, which offers well-researched and well-designed units that can be taken directly into the classroom as teaching aids. As another example, the Fort Worth Children's Museum supplies vast numbers of prepared mammals, insects, birds, and plants to local junior high classes—professionally evaluated specimens which have accompanying scripts and all the interpretive information needed by the teacher. Several museums have tried the roundtable discussion, initiated by the Charlotte Children's Nature Museum, to expose junior and senior high school students to the country's leading scientists, on subjects ranging from the weight and density of planets to the effects of radiation on human tissue. Here the intent is to supplement what the schools have to offer, for at no time do youth museums compete, or want to compete, with school systems. When there is good cooperation between school systems and museums, the community as a whole is bound to be rewarded.

Another activity that may seem unrelated to a museum's basic purpose is the careers program. Several museums have arranged to assist youngsters in selecting a career by bringing the local talent in business and science to sit down with them and offer professional counseling, a program which has proved extremely successful in both Charlotte and Fort Worth. The Charlotte sessions are televised and, thus, reach many thousands of high school students; the Fort Worth sessions handle as many as seven hundred at one time, with over one hundred counselors available.

Many communities do not have the facilities to give teachers in-service training, with the result that several museums have taken on the task. Charlotte is, again, a good example: the State of North Carolina gives teachers credit for their museum courses, which are given by the best and most experienced teachers in the school system, but within the museum and with museum equipment.

At one time or another, all youth museums provide a lecture series.

Two of these are the "National Audubon Screen Tours" and the "World Around Us," and some museums even make a little profit from them. Supplementing the series in a well-rounded museum program would be the outside lectures given by museum specialists, which extend the museum's benefits to school science clubs or summer youth camps. For all intents and purposes, marionette or hand puppet shows would seem equally unaligned with basic museum philosophy, but they have been employed experimentally to get ideas across to children. The East Bay Park District Nature Center in California has used them to teach nature conservation and to describe scientific concepts.

Youth museums are, unfortunately, far from perfect. One of the most acute problems is the emphasis on quantity rather than quality. Quantity does more for immediate financing, because to a community and board of trustees, attendance figures are more tangible than the long-term results. Youth museums desperately need research on their programs, so that the museum professionals can have concrete evaluations to offer of their accomplishments or failures. Otherwise, the complaint most often heard from museum personnel, aside from the lack of money, will continue to be the shortage of trained personnel and the inadequacy of educational opportunities to train new or improve existing personnel. A solution to these deficiencies must be found before the total incorporation of the youth museum and education can be completed.

Among the youth museum's current problems is its name. The titles "Children's," "Junior," or "Youth" carry a connotation that is misunderstood by the public. Adults believe it is only for children, teenagers feel they are too adult, and more knowledgeable individuals feel it is beneath them. A general name change would be advisable, in any event, because in fact youth museums do not exist. No community can afford the luxury of a museum just for children. Activities must be programmed for the older student and adult, not only because of community need but because adults do the financing. Youth museums could be better defined as *family* museums, where activities are geared not only to reach our curious children but also citizens of all ages who have a similar desire to learn. Regardless of their faults and various titles, the youth museums are here to stay, for they fulfill an obligation to the adults of tomorrow in their great incorporation of the museum ideal with an ideal of education.

1. Kamenitsa, Maxine Elliott, *Planning, Teaching, and Evaluating a Preschool Science Program for Children's Museums,* Denton, Texas, Texas Woman's University, August 1958. (Thesis for M.A. degree.)

Museums and Education: The Role of the Art Object

SUE M. THURMAN
Director
Boston Institute of Contemporary Art

The Smithsonian Institution Conference on Museums and Education gathered together for a week in Vermont in the name of STUFF—the goods of the universe, things: old or new, typical or unique, essential or optional, etc. What unites us as conferees is the fact that we *all work at showing things to people* on a nonprofit—and presumably, educational—basis. Whereas other sectors of the world of education now focus upon living human beings (even children's dentists proclaim the treatment of "children, not teeth"), it is generally understood that our sector may focus unabashedly upon things—provided they are presented in behalf of people, or as a record of people. (Think how this sets apart our specialist, Richard Grove, from all his cospecialists in the Arts and Humanities Branch of the Division of Educational Research at the U.S. Office of Education.)

Excited by the prospect of our multitude of unresolved issues finally being joined—at the nation's expense and for the general benefit—I agreed to do a portion of the advance homework. My assignment is to try to clarify *the role of the art object* in our overall considerations. I suspect that I won this job as the direct result of always having argued, often beyond the protection of my own professional circle, that art museum "education" worthy of the word emanates largely from the works of art, sensitively offered—that it is not a hubbub of supportive activity, as such.

My view, in brief, is that *all* members—not just a designated few—of this rare tribe of professionals who work in art museums are involved with education. Hopefully, each one is "called" there, whatever may be the exact specifications of his daily job, by the nature of what can be *seen* there, for that is the paramount distinction of an art museum.

Otto Wittmann has recently reminded us that art museums are still this country's newest form of educational institution, the great majority dating within the twentieth century. Only a couple of centuries ago, there was not an art museum anywhere. All of us are aware of the major conceptual changes through which art museums have passed but it may surprise you to note that this has all occurred in so short a span of time.

Under any circumstances, it would be natural to expect that our future would hold many possibilities not yet realized, nor even touched upon. In view of the particular directions in which the extensions of man are moving today, our tomorrow seems particularly promising. I cannot see how visual-arts museums can fail to play tremendously important educational roles in the future, unless we refuse to nurture them, day-to-day, with an eye toward their unique potentials.

What is an art museum? What are its unique educational potentials?

Educationally, an art museum is unlike a school of any type, even an art school; and, essentially, it is quite different from other kinds of museums (science, history, etc.) in terms of the kinds of learning it offers, and the ways these are best induced. Indeed, homes of the visual arts seem especially incompatible, as realms of exploration, with those of the collateral arts (music, theatre, dance, etc.)—though roof-sharing "families" are now being established everywhere.

Art museums must shape their role in and with the larger arts clan, where performance is the thing, and they must sharpen their focus within the larger museum community. I shall, however, defer our complex "arts family" problems to the conference discussions, where they are sure to arise in connection with scheduling educational events in museums.[1]

As I began to ponder the basic educational aspects of the art museum calling, I made it my business to study, for comparative purposes, the voluminous report of a major antecedent to this present meeting: namely, the Seminar on Elementary and Secondary School Education in the Visual Arts (1964). Those sessions were also financed by a grant from the Office of Education, and likewise constituted a giant step forward, by the very virtue of being called.

On page one, the school art educators voiced their conference plea. I was delighted to find that school art goals had become twofold—not only "creative expression" but also "cultural understanding." Can you imagine my disappointment, 234 pages later, at having found a total of only four minor mentions of art museums?

This seems to me to be one of the loudest silences ever recorded.

In actuality, their conference was heavily weighted toward creative expression, and when intervals of attention to cultural understanding occasionally occurred, they did not center upon the local art museum, though we might justifiably have expected that they would. This, as I said, was disappointing, mostly because the report was otherwise exemplary. But my mention of it is intended only as a warning, lest this conference, too, become distracted by (and I quote) "a sense of compelling professional responsibility." With apologies to our friends in the schools, it is no wonder they overlooked—quite inadvertently, I am sure—some of their favorite institutions. Nobody can think creatively about his role in the art field unless he can, upon occasion, blank out the administrative burdens of his office and concentrate totally—and with real joy at the chance—upon ART.

To prove to any doubters that I, too, boast folios full of very practical operational concerns and reams of urgent research proposals, and also to get these out of my system without spoiling the mood for thinking about art per se, I have drafted some rather formidable procedural outlines and added those documents to my conference paraphernalia, for any shareable value they may have to anyone. Having been so diligent, I feel I have earned my right to indulge hereafter in the most casual kind of reverie touching base with art, and hence—indirectly—with any educational values it offers.

Since I have the best intentions of finding fresh relationships to matters we all hold dear, and since any "dethroning" which may occur is really approached in so sentimental a spirit, I think you might label the style of my presentation "Camp"—innocence, fantasy, attenuation, exaggeration, flamboyance, annoyance, passion: *why not?* We may uncover some new clues or some fine old ones we had forgotten.

If anything could be wilder than to have agreed to write a conference warm-up paper on the subject of ART AND MUSEUMS AND EDUCATION, it would have been to settle for THE ROLE OF THE ART OBJECT IN MUSEUM EDUCATION, which is what really happened. Every time the Smithsonian nicely revised our program outline, some crack proofreader struck off my vital word "object,"—without stopping to comprehend the agonizing validity of this inconsistency.

Even a sidewalk poll would establish the point. We could ask people, "Why have art museums?" Without batting an eye, most of them would tell us: "for art objects"; whereas, with counterpart questions, they would not be apt to say "for science objects," or "for history objects." With both the latter, the thing-units consolidate to compose overall lessons. In the sciences, the lesson may deal with a principle; in history, the lesson may deal with an epoch. People visit art museums, however, to see the thing-units, the art objects, which sometimes tell stories but only as bonuses.

WHAT IS AN ART OBJECT?

From this page forward, it is: not a responsibility; not a valuation, an accessions number, nor a storage problem; not from a special collection, nor for a certain exhibition; not the necessity for a label, nor the urgency for a press release; not lure for endowment, nor bait for attendance; not, even, a seed for the core curriculum.

For taking on those responsibilities, we receive our paychecks. From looking at art, we gain a very pure kind of experience.

Art experience is of a type which can, in the best instances, bring understanding which is not to be had otherwise. It is basic education, applicable in all subsequent sight and stance, anywhere.

You will see.

ART OBJECT SCOPE

Art objects are the makings of artists. I am sorry, but I believe this encompasses everything we know for sure, and—as you are already aware—it is hard to know who is an artist. To show that I am not ridiculing definitiveness—I am only unable to provide it—I shall give you a few helpful comments found in the manuscripts and books which now happen to be on my desk. At such an institution as mine, the passing batches of working materials tend to offer a useful range of current thought. Quoting them will spread the base of art voices beyond my own and those of the four or five other workaday art museum types who are present here.

At the risk of inciting in-rioting—among Victor D'Amico, Carter Brown, Bartlett Hayes, Edgar Richardson, Hanna Rose, and myself —I am going to start out by quoting Marshall McLuhan. M. M. (*he* calls the Virgin Mary "V. M.") says that art is things done as well as possible, reminding us of the Balinese, who say they have no art. Susan Sontag assures us that a work of art is first of all an object, not an imitation of something else—which I hope we can take as a basic, though it will always bother us later, when we consider the deeds we may do.[2]

Transcriptions of artists' panel discussions held recently at the Institute provide the following contributions—extemporaneous, and out of context:

Ulfert Wilke: "What is art? Not just an ordinary word, but a very broad word. It can be a self-portrait of Rembrandt, like the one in the Altman Collection at the Metropolitan . . . a late portrait which invites the entire human participation, compassion, a feeling of tragedy and sentiment. Or, it can be a hard-edge painting with only three colors in it. Or, it can be a work inspired by popular or even commercial art . . . all the way from works which invite the entire human compassion, the understanding of life and humanism, to segments which deal, to speak with the words of Delacroix, an invitation just as a feast for the eye."

George Segal: "Good art offers a certain kind of illumination, and sometimes an intensity of image. When it offers both, we value it even without the right [historic] context for it. We do have the right context for seeing today's shaped-styrofoam packing forms [the focus was Found Objects], but we can't say this about them. . . . [Later, about whether every man could be his own artist, on a 'selective trash' basis.] Obviously people differ greatly in their ability to make images."

The listener could hear a kind of agreement: that the more sensitivity the person has, the more likely he is to see art broadly, and in its own terms.

> *Varujan Boghosian:* "It is the artist's duty to show the observer something more than he or she is (otherwise) capable of seeing. Right?"

One panelist went so far as to doubt that it is the artist's duty to leave visible evidence in any form.

> *Allan Kaprow:* "What is the difference between a manually transformed object and a mentally transformed object? . . . Who says the artist has to carry it all the way? . . . Can an artist create something by claiming it? Can an artist claim something by creating it? Traditionally art-making is considered the 'action,' and art appreciation is considered the 'response.' Why are art actions more signable than art responses?"

Kaprow says responses are also acts. For him, "happenings" are replacing objects as art form. He says that artists might ultimately spend their creative time conducting visual tours.

Obviously, no one agrees with *all* of the foregoing comments. But it bears noticing that even Art Object Scope is not among the fixed certainties, as registrars in art museums have always realized.

What gets art objects across to us? This, too, is a long-standing and fairly unresolved problem. Art is considered to have values of some pure sort, with direct, personal impact being among the highest. But what is the transmission like? What is the nature of whatever can transfer? To be utterly practical, we need to discover whether anything about our branch of education is, indeed, "instructional." A nationwide art museum necessity relating to Education, is *to discover to what degree we can assist in the understanding of art.*

To dive in headfirst, I will ask a corollary question. Could there be any such thing as "instant education" via an art object? Can it be scheduled, allotted, parceled—for beginners, or for connoisseurs; always, sometimes, or never? Nobody who spends most of his waking hours inside an art museum is in a position to know what would happen if he stopped in twice a year and, even then, never stopped walking.

Just about now, it may be that I am nearing my first million "treasures," counting those seen in other people's museums and my own, in artists' studios, in commercial galleries, and in jury warehouses. If I were to go into retreat to recall my close acquaintances from all those introductions, I expect the results would be indicative of something we need to know. With rare exceptions, the best remembered would certainly be among the best seen, and the best seen would usually correlate with some considerable span of association-time. For me, this has been every day—for several weeks or months—because the majority of my years in art museums have been spent with temporary exhibition spans. Though convinced that long, thorough exposure is essential, I am going to risk adding that I think there is—working in the other direction—also some kind of cutoff: a plateau, on which no more can be seen, at least for a while.

I hope that the implications are not too disillusioning; after all, the notion that every "masterpiece" grows dearer with every passing day of association is a claim which is otherwise reserved for loved ones. Whatever may prove to be true about aesthetic attention spans, I think that a great deal more than we know today *is* ascertainable, probably by skillful testing. Despite all the complications, it does seem safe to acknowledge that there is such a thing as appreciation time among the essentials for art object conveyance. I have come across a seasoned (1949) quotation of Mark Tobey's which sounds uncannily prophetic of the "depth involvement of faculties" statements of M. M. and others nowadays.

> *Mark Tobey:* "Who can say what we get out of meditating on a work of art, or who can say how long it will take to digest a work of art? If the thing isn't a work of art, I think it is digested very quickly; but I think that a painting which is a work of art is digested very slowly and must be lived with a long time."

> *Ulfert Wilke:* "Why not let the object work on you? It will be nice to change your experience. . . . Filling in too much destroys what is there . . . so why not try the low-resistance theory? Schopenhauer tells us: 'before a work of art, be as in the presence of a great man; wait until *it* speaks.' Very often it speaks very late. Or we are too preoccupied to respond. One of the beautiful things about art is to respond whenever you can bring yourself about it. Just waiting can be very hopeful and rewarding."

André Malraux reminds us that in the Orient the role of art has been seen for fifteen centuries as a deepening and adorning of communion with the universe. There art is to be viewed privately, in a proper state of grace. I would add that the Oriental manner of putting works of art away between sessions undoubtedly has as much to do with heightening the contact of each occasion, as it has with protecting the especially vulnerable media. All things considered, it does seem rather strange that we Westerners (and other peoples we have influenced) assemble hundreds and thousands of art works under one roof and invite the interested looker to come in. As perception fatigue necessarily precedes foot fatigue, it is small wonder that the average unsuspecting visitor suffers a severe aesthetic overload —if not aversion, or even antipathy.

In view of the likelihood of repletion, why does any art museum educator ever allow himself to be impressed by complaints from the public about the art works? Compatibility, i.e., "public relations" between the art work and its audience, is an area which we as professionals—yes, even as professional art educators—do best to ignore. Frank Lloyd Wright, who was always allowed to be blunt, announced a long while back: "It just simply doesn't matter what the public's reaction to works of art is." Ortega y Gasset points to what he calls the "distances" of art, urging that they be fully respected. Ortega, calling art "dehumanized representation," regrets that most people miss most of what is to be had from aesthetic experience by taking it too much in stride, treating it as if it were just another pleasure.

This brings us back to those questions we must ask, if we are to remember even vaguely that we are art museum educators. What can art cause to happen to people who experience it? What does art convey, granted favorable conditions?

Susan Sontag: "A work of art encountered as a work of art is an experience, not a statement or an answer to a question. . . . Art is not *about* something; it *is* something. . . . A work of art is a thing *in* the world, not just a text or commentary *on* the world. A work of art makes us see or comprehend something singular, not judge or generalize. . . . Comprehension, accompanied by voluptuousness, is the only valid end, the only sufficient justification for a work of art. What art gives rise to, properly, is excitation, a phenomenon of commitment, a state of thralldom or captivation. Art is seduction. To become involved with a work of art entails . . . detaching oneself from the world. But the work of art itself is also a vibrant, magical, and exemplary object which returns us to the world in some way more open and enriched. Art is a mode of nourishment."

Thus, far more than being part of the look of the place which it dominates (this could very loosely be called the "decoration" role), and also beyond helping to satisfy the familiar deficiences of people who see it (this parallels other entities in the "reduction of uncertainties" role), art can go farther—much farther.

George Segal: "Art can even set up situations [he cited Kaprow's 'happenings,' which are all participation and no audience] where each person encountering whatever it is walks away with a largely intensified view. . . . This is super-teaching, wanting to effect a deep and profound change in the lives of people."

Robert Motherwell: "The ultimate value of what we're involved in is the degree to which the world of sensed feeling is extended, refined, internalized, and incorporated in every human individual [he addressed the school-art seminar]. . . . The capacity to compose is really the capacity to give coherence to sensed experience."

My final questions on conveyance are the ones most human in focus, those which would relate beings to each other.

First: can we get to the artist himself through his work? Two extremities of opinion about this matter.

Marcel Duchamp: "We don't emphasize enough that the work of art is independent of the artist. *The work of art lives by itself,* and the artist who happened to make it is like an irresponsible medium. No artist can say at any time: I am a genius. I am going to paint a masterpiece. . . . The artist pulls out of the canvas the work of art."

George Segal: "It has just occurred to me what a work of art is. *Art is a form of superior gossip.* So at best when we look at the work of an interesting artist we get a very uncanny kind of quick shortcut into what kind of guy that person is, or girl. . . . Our intense interest is in other people that we can respond to somehow, and more than on the level of cocktail party manners. . . . A lot of us get drawn to art

> because there is that honesty revealed without pretense. . . . A lot of lying goes on in art; we take that for granted. In spite of the lying, there is a human being behind all that business. I was more than joking when I said art is a form of superior gossip."

And always there is the question: does the artist have the spectator in mind? I must confess to consciously demoting this feigned union into the lowest position. What is the artist "trying" to say? Most are saying *nothing,* especially to "that" inflection. The idea that the artist has sent the art work because he himself was unable to be present is flattering but false, and I abhor it for the travesties it causes in the name of education.

ART OBJECT INTERPRETATION

So, people called artists make altogether impractical but wonderful objects called art. And these really can get over to receptive human beings, one way or another, and deliver—more than anything else—very uncommon sensory impacts, or impacts common only to this given realm. Now, what more is to be added by us, the educators, or what is to be avoided? Need objects of art be interpreted? *Can* objects of art be interpreted?

THE LOW ROAD

Susan Sontag traces this "itch to interpret" (her phrase) back to the coming of scientific enlightenment, pointing out that new information automatically set aside myths which had been credible until that time. This brought the necessity to reconcile the past with the new times. Reviewed in this light, interpretation blurred rather than clarified. It "revamped history and altered heritage"—strong words—again, in the name of understanding.

> *Susan Sontag:* "Interpretation . . . cuts out sensory experience altogether, by taking for granted that such experience happens, and getting on to 'more important'—more discussable?—matters. We are reminded that in the greatest art, one is always aware of the abundance of what cannot be said."

I thoroughly agree with her view that the most potent elements in a work of visual art are often its silences. I believe that every art museum worker everywhere—including especially the newest volunteer docent—should hear and heed Miss Sontag's principal cry: that it is over-emphasis upon the idea of content which brings on "the perennial, never consummated project of interpretation."

> *Susan Sontag:* "In most modern instances, interpretation amounts to the philistine refusal to leave the work of art alone. Real art has the capacity to make us nervous. By reducing the work of art to its content, then interpreting *that,* one tames the work of art. . . . Interpretation makes are manageable, comfortable."

Surely there would be no "art-tamers" present here. But are there ladies-bountiful back home, primed to explain, or lay executives, starved for art investment advice? Malraux places the blame for these appalling expectations—which are only typical of the inappropriatenesses which education in art museums can create—upon the concept of *museum establishment* as such. Though surely the enlightenment forced reconciliations to a new degree, the real basis of our troubles remains, for Malraux, the fact that we dared to assemble art as it was not made to be assembled: that is, as museum exhibitions and collections. So far as he is concerned, this brought on all our woes of justification.

Since we were indulging in unnatural order, we soon had to arrive at categories for sorting and storing: crucifixes became "sculpture"; chalices, "decorative arts." Portraits became paintings, then soon they became their painters. Some works were detached from their surroundings and thereby lost all significance, whereas others, being undetachable (overweight, out of scale), fell totally out of "art range" by default. Thus, wholly new attitudes were imposed upon the spectator, and perpetual explanations seemed to be in order.

This seems to be undebatable and, to some extent, uncorrectable. None of us, least of all Malraux himself—as French Minister of State, Responsible For Culture—would lightly cancel out the total achievements of today's art museum complex, not as a cure for misstating the case for their contents. In a way, I am sorry to have been the one chosen to open up these educational anxieties, to review realistically the picture of how badly the best intentions can miss the overall mark—to state how anti-educational the predigestion of art for its audience actually is. Trusting that so painful a diagnosis may be followed by a equally emphatic recovery, I shall conclude by dwelling upon the positive side of what lies before us.

THE HIGH ROAD

What type of guidance—evidently something subtler than has been practiced by those most effervescent third parties—*does* appear to be legitimate for the museum art education situation? Do any appropriate educational avenues appear to be open, or able to be cleared? Reorientation of our thoughts is in order.

Think back to the art-prone viewer—the one who was always getting along fine with the art he approached, given sufficient time and tranquility. (Obviously, his creative mind was "running for its own goals," which would gratify M. M.) Was that art-prone viewer ever a not-prone viewer? *Every* living mortal was.

Usually we find that the more ready the looker, the longer he has been at such things. Seldom, it appears, does a person who gets all the way through childhood, adolescence, and young adulthood without artistic involvement suddenly—in established adulthood—become a communicant of real substance. (If blitz training courses will ever achieve this, indeed we have not hit upon the right kind up to now.) As it is risky to establish any ideal, early-life starting time on present evidence, it would seem safest to expose children all along the way, and follow up indications of genuine interest whenever they come.

Obviously, the very most "prone" art viewers are artistic. So how do people become *artists*? Probably along the same kind of path, with some special intensities and aptitudes added. It is definitely true that good teaching in the schools and the activities of art museums have set some artists on their way. But conversational research (which deserves checking out, and would readily adapt to scientific method) holds that the most prevalent incentives for getting really close to aesthetic experience are even more direct. The person gets to know an artist and comes to respect the approach firsthand; or, the person sees an art work which he would give anything to have produced.

Clearly, if art museum educators could know that all visitors would arrive already "art prone," everything would be ideal: we would know how to let well enough alone; or, if we knew how to *get* all our visitors into that state suddenly, we could then step aside. Failing either miracle, we can at least adopt the framework which is indicated; we can at least remember that their independence is our goal in whatever we do. To paraphrase, not failure but *contrived dependence* is our crime. Developments of the type we seek are commonly extremely gradual ones, whatever the realm of learning. Accepting gradualism, we do find avenues whereon *educators of superior qualifications may do some leading* from non-prone into art prone, via the art object.

Rudolph Arnheim feels that "untalkable" theories are tempting, but that they are taken to excess by purists. He finds that art is extremely hard to deal with in words, but that almost everything else is also. Arnheim is his own best proof that words per se do not have to paralyze creative dynamism if granted: constant balancing—looking, then words, then looking; giving and taking; working "for the object as well as on it." Though Arnheim speaks mostly about perceptive insight on the part of the viewer, working alone with the object, his system does adapt itself to the minds of others—though surely to a lesser degree than to his own, the party of the first part. Thus, it indicates that educative experience can be aided via excellent, individualized commentary.

I believe that Arnheim sees response as one part becalmed, hanging loose, *giving* (Eastern conveyance), and one part *tension* (rapt person to fixed object)—both essential halves, thus the total. But he clearly also allows for heightening: extra *attention* (succeessful leading). This suggests comparison with "slipstreaming" in racing cars, with the driver of a less powerful car following immediately upon a more powerful one, thus being able to exceed his own established maximum speed.

As we know by now, Susan Sontag stands officially against interpretation. But even she concedes that extremely good criticism can serve an art work and viewer well. Good criticism, very rare according to Miss Sontag, concentrates upon super-*description,* not upon subjectivity, and is definitely worthy of the viewer's attention.

James Ackerman, in appraising what kind of approach can actually be of some help, seems to me to set the toughest standards of all—in terms of the expectations they place upon art educators. Speaking of the art historian's goal as educator, he says that it should be one of removing obstacles, of revealing in an all-out way the genuine uniqueness of the art work. For Ackerman, the supreme good would be to teach in a dual context. An art work would be looked at as the product —via the artist—of its co-affectors: the "internal continuity of style" and the "external current stimuli." Thus, he accommodates pleas for both the cultural and the physical settings.

If art museums can ever be staffed to the point where they can practice such time-consuming systems—perhaps with corps of graduate researchers assisting every front man, as happens now on campus— they may be able to apply the best of Ackerman, Arnheim, and Sontag in documenting art objects fully: both as direct plasticity and as tangible evidence of the cultural milieu. Meantime, it is imperative that each of us examines his own convictions regarding the art object in the art museum.

IS THE OBJECT ITSELF TO BE THE VORTEX?

If it is, present educational practices will have to be reviewed; generally prevailing emphases will have to be reversed; and new possibilities for proceeding to present art objects educationally will have to be researched with all due haste and support.

1. They did (Eric Larrabee, editor).
2. It did (Eric Larrabee, editor).

Does the Museum of History Teach History?

JAMES J. HESLIN
Director, The New-York Historical Society

It is fitting that a Conference on Museums and Education should take place in Vermont. This is the state once represented in Congress by Senator Justin Morrill, father of the Land Grant College Acts, by means of which many Americans have been able to attend college. It was a Vermonter, Samuel Reed Hall, a schoolmaster, who introduced that homely but useful teaching tool, the blackboard, and it was Hall who wrote the first teacher's manual. Burlington, itself, was the birthplace of the man identified with the philosophy of education —John Dewey. The participation of the American people in cultural pursuits was one of the ideals of the sages of the eighteenth and nineteenth centuries. The manifestation of this participation, evidenced in the statistics relating to museum attendance—to use an example most immediately important to those attending this Conference—would appear to justify the hopes of all who have believed that the American people would one day realize their aesthetic and educational potential.

The information that more than one hundred million people in this country (between one hundred and two hundred million is one estimate) attend museums annually is remarkable. This, it appears, is more than the number attending the baseball games of all the major league teams in a year and—with the possible exception, one supposes, of the entrepreneurs and participants connected with professional baseball—there is general satisfaction with these statistics.[1]

A study of tourist interests in New York state in 1965, recently published by the state's Department of Commerce (the first such study in a projected series about New York's tourist industry) presents some further figures concerning museum attendance. Art galleries and museums, historic sites, and battlefields are among New York's most popular attractions. The figures represent attendance in general and are not limited to vacationers or tourists specifically, but they do indicate what people like to do in their leisure time and can act as a guide in reflecting the preferences of vacation travelers. Of a total of more than 115 million visitors, nearly 17 million went to art galleries and museums. The 16,824,974 visits to these institutions, plus the approximately 8.5 million visits to historic sites, exceeded attendance at the next most popular attraction—horse racing—by almost half a million.[2]

Museums have triumphed nationally over baseball and, in the second most populous state in the Union, are victorious over horse racing. Surely, if we were reasonable people we could rest and congratulate ourselves. As it happens, we are not reasonable people but quite the contrary, as in George Bernard Shaw's remark that: "The reasonable man adapts himself to the world: the unreasonable one persists in trying to adapt the world to himself. Therefore all progress depends on the unreasonable man."

Perhaps, after all, we are not so unreasonable. Despite the attendance boom, according to an article in *The New York Times* on 18 July 1965, museum costs have risen while endowments have shrunk. In addition, scholarly publications and research have almost disappeared, and such money as is available for scholarly study has been eaten up by the expense of new educational programs for the proliferating public. About two weeks later, on 1 August 1965, *The Times* carried an article outlining the protests of some of the large museums which claimed that scholarly research has, in fact, risen and that endowments have grown, although there was no dispute about museums' need for more money. In brief, the big museums claim to be able to make their funds go further which still, of course, leaves the smaller museums in a less favorable position; as we well know, there are many small museums in this country.

It may not be so "unreasonable," then, to consider history museums —those institutions which have been described, alas, as the poor relations in the museum family.[3] Of the total attendance at museums, however, over 25 percent is accounted for by visitors to history museums and historical restorations. Undoubtedly, much of this reflects an increased interest in American history—an interest which has accelerated sharply since the end of World War II. The war itself, as is probably inevitable in times of national stress, stimulated interest in the history of the United States. This interest is also demonstrated in increased graduate study in history in the universities, and in heightened popular interest not only in museums of history but in the presentation of historical information in other ways, such as novels, television and radio programs, and the cinema. It may be also, as has been suggested, that as the American of this second half of the twentieth century has become less zealous for the future, he has become more concerned with the past.[4]

There has, really, never been a period in which Americans have shown complete indifference toward their history. Even when the states were colonies, there were historians narrating the genesis and development of those regions. The Revolutionary War prompted the subsequent generation to read about that great event and, in the growing nationalism following the war, history was assigned a special place in schemes for a national education. Daniel Webster, for one, believed that the principal schoolbook in the country ought to be a manual of American history.

Just as there has always been an interest in American history, so too have there always been museums in the United States with some orientation toward history. In 1773, before the states were united, what is now the Charleston Museum in South Carolina was engaged in collecting natural history specimens relating to that colony. The historical societies, although largely library centered, had their "cabinets," as collections of various objects were called, and while there was strong emphasis on natural history during the first half of the nineteenth century, nonetheless, historical societies preserved considerable important Americana which might otherwise be lost to us today.

In the early days of the American Republic there were, of course, those who deplored the seeming indifference to American history. John Adams, for one, complained in 1813 that there was no interest in history on the part of Americans. "Can you account for the apathy, the antipathy of this nation to their own history? Is there not a repugnance to the thought of looking back? While thousands of frivolous novels are read with eagerness and got by heart, the history of our own native country is not only neglected, but despised and abhorred."[5] The situation was not actually as grim as Adams pictured it, and what Jefferson once described as the "Declaration-men" clearly had a deep interest in the spread of knowledge about American history. Naturally enough, they expected others to share this interest.

The Civil War acted as a catalyst in increasing interest in American history after the middle of the nineteenth century but, curiously, the colleges and universities, where one might expect the study of history to flourish, were slow to develop a professional approach in this field. The first seminar in history began only in 1869, at the University of Michigan, a date which marks the arrival of a more "scientific" approach. As we glance backward at these developments, so slow in coming to fruition, it seems even more impressive that the past two decades are characterized by such an increased interest in history—especially on the part of a large segment of the general public.

Nonetheless, one cannot avoid a nagging sense that there is more to be done today in history museums—in the visualization of history, so to speak—if we are to educate and instruct the public more effectively. In saying this it is necessary, not by way of defense but in explanation, to note that history museums also have their peculiar problems. Assuming that the museum of history has an educational function—indeed, assuming that museums in general have primarily an educational function (and I am not altogether sure that this is an assumption universally shared)—we might agree that the trinity of *collection, preservation,* and *dissemination* continues to pose questions as to how these activities can be best accomplished. I doubt that *collection* is the major problem in the history museum. When I say this, I am assuming that our efforts and energies are constantly directed toward the enrichment of our collections. I strongly suspect that whatever we do in the way of education, or in creating new buildings, or issuing publications, our institutions in later years will be important in relation to the collections they house. It is the material we have which justifies our existence in the first place. There are, obviously, occasions when the lack of funds which plagues nearly all institutions makes some acquisitions difficult. By and large, however, there is a distinct feeling today on the part of owners of material of historic interest that such items should be saved, and the reasonably active history museum profits from this attitude. (A less happy corollary of this attitude, regrettably, is the offer, and frequently the acceptance, of miscellany without any but the most tenuous relation to the elucidation of American history.)

To some degree, we all collect historical objects as we save the things of daily existence, and let time bestow its own historical value on them. But if we recollect that active museum collecting in history dates from the middle of the nineteenth century, we can see that the history museums have managed to gather a substantial amount. Some of it, to be sure, demands weeding and much perhaps never deserved to be collected in the first place, but the combined resources of the history museums are quite impressive. Perhaps they would be more so if these institutions *were* consolidated and less fragmented. Collecting might then begin to be more efficient and fewer local history museums would attempt to acquire material on every facet of American historical development.

Preservation obviously includes more than mere storage, whether hidden away or, in the form of "visible storage," ranged in tedious ranks throughout the building. Preservation, among other things, demands expertise—the knowledge of the painting restorer, the skill of the craftsman concerned with the decorative arts, the researcher who can distinguish, in effect, which items merit priority in care and display and which do not. Here, unhappily, most history museums also suffer from the lack of a trained staff, or indeed from the lack of staff generally. Thus, even minimal preservation is difficult to achieve. In the museum field, as a whole, we are often told that we lack the tools characteristic of the libraries: the indexes, catalogs, union lists of holdings, and descriptive matter generally, so useful in everyday practice. This is true, and a central organization which functions as does the Library of Congress, or some of the large university libraries, would be most helpful. Even lists, with the briefest descriptions of the holdings of history museums, would be mutually helpful and of assistance to the scholarly world. But how many institutions have published such guides to their holdings? If we think of "preservation" not only as the preservation of the actual object, but also the preservation of knowledge gained about the object, we are lagging indeed.

It is the area of *dissemination*—by means of interpretive exhibits and publications—that most directly affects the general public. We can collect material and we can, as well as possible, preserve it, but basically we conceive of the museum function as the presentation of material for educational purposes. We do this in order to help visitors try to reconstruct the past. The preparation for the installation of exhibits varies in depth depending on the available resources, staff, and material. Prior to any exhibition, there is *some* research, depending on accessible facilities. There are history museums fortunate enough to possess libraries of consequence or access to such libraries. Whatever the size of the institution, however, even if only a minimal checking of dates is involved (and this is hardly research) some background preparation takes place. But the more extensive the research, the more complicated may be the problem of exhibition. How, for example, does one present adequately, such an important event in American history as the struggle for independence?

John Adams said that the true American Revolution was in the minds and hearts of the people, and in the union of the colonies, both of which were effected before actual hostilities began against Great Britain. Adams observed further that "a history of military operations from April 19, 1775, to the 3rd of September, 1783, is not a history of the American Revolution."[6] Adams viewed the military campaigns as but one phase of the War for Independence, and—although it is most unlikely that he would deny their importance—it is evident that other less tangible factors were of consequence to him. How then *does* one present the story of the American Revolution in order to emphasize its varied aspects to a public of different educational levels—by a display of documents, either original or in photocopies? But we are told so often that people dislike to read long labels and, if this is so, would they then read extensive, or even less than extensive, documentation? Can it be done by issuing succinct explanatory leaflets to visitors? But then are we not verging on the function of the library? (It has been my observation, incidentally, that to the degree people are interested in *reading* history they are less interested in museum displays. Certainly this seems to be true of professional scholars in the field.) Does a likeness of Franklin, a portrait of Jefferson, or an engraving of John Adams—the three men constituting the committee appointed to draft the Declaration of Independence, the apex, so to speak, of the Revolutionary War—aid in illuminating an understanding of that significant document? Are examples of the uniforms and weapons used in the military campaigns of the war sufficient to help the public grasp the political evolution in the colonies which culminated in armed rebellion? Are dioramas or mechanically operated devices, however ingenious, relating the history we ought to present?

If, for example, we attempt to treat one part of the War for Independence, whether it be economic, political, military, or naval, are we portraying a reasonably comprehensive picture of this conflict? If, further, the exhibition is intended to be instructive, as I judge its purpose to be, are the ideas perhaps much better developed in a text book? It may be that political and constitutional developments cannot be treated successfully other than in a book—a thought which I surmise would strongly appeal to academicians—and the presentation of what we call "social history" is the proper province of the history museum. But one has the uncomfortable feeling that social history, with its many ramifications, cannot adequately communicate the history of such an event as the American Revolution.

A fairly common display in many history museums attempts to present the demographic, economic, and industrial development of an area, perhaps a whole region or, sometimes, of the entire United States. Can this be adequately presented in a truly educational sense by the exhibition of the wagon or wagons which carried people westward? Is this growth presented convincingly by an exhibition of the individual tools which aided in taming the frontier? Does such an exhibition, for instance, take into account the rise of cities which in their turn were important factors in the interaction of urban life on that frontier, and vice versa? Is the whole panorama presented, with at least some suggestion as to its complexities, in the usual manner of history museums by means of prints or photographs or objects? In sum, can the surging vitality of post-Civil War America, expanding as it did in nearly all directions, be presented in any more profound way than the usual exhibition clichés so common in most of our history museums?

Are we apt to forget that this presentation, as I indicated previously, may occupy a full-length book, or a complete semester of study in school or college? We can use taped narration, we can use films to supplement these exhibits, but these methods basically lack the sensory impact of the authentic material. Is there possibly an inherent conflict in interpretation between those with a comprehensive knowledge of American history and those with less? What image of American history *does* the public receive—this public that includes school children and adults motivated by reasons about which we really know little? Does the general public—assuming it does not read with any particular consistency, if it reads at all, the products of professional historians—obtain its ideas of American history from a mélange of museum exhibits, from popularization (and frequently simplification) of complex issues through other media, all loosely tied together with some memories of history courses in the formal school setting? One cannot but wonder if the tendency of so many history museums, to present an over-simplified approach to American history, is based on the theory that this approach is automatically more acceptable to the museum-going public.

The problems of historical interpretation are difficult. I am fully conscious that museums of fine arts, for one, have their problems, but to a considerable degree, a work of art may speak for itself. It is, in one sense, timeless, and thus may elicit an immediate aesthetic response—here, also, with reference to the background of the visitor. Even the most fervent historian can, at times, abstract the painting, sculpture, or drawing, from its period and savor his reaction to it. It may, indeed, cause him to speculate later on the vagaries of Venetian trade and politics, or on the social circumstances characteristic of the period in which the work of art was created. Still, a work of art may succeed in communicating without these considerations. The complexity of history, which every historian acknowledges, is not easy to translate into the form of museum exhibitions. Doubtless, in recognition of this, other factors often are introduced in an effort to enhance the material on display. In an effort to add another dimension to the exhibition, we are frequently confronted with an elaborate setting which may overpower the authentic object.

Previously, I observed that dissemination also included publications. The larger history museums, with trained staff supported by useful libraries, have a positive duty to publish the results of their research. By and large, museums of history are not active in producing scholarly publications. Most of the useful publications issue from the historical societies which have museums and libraries. The universities, as we might expect, are the main sources of historical publication, but the knowledge gained in a museum from a study of a Colonial painter, a nineteenth-century craftsman, or the transformation of a region through the artifacts in the possession of the institution, can add immeasurably to the scholar's knowledge. Surely, by osmosis at least, the staff of the history museum, however untrained initially, can make some of the information it has acquired available. If this is too difficult by way of formal publication, the history museum ought, at least, to emphasize and enlarge its informational, if not its educational, function by replying to telephone inquiries and answering written requests for data.

How much dissatisfaction exists with the current role of the history museum is difficult to say. That all is not well is evidenced in the recent announcement of the National Endowment on the Humanities that it plans to raise the caliber of the staff of historical societies and museums of history, on the grounds that this is an area to which the foundations have paid insufficient attention. The fact is, in any case, that we do not really know whether the history museums *are* doing what they ought to do. Does the news that millions visit these institutions indicate that these millions are satisfied with what they find? For that matter, do we really know what people are looking for when they visit history museums? Here again, we must stress the unusual aspect of the museum public—a public that literally encompasses all levels and degrees of education. What does motivate visitors to come to history museums is certainly a relevant question. Obviously, not all of them are in search of cafeterias or restrooms. We talk of education, but what kind of education are we providing, and for whom? If nearly two hundred million people visit museums, and of that number 25 percent visit history museums, we are dealing with a population which exceeds that of many countries in the world. These are large figures. Assuming that they may grow larger, surely we have a responsibility to determine what our function is and not be lulled by the spiral of attendance inflation into believing that we are accomplishing our aims.

At the end of the second and early part of the third decade of the nineteenth century, railway construction began in the United States. Despite this, far more people were interested in canals as a means of transportation, though we should suppose it to have been evident that canals, subject as they were to the vicissitudes of weather, were potentially less efficient than railroads. Eventually, of course, railroads proved themselves, and a new era was born. As the result of this development, new attitudes came into being. The railroad itself and its by-products, the telegraph to mention only one, changed methods of communication, of doing business, and of daily life. Today, we may be, and many insist we are, entering upon a new era in the transmission of knowledge and information.

Although we now have more books published than ever before, we learn from a speech delivered by Dr. Gordon Ray, President of the Guggenheim Foundation, before the opening session of the American Library Association in New York City on July 10 last, that according to a Gallup Poll, 12 percent of the American population reads 80 percent of the books published, and that half of the population has never read any book at all. Dr. Ray observed that Elmo Roper, another pollster, as a result of a study of American reading habits, concluded that 51 percent of Americans are culturally "inert" and another 26 percent culturally inactive.[7] And so, analogously, as once happened in the canal versus railroad era, we are faced with a new situation requiring new attitudes from us as museum people.

The figures just quoted appear to indicate that we confront a situation in which visual and aural impact may be dominant in the spread of knowledge. It does not mean that people no longer need to read, but it may very well mean that a sizable percentage of the population feels no need, nor urgency, to read books. It may mean that we must concentrate almost exclusively on other methods of presenting knowledge. I am quite aware that other methods have been, and are being used, but we still tend to rely, at least subconsciously, on the authority of the book, and I wonder if this reliance will continue. It is, I personally believe, a dreary prospect, but since many college students manage to survive their academic training without ever reading a book from cover to cover, there is no reason to assume that this situation will change simply because, in the future, more people will be going to college.

Changing values are not new in history. By "changing values," I mean the transformation in people's minds and attitudes toward aspects of living which result, ultimately, in what we call a "culture." It is entirely possible, therefore, that we, in the history museums, may be proceeding on false assumptions—that the memories of history courses, or the remnants of readings of books dealing with history, which we think are identified with a large percentage of our visitors do not, in fact, exist. In brief, we may be presenting material which, if not utterly new, at least may not accord with the variety of impressions of history constituting the background of historical information our visitors possess. This situation, need I say, has tremendous implications for the educational function of the museum.

In a recent study by a team of sociologists attempting to determine audience reaction to free performances of Shakespearean plays in various neighborhoods of New York City, it was reported that audiences appreciated the performances more than they understood them. The playgoers responded more to action and comedy than to thought. This finding was not pleasing to the producer, who maintained that there was no essential difference in response between various audiences, of different economic—and thus, one supposes, of different educational—backgrounds. Social scientists, who base their conclusions on samplings, collide with artists who, according to sociologists, are like all the humanists in that they either misunderstand statistics or are terrified by them.

The sociologists declared that central to the discipline of sociology is the proposition that persons situated in one social position have different attitudes from those in another social position. They argue that this concept runs counter to the instinct of the artist who is convinced that true art communicates to all, regardless of social position.[8] It may be, nonetheless, that sociological studies of the public visiting our history museums could be most helpful to us. Possibly the results of such a study might astonish or even dismay us. In a survey of the public library some years ago, the library was considered to be a useful and needed cultural adjunct to the community. It represented a cultural symbol which our society accepts as "good," and I suppose that this attitude also applies to museums. I think, however, we ought to attempt to discover what people do get from museums, with as much emphasis on adult reactions as those we more or less attempt to get from children, and whether their visits are aesthetically and educationally satisfying. It should not be our role to wait passively for a public which comes to us in search of something neither they nor we have defined.

If I have stressed the need to investigate the motivation of that 25 percent of the museum-going public that visits museums of history, it is because I believe that only by trying to fathom what they seek can we chart our own course. I do not advocate, necessarily, that we adapt ourselves completely to the needs of our visitors, since our role should rather be largely one of guidance into new educational realms.

Having begun by hailing the significant attendance figures, it may seem perverse to end by wondering what they really mean. But "museums and education" *is* the theme of our conference and if only because we are concerned with the educational aspect of museums, we must be careful to remember that mere enthusiasm for education has risks. We may use the ideal of education for objectives which are not essentially educational. We need enthusiasm, to be sure, but we also need scientific objectivity as a salutory corrective.

It is the intention of the National Endowment for the Humanities to support inquiry into the unknown, the unidentified, and the misinterpreted in man's humanistic heritage. It is also the intention of the National Endowment to serve the public educational interest in ways not always possible through the teaching media of our schools. It will give assistance to the two great arts of education—discovery, and teaching what is discovered—as it expresses the will of Congress. This statement of intention by the National Foundation on the Arts and the Humanities is eloquently expressed. On a more mundane level, one announced phase of implementing this objective is the support for educational programs in what is described as "humanistic museums." When I have talked about the need to define our audience and *its* objectives, I wonder about the possibility of specific support for such a study by the National Endowment for the Humanities.

It is clear that more and more people will be attending our history museums, and this prospect heightens the need to use the skills and talents of those institutions so as best to enlarge the knowledge of our visitors. If we can determine what people are seeking from us, we can plan accordingly. Somehow, we must increase our efforts to explain, not only the achievements of the past, but just as importantly how these achievements were brought about. I am convinced that once we know what we should do, in relation to what is expected of us, we are not likely to adopt the attitude attributed to Frederick the Great, who is supposed to have said of his Prussian subjects: "My people and I have come to an agreement which satisfies us both. They are to say what they please and I am to do what I please."

1. *The New York Times,* July 6, 1966.
2. "Study of Tourists' Interests in New York State, 1965," n.p., Albany, N.Y., 1966.
3. Jordan, Joye E., "The History Museum: Poor Relation?" *Museum News,* November 1964, pp. 17–19.
4. Commager, Henry S., *The American Mind,* New Haven, Yale University Press, 1950, p. 411.
5. *Works of John Adams,* August 31, 1813, vol. 10, p. 62. *In* Kraus, Michael, *The Writing of American History,* Norman, Okla., University of Oklahoma Press, 1953, p. 89.
6. Kraus, Michael., *op. cit.,* p. 90.
7. cf. *The Antiquarian Bookman,* July 25, 1966, p. 379.
8. Kadushin, Charles, "Shakespeare and Sociology," *The Columbia University Forum,* Spring, 1966, pp. 25–31.

The Role of Science Museums

FRANK OPPENHEIMER
University of Colorado

Denver has an Art Museum but no Science Museum; the same is true of Colorado Springs. The small museum on the campus of the University of Colorado has exhibitions of paintings and sculpture, of Indian rugs and Japanese figurines; it has anthropological displays but it does not include items of technology, or of pure science. The closest to any science that it approaches is through its natural history of minerals and rock formations.

One wonders why this division exists. In some way it would seem to be a genuine scandal, in an epoch in which science is so important and technology so complex and ubiquitous, that museums do not play a role in making science and technology more available to the public. Surely it should be possible and appropriate for museums of science and technology to exist even in relatively small towns. Yet, one finds only a handful of science museums throughout the world. The smallness in the number of these museums is all the more surprising since, wherever they do exist, they seem to be well attended, and they offer many programs that are coordinated with the schools and adult education classes. Furthermore, those scientists who had some contact with science museums as children usually maintain that the museums played a vital role in developing their interest in the pursuit of science.

It is a scandal that there are so few museums of science and technology. We live in an age in which science dominates a very large fraction of our efforts and our surroundings. Yet, despite the predominance of technology and the efforts devoted to science, it is not unusual to encounter a strong anti-science attitude in the general population. When, for example, I describe to people the current development of new science curricula for elementary school children, I frequently detect a reaction which borders on horror, and which in one way or another is equivalent to the statement: "Oh my God, now you are trying to corrupt even the young children."

There is an additional need which science museums can, at least in part, satisfy. They can portray a model of the whole. We live in a society which is, in fact, a whole, but in which the holistic view is becoming increasingly obscured, and in which fragmentation and departmentalization seem the norm. At the same time that the interrelationships between the sciences are becoming important, specialization is becoming more important still; at the same time that the role of fundamental science in technology is becoming more immediate, scientists know less and less about the details of industrial processes and devices.

Artists make use of acrylic resins, interference patterns, and the new understanding of optical perception theory in their work; and scientists create works of art in their bubble chambers, scintillation counters, and quadripole magnets. One has only to visit, say, the CERN high-energy physics laboratory near Geneva to realize that such labs are in some way the contemporary analogue of Gothic cathedrals. Yet, the deeper connections between art and science are ignored.

A good science museum, even though it is departmentalized, somehow makes one aware of the wholeness and the unified concerns of science, technology, art, history, and people. In one building one finds ship models from all areas and epochs, a collection of ancient and modern stringed instruments, a history of the technique of steel-making, Van de Graaff high-voltage generators, paper chromatography for protein analysis, and the beautiful interference patterns produced by lasers. The scale is such that, although it may tax the imagination, one can still conceive of all this diversity fitting and belonging together.

There is an additional aspect to the fragmentation and technological complexity of our surroundings. As a result, most of us are in daily contact with at least as much that we do not understand as were the Greeks or the early Babylonians. Of course, there is a difference; we can assume that at least someone in our society knows how the power steering on our car works, or what the little vanes on the surface of a jet airplane wing do, or how polio vaccine is made, or what is involved in freezing orange juice. Most of us, however, are surrounded by these and thousands of other mysteries. In general, we do not even *ask* questions because there is no meaningful way of absorbing the answers. We have learned not to ask questions about jet engines, the C.I.A., or Dick Tracy's space ship. We end up in the paradoxical situation in which one of the effects of science is to dampen curiosity. This effect is all part of the scandal. Here, too, science museums can provide a partial remedy for the defect.

We ask why there are so few science museums. Perhaps one of the reasons is that not many people are aware of their important and multiple functions and of the delights they can offer. There are, however, more concrete reasons:

1. Science museums are certainly expensive and there is no obvious source of funds with which to build them. Even the greatest science museums in the world, such as the ones in London and Munich, are severely strapped for funds.

2. There is no automatic recipe for building a science museum. One cannot simply buy or collect existing items and set them out for display. Even the conception and setting up of the enormous *Deutches Museum* in Munich seemed to depend crucially on the skill and ingenuity and patience of a few individuals, who were in turn dependent on a mere handful of extraordinarily skilled technicians. Such people are certainly rare, and it is not at all certain that they exist in sufficient numbers to develop science museums in all the communities that could support such museums. Even good modelmakers are becoming hard to find. The making of a good exhibit is not easy. The science of the exhibit must be accurate and must be integrated with some broad plan. The display must be attractive and rugged and accessible or, at least, visible to all. Furthermore, museum pedagogy involves its own special flair.

3. Finally, there is an even more difficult point—it concerns the development of a museum technology appropriate to the teaching of science. There is a tendency in museums, although certainly not a requirement, to make use of a passive form of pedagogy in which

the student makes no particular effort on his own, and does not participate actively with the material.

I would like to put forward some ideas connected with the solution of some of the problems that arise in the development of science museums.

THE DEVELOPMENT OF SCIENCE MUSEUMS IN MEDIUM-SIZED CITIES

Despite the fact that science museums have depended crucially on the dedication and the ingenuity of relatively few individuals, I believe that one can envisage the growth of science museums on a much wider scale than at present. Undoubtedly, no one approach to the problem can provide a complete solution. Highly competent, local personnel will eventually have to be involved in the museums, but one may be able to get museums started without having such people available at the outset.

In the first place, it may be possible to develop some core materials which could be mass produced in sufficient quantity to render the cost practical. The core materials could include demonstration apparatus, models, and reproductions of significant experiments of historical interest. They could involve not only independent designs but could rely heavily on exhibits in existing science museums. In addition, the museums could incorporate many of the new curriculum developments in the various sciences, including the commercial products that have resulted from these developments. In this way, the materials could be made available to students in the school systems and the teachers could work with the materials before ordering classroom quantities. (In this same context there is undoubtedly a need for a national center for the display of curriculum materials and apparatus; this could be of value not only to teachers in America but also to visitors from abroad.)

It would, however, be unrealistic to believe that such core materials could provide more than a starting point for science museums throughout the country. It is clear from current experience that the life of the museum must be derived from local efforts. There are, however, sources for this life in most communities and I would guess that any city with a population of a hundred thousand or over could find the interest and the quality of personnel needed to develop, perhaps quite slowly, very useful museums.

Local material for museums could certainly stem from the same kinds of efforts which have led, during the past decade, to excellent projects for science fairs. The science fair exhibits indicate an enormous resourcefulness on the part of students and teachers and parents. Much of the material that has been developed could well be put on permanent year-round display. Furthermore, if the exhibits were built and designed with museum display in mind, the individual projects might be incorporated into some larger plan. The sense of community utility for these projects would not interfere, necessarily, with the competitive stimulus involved in the science fairs. In addition, copying exhibits from existing museums in other places could provide an outlet for craftsmanship even for students who were not scientifically motivated. One would not expect that contributions to the museum would be derived wholly from students of high school age or younger. The students in the colleges and universities, including graduate students, could make contributions that would be most valuable both to the students and to the museums.

In fact, such contributions to the growth of a museum might provide one avenue in which students could play some useful role in their society during the long period in which they are being subjected to an education. It might partially alleviate the present situation in which education is regarded merely as a twenty-year-long preparation for a useful life. Such activities might well become a part of scientific training. Certainly all of those who have been engaged in building laboratory and demonstration apparatus have found this process enormously rewarding and instructive to themselves. Undoubtedly, locally produced efforts would also create a considerable amount of unsuitable material which would have to be stored or modified or discarded, but even the best museums seem to have their share of junk stored away in their catacombs. In fact, one would have to plan a museum so that the ratio of storage space to exhibit space was quite large.

The conception of a science museum exhibit and its fabrication is, of course, only the first step. It is necessary to set the exhibits up in a clear and attractive way, provide collateral material, write clear explanations, and keep them in repair. There must be attendants to protect the material and also to present demonstrations and answer technical questions. I believe that even this phase of the museum work could be developed in relatively small communities. The example of the science museum in Paris indicates a possible direction. In this museum a group of young men and women are employed who demonstrate selected groups of apparatus at regular intervals. In the intervals between the demonstrations they are available for answering questions or for keeping the apparatus in working order. Some of the experiments that are demonstrated are accessible to the general public after the demonstration. Apparatus that is too delicate or hazardous is on display but kept locked in a case or cage until used in demonstrations. As I understand the situation, these young demonstrators were, at the outset of the program, primarily college students; however, over the years a profession of science museum demonstrators has come into being. This would seem to me to be an honorable profession and one on which many young people would like to embark if there were employment opportunities.

In fact, in many fields one of the outcomes of a liberal arts education could be the development of professional explainers; people who would be able more successfully to bridge the gap between the research into the inaccessible by the specialist and the need for understanding by the public. This kind of explaining is extraordinarily hard to do with words alone. It is even hard to accomplish in college courses. The ideal milieu for this purpose, whether it be in art, anthropology, or science and technology, could well be the museum. The problem of building demonstration apparatus, that will be clear to the general public and which will withstand the wear and tear and abuse to which it will inevitably be subjected, is not one which can be solved at the first go-around. I believe that one would have to count on having a group of people in the museum who would continually be busy redesigning the apparatus on the basis of the museum experience. Even in the University of Colorado demonstration laboratory with which I have been connected, this process of redesign seems never ending. Perhaps, in some cases, local industries and machine shops would be willing to lend their facilities for this purpose.

In addition to the core materials and the local development of materials, traveling exhibits supplied by large city museums could contribute to the smaller museums throughout the country. At the moment, the London Science Museum is inaugurating such traveling exhibits, but they continually run into the problems of how and where to display them. If each local science museum had a special area set aside for such exhibits with standardized facilities, the traveling exhibits could be made more versatile.

SCIENCE MUSEUMS IN THE EDUCATIONAL SYSTEM

I would now like to turn to a discussion of the ways in which science museums can be used in the educational process. There is a new element which enters into this role because of a direction which is apparent in many of the new curriculum development projects. In general, these new curricula are attempting to present the various subjects to the students in a deeper and more meaningful fashion than has been adopted in the past. In order to accomplish this, they must devote more time to those aspects of the subject which they consider fundamental and must, therefore, leave out of the course an enormous amount of material which, although relevant and fascinating, nevertheless is either not essential to the development of the main theme or is too complex to be explained at a fundamental level. Thus, although the new curricula are intellectually richer, they are in some respects more barren. I believe that this current trend is the correct one for the classroom, but that much of what must be sacrificed there can be restored to the student through a greater use of museums.

The role which science museums can play in the educational process, however, is certainly a multi-faceted one and any narrowly restricted view of this role would detract from their value. It must include the visitor who quite randomly wanders through, and the individuals who are interested in some specific aspect of the exhibits, as well as the serious student who wishes to investigate in depth some particular aspect of science or technology. The museum must be of value both to children and to adults, and it must be capable of direct integration into community educational programs whether these are in the schools, in extension and correspondence courses, or part of educational radio and television programs. Although museums traditionally practice a passive type of learning, it seems crucial that a science museum also provide an environment in which people can ask questions and answer them by their own experimentation.

There is certainly a great variety in the patterns with which people use museums. Even the passive pedagogy of a museum can be extremely valuable. For example, if one walks through an art museum without looking at any of the paintings very long or thoroughly, one can still gain an enormous amount. One can appreciate the variety of styles and subject matter, the gradual developments of technique, the variations with time and place; and one can become aware of richness in color and form, and of the amazing interplay of fantasy and imagination with reality. Even in such a casual trip, one can find some style of painting which one had ignored, or even disliked, and which suddenly makes a fresh appeal. Usually after such visits, one finds a few or even just one painting which will bring one back to the museum over and over again. I believe that this same pattern is valuable and appropriate to science museums.

In addition, in an art museum one invariably sees small groups of people, accompanied by either a teacher or an attendant, who are standing around a painting listening to a wealth of anecdotes and a detailed discussion concerning the painting. If then, later, a person returns on his own, what he sees can become much more meaningful. And finally, in every art museum one finds one or two art students with an easel copying some picture. I have even seen quite a few people making drawings of the apparatus displayed in science museums. I believe that these have been, for the most part, graphic art students, but I see no reason why they could not be teachers and students of science who were interested in making records or copies of the exhibits for projects of their own. These types of activities are typical of what I would call a passive type of pedagogy.

In both science and technology, however, things happen; there are changes which one needs to observe and measure in order to understand the phenomena. One of the problems of a science museum, therefore, involves finding ways to make things happen and to understand what has occurred. The traditional answer to this problem is to arrange push-button and remote-control displays which are accompanied by written material describing the phenomena and pointing out what to look for. Although such displays are certainly a delight and can frequently be very instructive, they usually remain a passive form of pedagogy. There is no doubt that such displays are a delight. I recall an incident in the London Science Museum which houses an elaborate display of mining in the basement. The display is very realistic, with tunnels and mining tools and helmeted miners; but almost nothing moves. When I was in the hall, just outside the display, however, a small boy came running out of the tunnels shouting to his playmate in the hall, "I found a button, I found a button." They both went back in to push the button.

I have forgotten exactly what happened. I think a model mine car dumped some coal into a pit. But it is hard to believe that this delight is always instructive. One sees a great deal of random button pushing by children and adults in a museum, and frequently people walk off leaving the display to go through its paces unattended. Even when they wait for the apparatus to complete its cycle, there are many instances, as I have discovered by a little questioning, when the point of the demonstration remained completely obscure.

I believe that the problem with such displays is threefold: 1) that most push-button displays leave too little control for the observer, 2) that while the display is going on there is not enough to do or to think about, and 3) that the correlation between the written material and the behavior of the apparatus is seldom sufficiently clear or direct.

It is almost impossible to learn how anything works unless one can repeat each step in its operation at will; furthermore, it is usually necessary to make small changes which impair its operation. In almost all forms of learning, it is just as important to appreciate what does not work as to see what does work. Quite generally one can learn by mistakes. Even a comparatively simple phenomenon, such as the formation of an image by lens, is difficult to appreciate unless one can twist and turn the lens, and move it about, or put variously shaped diaphragms between it and the object or image. Such detailed control of apparatus does not necessarily preclude remote control, although wherever possible it is more instructive to hold and manipulate the items directly in one's hands.

In order to focus more attention on science museum exhibits, it should be possible to make use of some of the techniques of programmed learning, in which a question is asked and the observer uses the apparatus or the models to find the answer. Some attempts at using these techniques have already been made in the science museum in Paris. For example, in one experiment the rules governing the direction of the force between two wires carrying a current are explained. This display is followed by four or five setups with various arrangements of coils and wires which move when the current is turned on. Each display has a series of buttons labeled "left," "right," "up," "down," etc., and only if one pushes the correct button does the current go on to show the movement of the coil, and to light a sign exclaiming how clever you are.

I believe that it is more instructive if the exhibits in a museum can be demonstrated and discussed first and then turned over to the public. An excellent way of learning all manner of operations is to watch someone perform the operation, while explaining what he is doing as he proceeds, and then to attempt to repeat the operation by oneself. It is clearly impossible to have all the exhibits in a museum demonstrated either continuously or whenever someone wants to look at them. Yet, I believe that there is an adequate substitute for such "live" demonstrations in films or video tapes.

One can make—and we have tried this technique in our demonstration laboratory at the University of Colorado—sound track films of someone performing the experiment. In such films one does not have to go through all the variations or make the detailed measurements of which the experiment is capable; one merely has to illustrate the techniques and operations and point out what to look for and measure. In general, such films do not destroy curiosity but rather they whet one's desire to do the experiment. If used in well-constructed projectors, the lifetime of a cartridge film can be very long. I believe that video tape lifetime is even longer. Though the expense of such a program would not be negligible, I believe that it would not be prohibitive and that one could accompany a large fraction of the exhibits in a science museum with one- to three-minute cartridge-type film sequences. Certainly such films would foster a much greater attention to and skill with the experiments than could be achieved with the conventional written instructions and explanations.

It is essential, of course, that a science museum be integrated with the various educational programs of the community, though there are many ways in which this integration can come about. For example, the museum in Munich has a week long session for the teachers of the community every fall, during which time the material in the museum is explained and demonstrated to the teachers. This instruction makes it possible for the teachers to refer to specific museum items in their classes, and to make appropriate selections and give meaningful discussions for the groups of students they bring to the museum. It seems to me that this practice could be extended in two ways. On the one hand, the museums could become recognized centers for science teacher training during both in-service and summer institutes. Secondly, the museums might contain sections (not necessarily open to the public) which could be used as additional laboratories for all the schools of the community. The equipment in these could be quite varied and would not have to provide many duplicates; the apparatus might well be so complex or costly that it would be impractical to place it in quantity in all the schools.

The use of television programs for science education is increasing rapidly throughout the country. It seems to me that these programs could be made even more instructive if the equipment used were set out for people to view and work with after they had seen the program. This technique would provide an additional means of demonstrating the museum displays.

I would guess that local industry could make valuable use of a science museum for some of its personnel. Most industrial plants comprise only a small section of their respective industries. A science museum provides an excellent milieu to display the interlocking facets of a whole industry and its interconnections with other industries. In addition, at least a part of the scientific background for the particular industrial techniques might be available within the museum.

It would appear to me that the centralized facilities of a science museum would be an enormous asset, and even a financial saving, for all the science-oriented educational endeavors of a community.

SCIENCE MUSEUMS IN DEVELOPING COUNTRIES

In concluding, I would like to raise some questions concerning the building of science museums in developing countries, where all the difficulties concerning the building of science museums in America would be amplified. Premanufactured core materials would be less appropriate; the skilled and inventive personnel will be involved with other projects; and continued financial support might prove to be impossible to find. I believe, however, that the benefits from such museums would also be amplified. The one reason that might explain why we have so few science museums in America is that we are so surrounded by science and technology that we see no need to place any of it in a museum. As I stressed at the outset of this paper, I do not believe this a valid reason for eschewing science museums in any case, and it is certainly not a reason applicable in the developing countries, where they might be valuable to show merely the existence of various phenomena, products, and techniques. Although it might be possible to arrange for the display of commercial items that are made in and imported by developing countries, such displays would certainly not constitute a science museum; they would have none of the needed pedagogical effects, and they would not help integrate and synthesize science with the rest of the culture.

On the other hand, one of the avenues which might eventually lead to the building of science museums lies in the direction of teacher training. Certainly, the problem of getting adequate laboratory equipment introduced into the schools of some developing countries is an equally thorny one, and the two problems might be combined. If one could supply appropriate laboratory equipment for teacher training centers, these centers might become the nucleus of future museums, as well as institutions that could help build the schools. I do not have any adequate answer to the question of how America can contribute to the building of science museums in other countries, but I do believe that such museums could play a vital role in the scientific growth of developing countries, just as they can here at home.

Gawk or Think?

MICHAEL V. BUTLER
Associate Curator of Physics
Cranbrook Institute of Science

The results of education in science are easy to identify. They are: 1) the knowledge of facts; 2) skill in observing; and 3) the ability to reason (inductively) from observations. Note that the knowledge of facts, though not the most important, comes along willy-nilly, as the other two are accomplished.

Concomitant with these results are several others that are often easier to see than the essential abstractions above. These fringe benefits to the individual educated in science are: 1) respect for natural things and processes; 2) confidence in one's own reasoning faculties; and 3) the ability to store up or to comtemplate unsolved problems.

If my few suggestions are to deal with science education, I suppose that rare animal must be defined. I think that it is anything—*anything*—that brings about the above results.

Suppose for a moment that the student is a child. We all know that, next to his upbringing at home, the most important thing that happens to him in this country is his schooling. Schooling is a quick way to increase a person's experience. At school the child sees people who tell him about his language and its literature, about math and science, and, in the words of one teacher, about typewriting, tap dancing, and tomfoolery. The museum adds even more experience, I hope of a sensory rather than of a verbal kind.

Most of the child's learning, in spite of all of us, happens as a result of the experience that is peculiarly his. He learns about distance by suddenly finding that he can reach the light switch that was formerly inaccessible. He learns about dispersion by seeing the spectrum on the floor where the sun shines through the beveled glass in the door of his Victorian tenement. He learns about moments by swinging on the gate until he finds that his leverage is so great that the gate sags, scrapes, and no longer swings; but when he moves nearer the hinge his moment is less and the post supports him.

I once asked a fifth grade class to write why they thought that air was real. A girl wrote, "I know there is air because I can see it bulging out my washcloth when I pull the corners of the cloth down into the bath water." It is his or her own experience that makes a person what he is. It is experience that gives people their curiosity about nature and, indeed, their ideas about it. It is our education.

All children ask many scientific questions. In a sample of spontaneous questions asked of the teachers (not science teachers) by the children in the first, third, and fifth grades at Shady Hill School, all but one or two of each child's questions were either scientific or theological. Most were scientific, of this kind: "Where does rain come from?". By such a question the child is giving notice that he has seen something puzzling and is thinking about it. I suppose that such asked questions correspond to many, many that are not asked. But it is the internal asking, as well as the explicit asking, that has taught all of us the things we did not learn in school.

The ideas that we understand most clearly are, most of them, in this latter class. Understanding means, to me, having encompassed an idea intellectually or even experimentally; having glanced at the implications of the idea and knowing its relation to other ideas; and being able to apply the idea effectively in a situation different from that in which the idea was first grasped.

Tell any child that, if he spins a bowl on its edge, it will land bottom up: the child may politely believe what you say, but that is not understanding. He will try it out the first time that he can, and only then will he really understand the simple fact that you told him. If he had understood it when you told him, he would not have tried it out.

This same honest, scientific skepticism also applies to most adults. Those with whom I have talked in the physics hall of my museum, not trained in science, seem to understand things in the same way as the child; that is, sense-experience makes things clear as no words can. Adults' fears of their own ignorance are concealed more subtly than children's, and they are harder to soothe.

The question asked by the uninitiated really means much more than the words say. To answer the scientific question directly would be much less than the person expects. "Rain falls from thunderclouds," verbally satisfies the query, "Where does rain come from?". If the inquirer is a child of ten or so, and observant, he probably also means that he knows it only rains when it is cloudy; but he has seen enough water to know that water does not look like clouds. Therefore, the question really may mean still more: "Where does the water come from, how did it get there, why does it look puffy, and how does it know when to fall?".

I have tried to answer questions of this kind, and have found that people rarely know how deep their questions are, or more exactly, how to ask in words the questions that are in their minds.

Suppose now that the grown-up—parent, teacher, book, or museum label—answers the question that is asked. "Rain falls from thunderclouds." The youngster, who believes grown-ups, thinks that *is* the answer to the question that he had in mind, whether it makes sense to him or not. He has to conclude that his own stupidity is keeping him from seeing that the answer really did explain. That is an embarrassing conclusion; if the experience is repeated too often, the child usually stops asking questions.

On the other hand, the youngster who does not utterly believe grown-ups sees that the direct answer does not explain all that he hoped to have cleared up. He follows the first question with a second, "How is the water held in the cloud?" A direct answer to the second question will be less help than it was to the first, and less easy to give. In a few minutes, the child has the grown-up cornered and, for all the sensible questions and answers, the child knows that his problem is still not solved. He is dissatisfied either with the adult's answer or with himself for not understanding.

In the latter case, the child may have to memorize the verbal answer lest he appear ignorant later on. The child who thus memorizes soon comes to think that the verbal description of the process is all that there is to understanding it, for he has not been allowed to see for himself the phenomenon back of the description.

My experience as a teacher has made me enough of a behaviorist to know that if one tells a child the answer to a few questions he will then come to you for the answers to the others of the same kind. This dangerous fact is pathetically illustrated by many of the school children who come into my bailiwick. They observe the Foucault's pendulum, a ball swinging from a wire fastened to the ceiling. Asked what they see (not asked the name of it), some say, "I don't know;" but most just shrug, to indicate ignorance and that the question was too hard. All want the demonstrator to *tell* them what they are seeing. I suspect that, if they were not used to being told the answer, they would not expect it of me. And is my suspicion not confirmed by the teacher, who often answers for the children?

The response of the child who is used to being told goes from, "Tell me what I see," to, "Tell me what to conclude." It continues to, "Tell me what is right," and has been known to mature into, "It is right because the Joneses do it and I'm not obliged, or even able, to make a rational judgment." But that may not concern us here.

In other words, real understanding comes from direct observation of a process or an object; and it is such experience that museums should furnish as no school can, and as few individuals can.

We have all seen the tragic ignorance that follows inexperience in a grown person. We have all known the subtle ineptitude of the secretary whose only education has been secretarial school. It is even clear now that a person deprived of certain normal experiences as a child grows up without even the capacity to learn.

As schools and as museums, it is clearly our job to furnish experience that is the raw material of thought and is the stuff of judgment. We need to let people know the objects, the situations, and the processes that they might otherwise miss.

In my classroom, I used to have most of the space filled up with *things*. When a child, having observed some physical properties of several minerals, asked, "Why don't some minerals become eroded faster than others?" I might have given him a basalt beach pebble with a quartz intrusion protruding all around it. This answer is complete and useful. Having seen the object while the question was in his mind, the child knew as much as I did about the subject, and learned it in a few seconds.

There is some doubt about how many objects one must have on hand just in order to teach a few things. If a museum is an agency for the education of the general public, what is the difference between a museum and a school? If a museum is like a library, a repository of a scholarly collection, it is like a school restricted to the empirical scientist or the historian. But in either case, they are both like life—a source of experience.

The museum's part in helping people to understand where rain comes from, to continue the example, might be to exhibit the first loop in the cooling coil of a refrigerator. The label could ask, without begging the question, that one feel the pipe and notice the condition of its surface. Where did the water come from? If the pipe leaks, why is there not water everywhere? What is true where the water is and where it is not? One should also see a cloud forming, perhaps one's own breath blown over another part of the cooler. What do you see? Where else have you seen something like it? What is it made of? And so on.

This kind of usable, reasonable, unspoken, seat-of-the-pants understanding can come, of course, only if we have not already let the person learn the confusing verbal formula: "Steam forms when hot meets cold." That is, the verbal explanation is offered only after the person has the experience to understand it. Children and many adults do their real learning by watching what goes on around them. Until the store of observed facts has soaked into one's thinking, one may be confused by verbal explanations.

These propositions do not suggest that the science museum should be filled with examples of a polished technology. On the contrary, I find that space capsules and historic telephones add very little to the unpolished visitor's share of culture. The museum should provide objects for close examination by the individual: feeling, hearing, and smelling. The school, geared only for mass observation at a distance, usually cannot give its students that kind of access to knowledge. Hence, the schools have often had to fall back on description and memorization instead of experimentation.

To the question, "What is the difference between a museum and a school?" one of our staff said without a moment's hesitation, "One is optional." That does not say that school groups should not visit museums. It simply says that a museum visitor should be given the option to observe, and to ignore, what he chooses. It is the museum's responsibility to engage the visitor so that he does not waste his time.

Because museums are optional, failure to have visitors learn (in the highest sense of that word) from their visit is inexcusable. By what means we must avoid failure, however, is only intuitively clear to me. I should like to present a record of thousands of visitors, chosen at random, all of whom have drawn their own conclusions from observations made in my museum, and 90 percent of whom have become scholars, interested students, or accomplished mechanics. All that I really can say is that students who have an assignment to fulfill by looking at exhibits and, usually, by making a record of them, see very little. They rush, copy labels without looking at their subjects, and copy each other's notes. Asked an objective question about an exhibit, they say, "I don't know." Then they look at their notes, find no information, and then last of all, look at the exhibit. When the assigned time has passed, they rush for the sales counter. When a group of children is led past the tables in a line, the individuals cannot stop to look, so there is nothing to catch their attention and the hall is pandemonium. When students are allowed to examine the physics exhibition at their own speed, the room is quiet and conducive to learning (except for a few minutes at the beginning while small children try to see everything at once).

The visitor may see the museum only once. The student sees school continually for years. The subjects in a museum cannot be arranged in a sequence because nobody could finish. The school is furnishing techniques and information in the most efficient order—most efficient for the average person. The museum, because it can choose, may provide the unorthodox point of view, or the obscure fact, that a certain student needs in order to assimilate the school's sequence.

The children, that have had their questions answered in the non-verbal terms that all of us understand, have in their minds certain associations, even though they may not know the names. These associations are the memory of what the person has seen and felt and knows from having tried things. To such a child, rain is something very like the water that collects on the lid of a soup pot, and drops into the soup. Clouds are very like the stuff that leaks out of the radiator at school. With further thinking of that kind and with a few significant experiences in a museum, the child may see intuitively that the water on the lid came invisibly from the soup, as water in clouds might come invisibly from oceans. If one reminds him of the dew on the outside of a lemonade glass in summer, it will all be clear to him; though he may not be able to describe the relationship in the "right" terms.

In order to understand rain in the terms that most museum labels and school texts use, the reader must know something about kinetic theory, vapor pressure, adiabatic cooling, colloidal suspensions, and so on. Even if a child has the vocabulary, he can hardly understand it deeply. The museum can, if it will, provide the factual and conceptual knowledge that children seek, in language that they can use—the language of seeing and feeling. The school and even the parent usually have to use English, which may not help as much as we think it does.

There is no objection, I think, to memorizing the names for processes or objects not understood, provided that further learning can continue. Knowing the names of all the birds may make a person into an interesting observer or into an intolerable bore. There is danger that, having learned their names, the learner may believe that he understands the birds. If you think you understand something, you cannot learn any more about it.

Are we to admit that no verbal explanation will help the child? In most cases, children who have memorized explanations cannot solve problems with the concepts, and often cannot even identify the problems. It takes an educated mind to understand an idea merely by hearing it described or by reading about it. It is to that stage of education that good museum exhibits can bring people.

The objection is made that in a short visit to a museum we cannot expect students or Sunday visitors to learn more than the names of the things they see. I think we can. If one is allowed to learn only a little, is it better to learn that the plane of vibration of Foucault's pendulum makes one apparent revolution about the vertical axis in one sidereal day multiplied by the sine of the angle of latitude of the experiment: or to see that the pendulum and the gyro both determine unchanging directions in space? I believe the latter is immediately more fun, and ultimately more useful, than the former. The unexpressed sense impression applies to a greater variety of real situations than does the verbal formula, except in the mind already educated to scientific language.

A person who gets a phenomenon "inside" him nearly always repeats the action or rereads the label in order to check his understanding or in order to redemonstrate it to himself. The person's expression of delight is unmistakable. Piaget showed that behavior of this kind exists unambiguously in children. I have seen it often in grown-ups, as when I do it myself.

Another great point of Piaget's has been that a child must go through a definite sequence of stages leading up to his ability to induce general rules from particular observations. His elegant experiments speak for themselves. The pedaguese for our practice in the light of Piaget's findings has been *readiness*. We have heard for a generation, "Don't teach a child to read until he has Reading Readiness." I agree with Jerome Bruner, however, that a child's readiness depends on his experience. I conclude that exposure to good museum material may let youngsters understand scientific ideas at a younger age than if they had not handled and seen the exhibits. I do not know that beating the Russians to the moon is a good reason to carry out the idea; but perhaps giving each person a little extra time in his youth for his education is a good reason.

A youngster whose school offers him an impoverished curriculum, whose family offers him money but deprives him of culture, and who visits the museum in a class with his contemporaries, already has certain built-in objectives. They have sinister similarities to the objectives that *we* have for him. He wants his life and surroundings to be exciting. We want him to enjoy his surroundings. He wants something to happen. We offer him Batman at home and fossils in the museum. In the museum, the exhibit is behind glass; it does not do anything, so it must not be important. If he examines the label, he finds words that he cannot easily read. *His* purpose—excitement—has been thwarted; he moves on to another exhibit.

In the children's area of the United States Science Pavilion in the Seattle World's Fair, at one point five busloads of tough city tenth graders were unloaded without warning and with no preparation by their teachers. The exhibition had just opened, and only two demonstrators were on hand. We were both certain that the displays, which had not yet been child-proofed, would be wrecked. The noise was deafening, and I found that I could not get any individual to stop rushing around long enough to look at one thing. But the character of the do-it-yourself exhibits prevailed. After ten or fifteen minutes of bedlam, the noise dropped off and people began to concentrate. Since my rhetorical attempts failed, I am sure that the reason the racket stopped was that the children had just found the satisfaction that goes with learning—and there was no language barrier between them and the subject.

It should be said in this connection that, in spite of my own fears and the warnings of museum people, we had virtually no vandalism in that exhibition. Although the chips from the probability exhibit were stolen, the displays, though not solidly built, were never deliberately hurt. I suppose that, if one were being interested, one's aggressions would lose their importance and one would forget to make trouble. There was considerable vandalism in the adult sections of that exhibition.

Museums are moving in the direction of inductive thinking in their exhibits, just as schools are doing in their programs. For a long time, the Franklin Institute and the Museum of Science and Industry in Chicago have had physics displays in which the visitor could observe physical processes directly. The problem there has been that the conclusions were stated in the labels. I believe firmly that principles, if not laws, are conclusions that the observer should reach by himself.

A question which good teachers answer intuitively, and which I as a museum functionary cannot answer, is: "How little can you tell a person and still not scare him off?" In the classroom this problem is a matter of timing; the teacher asks a question: not, "What is combustion?" but, "If the wick is what burns up in a candle, then what happens to the wax?". Then, there is a long pause while nobody answers. It is in that pause that learning takes place—not while the teacher is talking, and not while a student answers. As the silence draws on, the natural-born teacher knows the exquisite moment in which either the question must be answered or a simpler one asked in its place, lest the students lose interest because they are frustrated.

As I watch people at exhibits, I think that I often see the same thing happening to them that happens to the student who could not answer the question within the period of his attention. A museum visitor of any age looks at a display and then either leaves it or reads the label. If he leaves the exhibit right away, the reason may be that he is already familiar with its content, or that he is frustrated by it. Few of our visitors are so learned in physics that they ignore demonstrations for that reason. Frustration may be the reason that he turns away. That fact alone justifies this conference.

The question is, then, "How do you arrange exhibits and labels so that a person can find out enough to feel the excitement and triumph that are the only legitimate reward for learning, and still not prevent learning by telling the answers?". I suggest that the method lies in the direction of museum exhibits that involve handling, hearing, or smelling as well as seeing; that involve puzzlement, with its inevitable consequence: thinking.

Exhibits should require the visitor to do something; to sense the result and to be impressed with it. In order to impress someone, an exhibit may have to surprise him. An example of a surprising exhibit is the small Foucault's pendulum hung from a bracket mounted on a disc that one can turn. When a visitor sets the weight swinging and turns the disc around, he is usually surprised to see that the direction of swing does not turn with the suspension.

A bike wheel, hung in a gimbal, is nothing special until the visitor tries to turn the gimbal while the wheel is spinning. Then, curiosity is plain on his face, and the museum's work is done. If the visitor reads the label, he will understand it; if not, he will remember what he felt, and may someday detect the family relationship in the "feel" of an electric mixer tilted to and fro when it is running.

As for administration, one should remember that the exhibits professionals cannot build do-it-yourself physics displays because of the high standards of mechanical soundness that are required. I do not know of any displays bought outside the exhibition, either in the U.S. Science Pavilion children's area in Seattle, or at Cranbrook, of the kind I describe, that have not had to be redesigned and rebuilt in the machine shop, under the supervision of a person who knew their purposes and their probable use. The capital investment in such exhibits is low, for they must be very simple. The investment of time is large, for they require trial and modification for months before they can be considered permanent. Their maintenance cost is higher than it is for static displays, but much less than I should have guessed.

The old synoptic collection of extinct vertebrates will no longer serve the general public. We must now have exhibits that show, for example, how fossils are collected, that show their relation to the neighborhood, and that encourage the observer to draw his own paleontologic conclusions. Again, we must now have exhibits that show, not what is the arrangement of atoms in the diamond, but how crystal shapes, cleavages and X-ray diffraction *imply* that arrangement.

Of course, the great research collections must remain while observations are still to be made; they are the grist of the scientific mill. But those collections have an obligation to the layman of which McGeorge Bundy gave a hint in his last Dean's report:

> "There is, I believe, a great need and opportunity today to reconnect teaching and investigation to each other. . . . The process of Science is learning; this is true for the Freshman "taking" physics and for the Professor testing a new idea. The enormous difference between these two activities must not blind us to their common characteristics: in each case a man is engaged in making his own what was not his before. . . . These two learners will always be conscious of their kinship, and the air of their learning will somehow be one."

To the layman and to the child, there is immense interest in knowing how "they know" what they think they know. There is also satisfaction, for it makes us see that we ourselves are capable of understanding the scientists' interests and problems, if not of doing his work.

Here the scholarly collection can contribute more than any agency, except the scientist himself, to the enlightenment of the layman.

Briefly, understanding of the kind that is permanent and useful, comes at first through experience rather than through words. Museums can and should provide such experience by means of exhibits that involve the senses and actions of the visitor, as well as his reasonable soul.

A Look at the Future

Implications of Technology for Museum Education

STEPHEN WHITE
Carnegie Commission on Educational Television

The request from which this report stems was for "a paper on technological innovations in education as they may relate to museum education." The title of the report itself, however, has been changed to the one the reader sees above. The distinction is an important one, and there is an obligation to make it clear.

It can scarcely be denied that the past few years have seen considerable technological innovation in formal education. Out of the development of electronic data-processing equipment—which can display information, register feedback and in response to that feedback govern the display of further information—have come elaborate teaching machines. The abrupt emergence of television as a medium of mass entertainment has been followed by attempts to make use of television in the classroom. The digital computer is in use not only for the routine clerical tasks that accompany education, but also as a tool of investigation into the process of education itself. On a somewhat less elaborate level, the tape recorder has been put to use for instruction in foreign languages, and the electric typewriter for early instruction in reading and writing.

All this is impressive; yet, it has surprisingly little to do with the revolution in education that has taken place over the last decade. To anyone who examines the list I have made, it should be apparent that the educational revolution would have taken place, virtually unchanged, if none of these electronic devices had ever been made available to the schools.

Consider them one by one. The teaching machine is one reflection, and only one, of a theory of the learning process that was developed after the war by various schools of behavioral psychologists, here and abroad. The theory can be put to use as a practical guide to instruction by the teacher in the classroom, unsupported by any classroom paraphernalia of any kind; it can be embodied in books; it can be embodied in a mechanical teaching machine, for which the technology goes back more or less to Sir Isaac Newton; or finally, it can be embodied in an intricate electronic device. To the extent that the theory corresponds to the real world of learning, any or all devices will be useful, but it is the theory that constitutes the innovation, and not the form in which it may be embodied.

Television in the classroom is the latest in a long series of attempts to enrich the classroom experience, and to bring into the classroom a higher degree of teaching proficiency than the average teacher is likely to command. It is, in short, a kind of textbook and can be supported for the same set of reasons that would lead one to support the notion of bigger and better textbooks. To those who believe that the ideal educational process is constituted by having Mark Hopkins on one end of a log and the student on the other, instructional television is not particularly inspiring; to those who believe that education is best effected by multiplying the student's resources and by appealing to him along every imaginable avenue of perception, it is an important weapon in the classroom armory. Again, it is the mode of education that is in question, not the particular device which may be employed.

There is no need to proceed in this vein. Each agglomeration of vacuum tubes and transistors, however impressive and however costly, is an embodiment of a theory of instruction. It is not impossible that a new technology or a new application of technology, by revealing totally new possibilities or by creating totally new desires, could lead to a new theory of instruction; so far as I know, however, it would be difficult to make the case that anything of the sort has yet happened.

Meanwhile, it is the theory that calls forth the machine, and not the converse.

Yet there has indeed been a revolution in education, and that revolution has been brought about, to a large and perhaps to an overwhelming extent, by technology. The point to be made is that the technology in question is not the technology of education. It is, rather, technology in the most general sense of the word, and it has operated not directly upon education but upon the society in which education occurs. The effect has been not upon the teaching process itself but upon the environment in which the process takes place. It is not irrelevant to discuss it here, for the environment is also that in which the museum has its existence. It is, essentially, an environment characterized by an enormous and ever-growing body of information, as well as by an equally enormous and ever-growing facility in displaying and transferring that information, and by a progressively increasing need for information.

Recall that this has not always been so. Not very long ago (and in most of the world, to this very day) the average man or woman required, for purposes of a useful and enduring existence, knowledge of the processes of animal birth and growth and death, and of vegetable growth and decay. He began to accumulate that knowledge as a child, drawing it from his immediate surroundings; he mastered it, to the extent of his own capacity, as a young man; and he could justifiably depend upon it during all his life.

Slowly, technology began to disturb this equilibrium. The time came when society was such that the average member was obliged to learn reading, writing, and arithmetic, and when for more and more people the daily task was something that could no longer be mastered out of the surroundings, but required some kind of formal or informal instruction. At the outset the demands were modest; what was learned in childhood was a sufficient base for maturity; life had become less circumscribed, perhaps, but was circumscribed still.

Then, as technology gained momentum the pace of change quickened. We stand today at what appears to be a climax of that process (although to another generation the sense of climax here and now may be absent). One technology, that of agricultural production, has ended for the vast majority of Americans the tie to and dependence on the land. Another technology, that of the internal combustion engine, has expanded beyond measure the space traveled over his lifetime by the average citizen, and expanded accordingly the variety of his primary experience. A third technology, that of electronic communication, bathes each one of us at all hours of the day in incessant secondary experiences. And all the technologies, working together, supporting one another, irresistibly create newer, more pervasive, and more powerful technologies.

Let me seize, for the moment, upon one aspect of this series of developments. At the risk of being so abstract as to verge on unreality, one might identify a preindustrial era, an industrial era, and an electronic era. In the present context, there appears to be a kind of spiraling effect.

In the first of these eras, information came to its recipient in a highly integrated form. What he learned about agriculture, for example, he learned as a whole, out of a set of undifferentiated experiences. To a degree, the information was presented to his perceptions in its totality and at all moments, in the form of a process and a structure.

As the environment became more complex and more differentiated, the manner in which information was presented began to be patterned by classification and to be presented serially and in detail. One does not learn to read by surrounding oneself with the written word; instead, the process involved in reading is one in which the data are treated as something to be classified—to be put in order, filed in their proper niches, examined according to plan. Formal education, too, fell into exactly such a pattern, from the earliest grades through the graduate school; informal education was forced, sometimes with great difficulty, into the same mold.

In the electronic era, we find ourselves immersed in information once more. There is a great deal more information than a farmer of the Middle Ages wanted, needed, or could find; and so the immersion takes a somewhat different form. It comes, most spectacularly, from television; it is accumulated and heaped upon us, still in spectacular form, by the digital computer. But it comes also from the book, which technology has remade into something quite different from the printed matter of the nineteenth century; from the telephone; from the Xerox machine; from the mobility provided by the automobile and plane.

The effort to place it in serial order is vitiated by the speed with which it arrives. The urge to classify confronts the reality that much of this new information comes to us integrally, in a form that resembles the direct experience, and the classification must follow our perceptions rather than organize them. To this extent, we are once again like the farmer immersed in the whole data of agriculture.

But today the information is bewildering in its scope and variety. Looked upon as raw data, no lifetime is long enough to grasp any significant portion of it. Information hammers at us, morning, noon, and night—at work and at play. There are even those who have proposed we organize means of submitting ourselves to it during sleep. An enormous amount of this data we need in order to go about our daily business; an even more enormous amount we seem to need because humanity is a breed that feeds upon information. It accumulates; it is rushed at the speed of light to our eyes and ears; we are inundated with it.

It is from this hard reality that the revolution in education has emerged. Underlying all the superficial phenomena of the new math and the new physics is the recognition that mathematics and physics no longer impinge on our senses serially, but as part of our total environment; that the sheer quantity of mathematics and physics that confronts us is too great to master in detail; and that in combination, these two characteristics of the electronic era require that education deal with process and structure, rather than with raw data. It is no longer enough to learn to compute: there are too many computations, too many kinds of computation; too many areas where computation is an integral part; too many ways in which we meet computation—too much, too often, too fast—for us to proceed step by step, fragment by fragment, through the art of computation. We must learn to look at computation as a whole, which is in turn part of a larger whole, and which will be comprehended, if it is to be comprehended at all, as process and structure.

It is in this manner, rather than in the provision of electronic devices for use in the classroom, that technology has affected education. And it is in this manner that technology is likely to affect that part of education which can be expected to take place in association with a museum. In the museum, too, twentieth-century devices have their place: it is convenient to be able to traverse a room with a private commentary delivered from a head set to one's ears. But this does not significantly alter the museum, or modify its function; if we are to look for more than minor refinements, in all likelihood we must look elsewhere.

It is wise to begin from fundamentals. A museum, my Webster tells me, is "a place where objects are exhibited." There is something vaguely deprecating about the definition, but it is not unreasonable.

Certainly, at one time, the museum was *the* place where objects were exhibited. To a man bound fairly closely to the neighborhood of his home and work, and whose flow of information from outside that neighborhood was the newspaper and other products of a far-from-glittering printing press, the museum was, perhaps, the only place where he could come into direct contact with the world outside his parish. The artifacts, the elaborate representations of other societies and other neighborhoods, the careful reproduction of antiquity—all these added inches and feet to his horizon.

Today the artifacts are richer and more attractively presented; the representations of other societies and other neighborhoods even more elaborate; antiquity more carefully represented than ever. But the museum has long since ceased to be the sole recourse for the curious. It has, to begin with, the real competition of the printing press: magazines and artfully prepared books do not, indeed, present the object, but they can and do present representations of the object that are in their own way quite as satisfying as anything seen within a display case, and their wealth of resource is far beyond the wealthiest museum's.

The moving pictures, first, and now television, in their own way, do even more. Television ranges the world, and if its subject matter is more often than not entirely trivial, its backgrounds appear all the more rich. Behind a trite dramatic series, the viewer does indeed see Africa, its people, and its flora and fauna. Under the proper circumstances, such exposure might stimulate him to see something of the real Africa in an appropriate museum, but unless that Africa can somehow be presented by the museum in a fashion that has the immediacy of the film or television background, the museum is more likely to be a disappointment rather than a reward.

Even more than these, in their own way, the automobile and airplane have competed with the museum. There are real experiences to be encountered today, a few hundred or even a few thousand miles away from home, and more and more we encounter them. The shadowy curiosities of the museum cannot begin to compete with the real curiosities of a new state or a new country.

It is not intended that there be any implication here that the museum has lost its raison d'être. Rather, one might say that technology has brought into being a host of competitors for that part of man's attention that once was attracted by the museum. It is irrelevant to argue that they are unworthy competitors—at times they may be exactly that, at times not. The hard fact is simply that they compete, and if the museum is to play its proper role, it must do so fully aware that it is no longer alone in serving its natural public.

It may readily be seen that the problems facing museum education, as a consequence of technology, are in many respects similar to those which have faced formal education over the last few years. The information available in the museum, as in the school, now takes its place within an enormously aggrandized body of information available anywhere and everywhere, and available in forms that envelop the recipient. The museum, like the school, begins to appear static in a rapidly moving world; intent upon singularities in a world that presents again and again perceptions of the continuous.

The schools have attempted to meet the challenge by reconstituting their curricula to emphasize process and structure. In doing so, they have called upon the massive curriculum reform, about which Dr. Frank Oppenheimer spoke during the conference proceedings (see page 215). Without wishing to invade Dr. Oppenheimer's territory—although, indeed, I may already have done so—I should like to comment briefly on one aspect of the major curriculum reform.

Each discipline has found it necessary to involve a large part of the academic community in its reform efforts. The physics reform, with which both Dr. Oppenheimer and I have been associated, was truly national in scope. It required the service of physicists from the entire country; the work was done on college campuses from coast to coast; California inventions were tested in Illinois and manufactured in Massachusetts; and, in the end, put to work wherever there were school districts. Nothing less would have sufficed for the very difficult task that was broached when the decision was made to rationalize the teaching of twelfth-grade physics in terms of the mid-twentieth century.

It appears to me that some similar massive attack is necessary if the museum is to play a part in education commensurate with its capacities. The museum which is content to draw only upon its own resources may have become, in this century, as anomalous as the school system which attempts to teach physics entirely on its own. The museum collection, however rich, is no longer adequate for its task. It is, primarily, a mass of items, and the item is no longer the primary element of education. Like the schools, it may be that each museum must look outside itself.

Since I am by no means knowledgeable about the management of museums, I present the following suggestion diffidently. Science and humanities museums might seek to pattern themselves after a procedure that is relatively common among fine arts museums: that of assisting in the preparation of carefully planned, coherent presentations that draw upon resources beyond the museum itself. I am thinking of the retrospective exhibitions which tour, from time to time, the country's large art museums—a Matisse exhibition is being shown in the neighborhood in which I am writing.

Such exhibitions are designed to present a man's work as process and structure. The visitor does far more than see great art. He sees, also, how it came to be; where it began and where it was directed; how it failed and how it succeeded. The artist is presented to him as all things are presented to him in real life, flowing and moving, growing and falling away. In the end, he has shared an experience, and not merely viewed the results of another man's experience. Because this integrated approach has significance to the man and woman to whom it is intended to appeal, it grasps their interest. The man who would not visit the local museum under ordinary conditions will make his way there upon learning it has purchased a new Matisse—not to see paintings by Matisse, but to learn about Matisse.

Finally, it brings the museum itself into a kind of rapport with our own times. Webster may say what the word "museum" denotes, but what it ordinarily connotes is all too clear: a grim building in which nothing ever changes; a timeless repository for timeless objects, in detail and in sum the same today as it was yesterday. The Matisse exhibition is something new in town, and the museum which houses it becomes, suddenly, a place where things happen.

An exhibition built around Sir Isaac Newton could have precisely the same appeal. It would present not only the man's physics and his mathematics, but also his alchemy and theology; it would present the society in which he lived, the fashions of the times, the music, the architecture, the thought; it would deal with both the giants on whose shoulders he stood and the men who followed directly after him, who began building modern physics and mathematics.

Every museum in the country would have to be ransacked to provide the material for such an exhibit. Every scholar of Newton and his times would have to be called in to tailor the exhibit. All the supporting dramatic and technical skills would be called upon to stage the exhibit and make it manageable and transportable. Yet, once all this was done, such an exhibit, touring the country's museums, might have a lifetime of several years.

I have singled out Newton, merely to exemplify a notion. The subjects for such treatment are inexhaustible. There is little reason to doubt that such exhibits could be prepared so steadily that every major museum would be able to change programs once a month, or once every six weeks, bringing a "new show to town" as often as the public exhausted its pleasure in the old. There are obviously problems in such a scheme. It is not comforting to contemplate shipping priceless objects from county to county, or to estimate the costs of preparing museums so that they might welcome such exhibits and show them to their best advantage. It is here that technology might well be called upon to aid the museum, for these are technical problems, and it is not unthinkable that they might be solved.

Clearly, what is called for is a national effort of a sort that is not perhaps customary among those who manage museums. But some such effort, of this sort or another, is clearly what technology implies for the museum. In this world, knowledge and information are no longer things which are conveniently stored in a building, however loving the care that is given them there. The world is a larger place than it once was, and the walls of the museum must be broached if the museum is to be part of it. In the end, the technological device of the first half century which is of most significance to the museum may turn out to be the ten-ton truck.

Discussion and Documentation

Summary of the Proceedings

❧

ERIC LARRABEE
Provost, Faculty of Arts and Letters
State University of New York at Buffalo

The Smithsonian Institution Conference on Museums and Education, in one way or another, managed to be a source of frustration to its participants. It included pleasant circumstances—most especially the hospitality of Mrs. Vanderbilt Webb at Shelbourne Farms—but they did not wholly alleviate our malaise. There were numerous reasons for this, most of them legitimate. First of all, the subject for consideration was forbiddingly open ended, made up as it was of two topics either of which alone could have preoccupied an even less articulate group for an even longer period of time. As it was, the pairing of Museums with Education tended to raise, all too quickly, the questions: "What is a Museum? What is Education?" and to lead discussion aside into a search for fundamental definitions. It may well be true, as Dr. David Abbey was forcefully to argue, that without some theory of learning one is powerless to examine museums in their educational role, but to have asked an assembly of such disparate people as these to agree upon any such theory would have been a quixotic endeavor.

Moreover, the confrontation of museums and education with one another has a way of highlighting the imponderable qualities of each, and of suggesting further subjects—for example, the polarity of art and science—which are endlessly productive of reflection and talk. Some of the best things said at the Conference were digressions of this kind, and it is a tribute to museums in their educational role that they stimulate thought in so many other fruitful areas of interest. But all of these admirably open qualities in the subject matter made it as difficult to organize as it was attractive to talk about, with the result that speaker after speaker seemed confidently to be handling ideas with which the Conference as a whole was unable to cope. We constantly threatened to come apart into our separate components of wisdom, and to fail in that degree of willingness to admit one another's existence without which no conference is worth holding, let alone reporting afterward.

Another source of frustration was the fact that the assembly represented such contrasting degrees of familiarity with the problems it was to engage. Since one of the objects in view was to bring museum professionals together with educators and others of similar concerns, it was nearly inevitable that people who were considering the question of museum education for literally the first time in their lives would find themselves in the same room with others who had devoted their entire professional careers to it. The latter may be forgiven if they were less than fascinated to hear announced in a tone of self-congratulation propositions which they had discovered thirty years ago, and had learned to recognize most of the arguments for or against in the interval since. They had to listen to earnest pleas for research in areas they themselves had investigated, and to laments over a state of ignorance which they—to put it mildly—did not feel they shared. Frederick L. Rath, Jr., for example, was constrained to comment on his surprise at hearing raised again, in 1966, questions which he could remember discussing in the U.S. Park Service in the 1930s. In his own field of historic preservation, the information might be scattered "but it is *there*," he said. "We *have* found some of the answers."[1] Mr. Rath remarked on the presence at the Conference of people like Dr. A. E. Parr, of whom it could well have been said (Dr. Parr himself was much too modest to say it) that he had written more on museums and education than some of the rest of us had ever read.

It should be admitted, at the same time, that there are at least one or two advantages in bringing a fresh eye to bear, in that the outsider can not only praise an institution as an insider may not, but can see it whole. Certainly no museum professional at the meeting matched the heartfelt statement of a museum's value which came, in an early session, from Dr. Frank Oppenheimer.

> *Dr. Oppenheimer:* First I wanted to say, as a non-museum person, a little of what I thought about museums, because they are terribly important; they are just always full of people, there is an enormous hunger for them. If one thinks of what would happen if museums were destroyed, the stuff in them destroyed, it would be the most awful loss to society. So they are playing some role, and have been for centuries, which is independent of the various programs they have—I think something we could not live without, though I do not quite know why. I can think of some of the things that they do: perhaps one of the most important is that they lay before one all the things that people take, or have ever taken, seriously—and that is perhaps the main reason why a museum has to be terribly careful not to be fake. But they do other things too, I think: they manage to fill in the holes in one's experience. In school, or in one's living, everything has to be fairly narrow, but in museums you can see this great variety spread out before you in some way that fits together. You go through the suburbs of a city and you see a factory here, or a school there, or a pub, and it is all just mixed up. In a museum, somehow, things that are laid out, in this great variety, can be synthesized.

Dr. Oppenheimer's words will do nicely to stand for one reference point in the Conference's overall pattern of moods, for it was obvious as we proceeded how awestruck we all were—professionals and amateurs alike—at the fantastic potential of museums as educative tools: their casualness; their tactile, kinetic, three-dimensional quality; their comprehensiveness; their freedom from pedagogical bureaucracy and doctrine. And this, too, paradoxically, was a source of frustration; for we, therefore, tended to contemplate the day-to-day realities of museum life—or, on occasion, to have our noses rubbed in them—in the light of those far-off, beguiling possibilities: practicality in the light of perfection. The exigencies of bus scheduling, the protection of exhibits against random vandalism, the—as Peter Caws called them—"cloacal" aspects suggested by Secretary Ripley's reference, in his introductory remarks, to the importance of washroom facilities; all operated to induce a sense of futility when seen against the far horizon where stood the Perfect Museum, the embodiment of all our dreams.

No doubt this conference was not unusual in its degree of behind-the-scenes griping, its head of steam built up of unresolved tensions, but by Wednesday morning the sense of repressed dissatisfaction had mounted to such a point that a number of us—the writer of this summary among them—made an effort to bring the covert discontentment out into the open. The normal conference overtures of deploying one's prejudices, of feeling one another out, had been exhausted; it was now apparent that what many of those present wanted was some clearer indication of what they were expected to do. The question devolved first on Charles Blitzer of the Smithsonian Institution, and subsequently on Richard Grove of the Office of Education, the Conference's ultimate sponsor, who replied:

Mr. Grove: This is a conference which is supported by, and is a unit of, the federal government, which is somewhat unusual in itself. One of the things that we would hope to get is this: we have the problem of administering and working with certain definite federal programs which can help museums. What we ask for is help, guidance in doing this wisely and well. The question has been asked: is [this Conference] research-oriented? I guess it is, partially because this is one of the resources. There is a program which offers support for educational research, which could be in museum education, which is largely unused —to date. There are also the programs that I mentioned the other day, under the Elementary and Secondary Education Act most particularly. These are involving museums all over the country and, from what I see, I do not think it is being done as well as it could be. Where should the guidance come from? I suspect from just such a group as this.

Mr. Grove's statement had handed back to the meeting exactly that burden of decision which the meeting was reluctant to accept, and the next speaker drove the point home by suggesting that we stop being so polite to one another, since if we did not confront the issues, no one else was going to.

Mrs. Thurman: What I think we need is to be a great deal gutsier as we work on this big question. Frankly, I believe in every one of you people—for caring enough to inconvenience yourselves to come here. This in itself shows that we agree there is a need to get something done. Now that we are here, can't we attack the question? And, mostly, can't we stop worrying about the side effects of attacking each other—as we obviously must—in the process. This is an appeal for honest conflict, here in the meetings. What I'm knocking is this over-abundance of educational friendliness: it is hurting this conference. Now I am not saying that we should just make a point of fighting with each other for the rest of the week. I only want us to be as candid and creative here as we are in our own little gangs in the elevators and buses. Courtesy has had its share, and the results speak for themselves. Let us risk letting heart and mind take over. Maybe we will find everybody wrong about everything. Maybe this will prove that the wrong people were invited. Whatever we find, let us not just review what we know already: that in both the school field and the museum field 'sweetness and light' can cut out a great deal of illumination.

It took time for Mrs. Thurman's words to sink in, but when they finally did—later the same morning—the result was a cathartic outburst of people talking all at once which the written record can only faintly reproduce. The immediate occasion was another impassioned plea for the acceptance of responsibility, this time from Mrs. Mary L. Sherburne, and it produced a degree of candor on all sides which Mrs. Thurman might well have been proud to have been the first to ask for.

Mrs. Sherburne: You people have really got me going—with definitions, and purposes, and papers before, and all this. I don't think we really need any of it. We are all here, and we have all come from backgrounds in which we have been intimately, intellectually, and feelingly concerned with all of this. How are we to define so much, and then knock it all down? We are defeating ourselves; we are defeating the creativity that is in all of us by doing this. . . .

I have heard so much, I think I shall die if I hear anyone else tell me why you cannot do something. . . . What would the museum be like if we had everything we wanted, if we could dream the dreams that are as big as what we are going to be able to handle in the future? I would like to have a moratorium, just for two or three hours, on the impossible . . . and let us just think, what would this museum be like, or whatever it is—I don't care what it is called—this place where the best that man has thought can be put . . . but apart from the limits we have set ourselves . . . we should be able to be free from some of the things that shackle the schools as institutions.

I am glad we do not have any direct commitment from you people. I mean, we have here what I spent three months trying to germinate in a group of teachers. We have a situation where we have got to work out our own system, and we are all fighting it like hell, which is exactly what we do not want in the teachers. We keep looking for the big father, you know. First we looked at Charlie Blitzer, and he would not do us any good . . . and now we are getting mad at Eric Larrabee because he has not told us what we should do, and then we looked over here at the Office of Education, and by gosh that big father has not told us what to do.

Douglas O. Pedersen: Well, I want to get mad at Larrabee. He just says, let us not try to define education. . . . I am not interested, frankly, in museums as an end in themselves, but in how they relate to the ongoing concerns of society, in which I think education—as it is now constituted and established—is central. And I do not think we have really hit the point: what the hell *is* education? If it is something, if we can decide what it is, and what is going on in it now, we can perhaps establish the relationship museums ought to have to it, which I think is what Grove here is trying to do, or it is why they financed this thing.

Eric Larrabee: Mr. Abbey offered eight models [of learning theory].

Mr. Pedersen: Oh I didn't buy that—that's a bunch of jargon I would like to fight with him about.

Duncan F. Cameron: Why *didn't* you fight with him about it, that is the—

Mr. Pedersen: Somebody used the word—this is a very genteel affair here. We came lots of miles to be genteel. Gee, I'm tired of being genteel.

Mrs. Sherburne: Couldn't we kind of get—

Mr. Pedersen: Everybody line up. Let's have a good fist fight.

Mrs. Sherburne: It's really too big to fight well. I disagree with you but—

Mr. Cameron: Can't get close enough to people.

Mr. Pedersen: —and we do not have much time left. I mean, I think Mike [Michael V. Butler] was right when he said there seems to be some effort to decide that all museums can be all things to everybody. . . . I've got the feeling that we have really been skirting the issue. Every time we say they are not the same [different kinds of museums] then we duck it, and go on to say they are the same. Didn't you get that feeling, Mike?

Mr. Butler: Yes, though I think there is another point that ought to be made . . . they are not the same. The art museum is not trying *at all* to do what I am trying to do, I know, and I am not sure whether the natural history museum is—I think not, saving your presence, Bob [Robert T. Hatt]—but the thing we are all trying to do is to get people to look at things, and this much we share. . . .

Mr. Larrabee: Let me ask a question: what would you do if you were trying to prepare a big, comprehensive exhibit on Leonardo da Vinci?

Mr. Pedersen: Cut my throat.

After this therapeutic bloodletting the Conference went much better. And Mr. Pedersen had been right, of course, to call attention to the casualness with which we had tended to generalize about "museums," without examining in any depth the essential distinctions between one kind and another. Dr. Parr had asserted a basic difference between an art museum and a science museum when he said that one is oriented to objects while the other is oriented to ideas. The art museum is devoted to the care and presentation of things ("stuff," as Mrs. Thurman called it in her paper), whereas the science museum is concerned with presenting principles or aspects of nature. This dissimilarity has historical origins, as Carter Brown pointed out, in the contrasting Northern and Southern European traditions out of which the modern museum came. In the North the museum's predecessor was the princely collection, the *Wunderkammer*.

Mr. Brown: Into these were put the bits of coral, the fossils, the fetuses in the bottles, the Holbein drawing, whatever happened to be at hand. On the other side one had the southern tradition, the Italian tradition, which really went back to Roman times, of the gallery—*galleria*—which was a wing added onto the country villa into which were put the bits of classical statuary, or later the oil easel paintings, to be considered part of—in and of—the salon, and this room in the house was not used for anything else; it was in effect for a kind of aesthetic contemplation. . . .

To Mr. Brown this was a difference between primary and secondary sources; "the stuff inside an art museum *is* the matter one is contemplating, and not an illustration of something else." In his view the problem—or, at least, our conceptual problem at this Conference—was that the two streams were drawing together and becoming confused, so that the distinction was no longer "crisp," the sort of confusion between art and science that may lead an artist to mimic bits and pieces of science because they are fashionable, without understanding them. At the same time, the pervasive "trend toward the visual" in our culture underscored the importance of the primary source, art museum tradition. The proceedings of the Conference took place mainly in Billings Center, originally a distinguished work of the architect H. H. Richardson, now sensitively restored, and it amused Mr. Brown to note a change in its function.

> *Mr. Brown:* I think it is of great symbolic interest that the building we are now in used to be a library; however, that beautiful room across the way is now occupied by an exhibit. In the room we were in yesterday, as you noticed, the book shelves had been converted into art exhibition shelves.

Gentle as this needling is, and unobjectionable as Mr. Brown's proposition may sound, it conceals within it the issue—or set of related issues—on which the Conference was indeed divided. It was not simply a matter of the art museum versus the science museum, or the old-fashioned curator against the modern, audience-oriented specialist in exhibit design—though these rivalries played a part. The inner core of resistance to Mr. Brown's idea came from those, like David Abbey, who violently objected to the "pernicious statement that the object is the message." Dr. Abbey, and many others, saw no reason for putting an object on display in a museum unless you had something to say about it—the same point which was made, in terms of exhibition technique, by Alma S. Wittlin, both in her paper and her presentation of it at the Conference. Even the curator who does nothing but assemble a distinguished collection is saying *something,* since (in the apt phrase of Edgar Richardson) his collection is a kind of "personal anthology" of one man's taste. One of the strengths of museums is to contain real things (not to be "fake," as Dr. Oppenheimer had said) but it may well happen that a science museum will achieve its most "authentic," scientifically exact effects with exhibits which are—Dr. Parr's figure—90 percent fake, one occasion among many in which the idea prevails over the object.

One way or another the Conference spent considerable energy in exploring this axis of alternative approaches to the question of what a museum is and does; and, the more we talked, the more apparent it became that idea and object are so bound together that none of us could successfully disentangle them. No statement could be made on one side that could not be countered on the other; and, from time to time, it would occur to a speaker that perhaps we all had more in common than was seemingly keeping us apart. "The thing we are all trying to do," as Michael Butler had said—and as Sue Thurman had written in the first paragraph of her paper—"is to get people to look at things. . . ." If the difference between an art museum and a science museum represents some fundamental distinction between art and science, then that distinction too could be considered in the light of the even more important similarities. There are a few, rare people who seem able to embody in themselves a degree of philosophical breadth and unity which makes the differences look trivial, and Frank Oppenheimer is one of them. The subject of what art and science share brought from him, extempore, this remarkable passage:

Dr. Oppenheimer: I think one of the things that both art and science do is teach one to be aware of one's surroundings, and they do this to a large extent by forcing one to pay attention to things that one has learned to ignore. In growing up one even ignores what people's faces are like, but by seeing paintings of people's faces you begin to look at them again, and I think that the same thing is true of science. You look at the sky and you see the stars, and it is just an amorphous mass; but suddenly somebody talks to you about it and you see that some stars move with respect to other stars. There are many examples of things that one just does not notice until either they are brought before one by a painting, or they are brought before one because one begins to understand them.

They both change in this way, the way one looks at oneself and the rest of the world, and I think this is one of the reasons that science, as it has been taught, is so unattractive to many people, because it has not succeeded in changing the way they look at themselves. But the whole development of modern physics—and especially the need for a sort of complementary and dualistic description of, say, light—changes one's attitude toward the many things one finds in one's own life, and in human life, in which you cannot describe reality by a single sentence; where you have to use sentences which do not make sense if you say them both in the same breath. That this can be a valid description of reality, so that you do not have to reject one description—you can say that there is a purpose to life and at the same time realize that if the earth were eliminated it would not make any difference—that these two separate statements, which do not make any sense, can both be a description of reality, is something that one finds from the study of atomic physics, and there it becomes very convincing and real. And you do not have to say you are not going to consider light as a particle, because that would be a sin, or it would be heretical. I can say, under the right circumstances, that either of these descriptions of reality is a valid one. This is just an example of the way science has an effect on what one thinks.

The other thing that both art and science have in common—or one of the other things—is that they are both increasingly concerned with the inaccessible, with things which are far away from the tactile, ordinary experience. I think that contemporary art, whether it is in poetry or in music, is hard to learn about, because it is talking about things which you can see with your eyes shut, it is talking about things which you can feel, it is talking about relationships which are not the accessible, easily formulated ones—and this means that for both art and science one has to start with the very familiar and work up [to the complex]. One cannot plunge into the inaccessible right away and have it be meaningful.

I think both science and art are now terribly involved in trying to find new techniques, and to explore all available techniques, and one sees this sense of exploration not just in science but in art. In order, I find, to become excited about some of the things that people are doing in art one has to say, "Well, they're trying to find out," and if they make a picture and they do nothing but squares, one must say that this is not so very different from what a mathematician does in trying to see what a given kind of mathematics will do if you just push it, and push it, and push it to see if it ever comes out any place.

Of course, [there is also the fact]—a trivial one in a sense—that both science and art have roots in the past and in the very familiar; and the final thing in common with them is that there is an awful lot of both of them, much more than you can really get hold of and know well.

On the formal agenda, Dr. Oppenheimer had been assigned the topic of curriculum development, since this was a matter in which he had personally been involved, and since the toughest *specific* question facing the Conference (one which had bluntly been put to it by Bartlett Hayes) was whether museums should make a deliberate effort to accommodate themselves to the formal curricula of the schools, or to intervene in the schools' process of arrival at curriculum requirements. It would be rash to say that the group as a whole responded to this, or that the question was answered in any other way than by being sidestepped—which is to say, answered in the negative. I doubt that anyone present would have been prepared to argue for such a formalized, restrictive alliance between museums and education, whereas many could surely have been found to endorse the supplementary image of mutual reinforcement between the two as it was—again—most eloquently described by Frank Oppenheimer, when speaking of the recent reforms in science curricula with which he happened to be familiar.

Dr. Oppenheimer: What most of them try to do is get rid of the idea that you can understand things by just throwing words at people, by making lists of nuclei and protons and electrons and transistors, and that this becomes modern science. Stuff has accumulated to such an extent that [we thought we were] adding to science courses by just adding all the new phrases, all the new symbols—but nobody understood anything.

So people have gone back, and they have said in the elementary school, let children just play with pendulums. Let's get familiar with the way they act, let's watch them as they swing, let's measure a few things about them, let's couple them together, let's invent and explore—and see what happens. In the high school, the PSSG course is a terribly narrow course; it aims really at trying to get some understanding of the Bohr atom, and to do this it has an extremely narrow channel. Many, many things are left out of the course that are important in physics, so that one can follow this quite narrow path aimed at trying to make real something which is inaccessible, namely an atom, to try to lay a foundation for this. And as a result one does not learn very much about sound, one does not learn much about crystals, one does not learn about friction—all the things that used to be in many standard courses are left out, because one wants to lay a foundation

> for some genuine understanding, and one has been very selective about this. . . .
>
> I think this is characteristic of modern curriculum development, that in order to produce real understanding, in order to have science come to something—so that it really affects the way one thinks about the world—it leaves things out. So this, I think, may be a connection with the role of museums, certainly not the only thing that museums can do, but if one is going to teach in this way—so that you leave most of everything out, in order to make something very meaningful—then there are enormous holes. Some of this can be picked up by reading, but I think most of it has to be picked up through props, and that the museum's role is to fill in these holes. . . . The school provides the narrow channel and the museum is the thing that broadens it, and without this broadening I don't think one can get a decent education.

It is impossible, as Dr. Oppenheimer said, to set up museum exhibits which will please or get through to everybody; to be comprehensive does not mean to aim at reaching the entire public. In the first place, there are variations in personality which make one type of exhibit effective for one type of person, but not for another; and Dr. Parr provided an illustration of how statistical analyses of exhibit impact could be completely misleading unless personality differences were taken into account—a subject which Duncan Cameron, among others, had also been engaged in researching. How much research, on what, by what method, and to what end were also among the questions facing the assembled company. Richard Grove had replied that yes, he guessed the Conference *was* "research-oriented . . . partially because this is one of the resources," because, that is, further research along some given line was one of the concrete results which might emerge from it.

This prospect did not entirely fill everyone present with enthusiasm. Perhaps we had all attended too many conferences which automatically announced "more research" among their recommendations. Perhaps too many of the museum people present had been badly stung in some past experience by ill-informed, inept researchers. (Robert T. Hatt gave several frightening examples from the rich repertoire of available atrocity stories on this theme.) Perhaps too many people believed (as did Drs. Oppenheimer and Abbey) in the right of the curator, if he is so permitted and inclined, to operate intuitively, "as an artist would paint a canvas" (David Abbey's words). Or perhaps there was some simple fear of rendering an already unsettled profession even more uneasy about its traditional practices. When it devolved that only two of the museum professionals present had on their staffs anyone qualified in social science research techniques, Mrs. Helen Bronheim asked why this was: not enough money, or what? Various answers were offered, none quite responsive to the question, until some minutes later—the very closing remark of that session—when Dr. Parr got up to say that there *was* one reason no one had so far mentioned, namely: "Too many museums are scared of finding out how wrong they have been."

The writers of papers, in putting them before the Conference, chose many and varied methods, but none provided a more startling contrast between the written word and the presentation of it than did Scarvia Anderson. In the first place, Miss Anderson's accent and attractiveness bore little relationship to the conventional image of a research psychologist and, in the second, what she wanted to say turned out to be far more than the restrained statement of research objectiveness which (if she will forgive me) her paper is. She began by telling what she does, professionally, and as she described the condition of vague, confused objectives—or total absence of them—which she and her organization have repeatedly encountered, one began to see that the real power (and object?) of research was to clarify the minds of the people who asked for it. She came to this theme so mildly and deftly that at first it was scarcely noticeable, but soon Duncan Cameron really opened up on it:

> *Mr. Cameron:* My experience has been that the definition of objectives is a very useful and very creative kind of exercise, that the museum professionals who sit down, either with social scientists or among themselves, to decide what they want to know—by means of a survey or some other applied social-science method—suddenly discover that they really do not know but thought they did. And they become involved in a very productive process which often leads them, not necessarily to a survey, but to a healthy reevaluation of what it is they are doing. Sometimes they wind up going in strange directions, concerned with problems they would have thought were irrelevant to their original intent. . . .

Mr. Cameron himself thought he had been aware of this fact, in the 1950s, when he first began doing museum audience research, but the full import of it was not brought home to him until "the most horrible year of my life," when he engaged full time in commercial marketing analysis and found himself enmeshed in such concerns as the proper thickness of peanut butter in a sandwich, or the "suds-booster level" of detergents. Asked what they were trying to do, his commercial clients often did not know, and time and again he witnessed research projects concocted out of thin air by ingenious marketing analysts, merely to provide the thick reports full of charts and statistics which boards of directors find impressive. Even so, he was again reminded of "how enlightening this problem of trying to plan research" was when he freed himself from peanut butter and returned to the problems of museums. "I think it might almost be worthwhile to do a lot of planning," he said, "and never mind doing the research, because planning is such a demanding and painful process, but such a productive one."

Mr. Cameron: I know that last spring, I'm embarrassed to say, I was unenlightened enough to propose to a state education department planning a new museum that they should attempt to evaluate, to estimate the potential demand which they would face for service from the state school system. It became apparent that there was no need to make a survey, or interview a thousand teachers or superintendents of schools, or look at the curriculum—that no matter how many docents they hired, or how large the education department, or how many thousand square feet in the museum, if they were serious in their intent to involve themselves in the school system, no matter how large they made it, they were never going to meet the potential demand. Their problem was to decide how much they could afford to do, knowing that they would then be doing the best they could, but that there would always be more to be done. And so the whole nature of that project was changed.

For Mr. Cameron, professionally, the continued evaluation of museum projects had "led, of course, to questions of why the kids were there in the first place," and had caused him to struggle with the view that bringing children to museums in buses might "have nothing to do with the problem," that perhaps museums should be scaled entirely to the individual, and that group visits should be encouraged only as a way of exposing the single child to the visual language, which only as an individual would he then proceed to learn and use. "Perhaps," Mr. Cameron concluded, "at this time of confusion—and I think it *is* a time of confusion; I think we know that very well at this Conference—in museum work, one of the most useful exercises we can involve ourselves in is an attempt to plan meaningful research. If we can plan it, and can define our objectives, then this is useful work—but, in the process, the by-products are going to be a bounty that is much needed."

The intention of the Conference planners, from the start, had been that specific proposals—as, say, for research projects—would come from the sessions on Thursday and Friday mornings when the participants would separate into three "work groups" and proceed independently. As an aid to their deliberations, the staff from the Smithsonian provided each of the three groups with a set of the same seven questions, to be answered if they wished, ignored if they preferred, but in any event to be regarded as posing problems which the Conference could not in good conscience evade. The questions were the following:

1. What are some of the special advantages of museums for education?

2. Are museums capable of an expanded role in organized, formal education?

3. If so, what are the principal arguments for and against?

4. If the role were accepted, what should or would the broad social consequences be?

5. How might such an expanded role be fulfilled in a specific instance?

6. What structural changes would be required in museum or educational organizations?

7. What would you want to learn about museums and education through research?

This series of yes and no alternatives had a disadvantage, as Dr. Abbey was quick to point out, in that the task of the work groups could be considerably simplified by answering "no" to question number 2, but in general the outline as offered was accepted. What follows here are the summations from each group as delivered to the final plenary session, either by the chairman or the group's selected spokesman. To the extent the Conference arrived at conclusions, they will be found in these statements, which have been only slightly edited for clarification and transfer to print.

REPORT OF THE FIRST WORK GROUP (HANNA ROSE)

We have a number of recommendations we would like to make.

The first is that every student who is preparing to be a teacher should, at some time in his or her college or university course, study museums—how they are to be used—and he should carry on work in museums. To do this we would like to suggest a demonstration program, to be set up in a city which has a museum or museums, preferably, with educational departments, the plan to be worked out with a college of education, a sympathetic superintendent of schools, and the State Department of Education, because accreditation is so important.

There are two areas in which this could work; one, a general area where the relevance of a museum collection is fairly obvious (this could be a program of what we call "saturation") and, of course, as I said, the teachers would be accredited for this work just as they would be for any other course. In a rather less obvious area, where the relationship to a museum collection is not clear, we would like to see experiments made, because we believe that there can be a museum collection which will fit into almost any school subject area. That, of course, means a budget. We would like to see museums set up exhibits, small but open exhibits—not ones in a closed, locked room—of educational materials relevant to the museum collections, including the most recent curriculum materials as they become available.

We suggest that museum educators should be on curriculum revision committees, and that this can probably best be done nationwide, with the backing and support of the Office of Education.

We should produce lists of supplementary materials which should be made very readily available to schools and to teachers.

Since museums' objects are in so many cases precious, irreplaceable, and cannot be moved beyond the walls of the museums, we discussed the possibility of a museum staff working with film makers to produce films of excellent technical quality, and as nonverbal as possible. Such films could be used in areas distant from a museum, or on TV, not as a substitute for the real object, but as Sue [Thurman] said, as a "temptation," or a promotion, to invite people, to make them want to come to the museum.

Since Americans are now so very mobile, we recommend that regional manuals oriented to the school curriculum be published, listing resources of museums in a particular area. These were not to be used necessarily for class visits, but for parents and children as they travel, and in this case it would be very important that the museum collections be cross-referenced, so that it would be very simple to see where one might find a collection related to the curriculum area in which the child is interested. In other words, if you wanted to see a collection on Africa, you would not have to leaf through all the lists for each museum, but you could look under Africa and find four or five museums that would have this sort of material.

We have all heard about Title 3 and supplementary educational centers. Instead of the schools building supplementary educational centers, would it not be possible to build a school near an already existing cluster of educational institutions such as a museum, library, university, or whatever happens to be there—many of our large cities have done this—and have the children brought from all over the city to spend a period of time in this building, where concentrated and at the same time casual and personal visits could be made to the museum collections? We would also hope that in some cases dormitory facilities might be included for schools which come to a large center from a distant area.

We felt that museums of industry and technology should be encouraged, in order that all of us might better understand our own technology, but that they should be set up and maintained by the respective industries, with the assistance and advice of professional people.

We discovered that the Bureau of the Census conducts a monthly survey of forty thousand families, a panel which is reconstituted periodically, and we suggest that funds could be provided to enable this survey to collect additional information on the use of leisure time and the use of museums. This could help to answer some of our own questions as to who our audience is and who our non-audience is. Such data could then be widely distributed among museum professionals, educators, and so forth.

We strongly urge the American Association of Museums to include, in *Museum News,* abstracts of research activities which are related to museums.

Then there were a number of areas about which we wanted to know more. We think all of these are research possibilities, but we could have used another three days to talk about some of them. One is the problem we all face with crowds. The suggestion was made that a very good study could be made of crowd flow and circulation problems within museums, as well as of attitude changes caused by museum visits, not only school attitudes but attitudes toward all the problems, the many problems of today. We need information about our visitors; some of us have acquired this, one way or another, but I think it still needs to be widely sought, and most of the people in the group felt this way. Who are the repeaters, the regular visitors at one end of the spectrum and non-visitors at the other? Then there are examples of theoretical research, such as, what is the museum experience? Can we separate the components of a museum experience and try to reconstitute it without the museum? Is this a possibility?

Our final two suggestions were that all proposals for research projects recommended by this conference should be circulated very widely among museum people, and among universities, because in that way we will find individuals or organizations interested in carrying on some of this research; otherwise it is going to be limited just to this small group. Any report that comes out of this Conference should be circulated as widely as possible to people in all levels of education—my own addition to that was, "to all museum directors and boards of trustees of museums."

For my group and for myself, I should like to add just a word of thanks to all the people who made this Conference possible. Beyond what we accomplish here today, I think it has done what so many good conferences can do: it makes you feel you are not alone in facing your problems, you have support from your friends, from your colleagues everywhere. I think this is extremely important to all of us, and it certainly has been to me.

REPORT OF THE SECOND WORK GROUP (E. G. SHERBURNE)

This is an interpretation of Frank Taylor's committee's comments, or my interpretation, I might add. I have already apologized to him, so I won't apologize again.

We went by the questions, but we interpreted them rather freely and didn't get too concerned about semantic problems. The first question is what can museums do that no other institutions can do. We felt that the characteristics of a museum, or the typical characteristics of a museum, are really the important thing here, and we felt first of all that a museum was something which had a visual emphasis, a place where you looked more than you read or listened, although reading and listening can be a part of the activity, but basically it is a place for looking.

Second, we felt that the resources of the museum are usually set aside from other institutions and usually in terms of the objects of which the collections were built. Also, a museum not only has objects but it may have these objects exhibited, or it may have exhibits which are not, literally speaking, rocks or "Netsuki," and so on, made especially for purposes of communication. I think this tends more toward the kind of thing you often get in a science museum, whereas art museums, of course, are based on paintings or art objects. We did not feel that the staffs of museums are necessarily unique resources, although in some instances they could be.

Third, we felt that museums, at least potentially, had a characteristic of independence and flexibility. They are certainly less formally structured than the educational system, and we felt that this might offer some opportunities for action which might not otherwise be provided. We also felt that museums had an open character which set them aside, in that they were open to everybody without registration, prerequisite, or anything of that sort. In some cases you might have courses with some kind of requirements, but by and large people can walk in off the street and look at exhibits; they can participate.

Second question: Are museums capable of an expanded, formal, organized role in education. We felt, again, that terms like "capable," "expanded," "formal," and "education" are a little restricted, so we did not hold ourselves too closely to them. The answer was yes. We felt, as far as the expanded role was concerned, that museums could, first, improve the quality of the experience which they provide by increasing the scope of their activities, and providing better preparation for looking at something in the form of films, or more objects, or something similar. Second, they could increase the quantity of people, have a greater audience size, and expand their role that way. Third—and this is not literally expanding, but at least it is a change and perhaps an improvement—they could change the audience focus, or composition or, if you wish, the audience mix. For example, they could concentrate more on deprived people, or they could concentrate more on people they thought might get something out of such activities, if provided. Fourth, they could expand and improve their role by changing the nature of the program—the types of experiences which they offer.

We noted that in some cases there will be problems—for example, if you reduce the number of people you service you may improve the quality, while if you increase the number of people that you service you may reduce the quality; therefore, expanding in the literal sense may actually be a retrograde movement, rather than a forward movement.

We tried to grapple with the question of what kinds of audiences museums should handle, and we gave up. Out of the two hundred million people in the country, who should be served and in what order? We simply noted that there are numerous groups—scholars, students, and various kinds of sub-publics within the general public—and at that point we gave up.

We noted that collections tend to be underused in museums, and staff tend to be overused. I, as a naive observer, felt this to be a profound point, one that might hold some significance for activities. And we also noted that, at least in some aspects, there is a finite limit to the number of people who can be served by some museums. With expanding population we are running into the saturation problem with some people, so that we cannot think of expanding indefinitely; only so many people can probably look at the Mona Lisa. I do not know what that limit is, but there is a finite limit somewhere.

Question three: If so, what are the principal arguments for and against an expanding role? As to the arguments *for*, I simply have a list of shorthand things here which I divided into idealistic arguments and practical arguments. The idealistic arguments are social needs: to upgrade education, to modify attitudes, to increase education in order to provide increased demand, to serve people not being served. Museums possess the best of all generations and should be available to everybody, to learn the visual language, to teach people a visual language, the learning of beauty—or, that is, learning more about beauty to get people to improve their environment—to increase the amount of firsthand experience, to improve cross-cultural communication, to improve the use of leisure time, to aid continuing education, and to increase the variety of sensory input and enrich people's environment. All of these have implications of one sort or another.

The practical reasons *for* include—there are simply statistically more people being interested in museums and, therefore, more people being likely to come. There is the economic support available for an expanded role; there are some opportunities to do more things than there have been in the past; self "interest"—the demand is there, you open your doors and people will come in. Museums have underutilized resources; the flexibility of museums makes pilot projects of various sorts quite easy. There is institutional desire: people simply seem to like to go to museums, you might as well help them out.

The arguments *against* an expanding role all seem to be practical; we did not have any other types. Shortage of trained personnel, budget, lack of imagination, lack of adequate objects or collections, insignificance of collections, the attitude and resistance of the staff and of the "establishment," an expanded role would interfere with research, the fragility of many objects, the possible penalty to individual experience (if you handle more people the quality of individual experience will diminish in many cases); museum education is superficial now, if we expand it we will simply dilute something that is already bad; a lack of knowledge of how to display and do exhibits, the political problems of getting things done, overcrowded curriculum (schools now have too much to teach, why should you teach more), and the possibility that museums will try to expand their role and be unable to live up to the expectations, to the promises.

Question four: If the role were accepted what should be or would be the broad social consequences? We first discussed the possible institutional consequences, the consequences to the museum itself; and there was some concern that the present level of knowledge in the staffs, and the size of staffs, must be bolstered; otherwise, there would be serious consequences, or interference with what is now going on, or inability to live up to commitments. We had a difficult time in defining other social consequences and pinning them down. We could talk in generalities, but in terms of specific social consequences we had some difficulty. We had a "better" category of consequences—for example, a richer active life. Perhaps we could get people to substitute museum going for some less desirable types of activity, and a result of this would be a richer environment: the home would be improved, the urban planning would be improved, the natural environment would be improved, the people would want a more beautiful environment. The effect on other media—advertising design, and so on—might be improvement. The world view of people might broaden: they would understand the changes that science is bringing about, and so on. So then we tried to tackle the sort of things that are concerning people today—the population, disarmament, and so on—and we decided that you could probably say that museums could make a contribution to these, and probably *are* making a contribution. But you would have in most cases a rather difficult time in pinning down, in a one-to-one relationship, the proposition that because you have an exhibit here everybody rushes to do something over there. So then we tried to discuss, though we did not have the time we needed, what would be the effects, and we focused more specifically on schools, for example, on individuals, or on the labor force; and we simply, as I say, were not able to do enough there to make it worth reporting.

Question five: How might such a role be fulfilled in a single specific case? We interpreted this, for reasons which I do not quite recall, to call for historic answers rather than a hypothetical answer. I notice my wife's group had a hypothetical answer. So we tried to look for cases where an expanded role, or some activity on the part of the museum, had made an impact. Here are some examples of the kinds of things that were discussed.

We discussed the economic impact of museums through tourism, and specifically the impact of the Baseball Hall of Fame in Cooperstown—bringing people in, hotels, everybody makes a lot of money. We discussed the impact of Williamsburg on interior decoration (apparently it has had quite a bit of impact on interior decoration, and has in some way affected the way people furnish their homes). We discussed the impact of museums as a part of the group of cultural institutions which enable industry to lure executives and scientists and engineers and people of this sort into a particular community, and we discussed—or I added this one myself: I think I'm right, though the art people may cut me down on this—that exhibits of abstract painting have certainly had some impact on people's perception of the world. I am interested to note that it is difficult to find any examples for science museums. Perhaps this is because science museums are, I am told, relatively new on the horizon, I do not know; I simply throw that in as an interesting comment.

What specific practical measures might be employed to provide an expanding role? First, the group supported: the proposal for the National Museum Act, if that is the correct title for it, where it suggested funds for training museum staffs; the development of regional centers which serve small museums, particularly in the case of preservation of objects and in authentication; provision for a roster of consultants who would be available to help provide funds for the support of publications. We also had some additional specific suggestions: the first of these, under the category of extending the activities of existing museums, was the possibility of developing new outlets for exhibits, such as community colleges, as Dr. Ripley suggested; the development of consortiums of major science museums permitted to make traveling exhibits; the use of libraries as outlets; the development of new technologies, particularly mass media, film, TV, slides, all of this type of thing for expanding the role of museums; the development and study of reproductions—what can be done in this area to improve and widen the use of reproductions? Also discussed was the possibility of starting new museums, particularly in respect to a proposal—apparently one which had been set out at one point and then got killed, I don't know exactly why—for package museums complete with staff and display materials, to serve as receptacles for exhibits from existing museums: it's like starting a new university, you just come up with the whole package.

We also discussed the need for birth control and selective breeding in museums. It may be that we do not want a lot of museums or that, if we do, we want to control who gives birth to these museums and the means by which birth takes place. Under the topic of development of new audiences, we discussed the need particularly to be concerned about the deprived; we feel that much more consideration should be given to the needs of the deprived, from their point of view and not our point of view. We must ask them what they want, or in some way try to find out, because they may not be able to articulate exactly what it is they want. We should be more responsive to *their* need as they perceive it, not as we perceive it. We discussed the possibility of using docents from their cultures—when you get somebody who speaks the language and can talk about "that cat Renoir," or whatever the best way to do it would be—to take these people through, rather than having it done by our upper- and middle-class types who probably do not understand these people at all and have difficulty talking to them. We also discussed ways of getting them to come to museums and exhibits by providing free transportation, or free meals, or even paying them to come. We see no reason why any of these should not be done, as in the very interesting research project in Boston, where a man pays people to participate in his adult education program.

We also discussed the need for development of humanities fairs, similar to science fairs; as the person in the organization who runs the international science fairs here at Science Service, I think this is a great idea. Another category was the development of services for audiences that you do *not* expect ever to come to your museum. I thought somebody made a very interesting comment, that there are some people you can expect to come to the museums, but of any particular museum it can probably be said that most of the people in the country will not ever get to it. So what is your responsibility to *these* people? This could, of course, involve the area of TV, film, reproductions, and so on. Under the category of miscellaneous, I have recommendations for a behavioral institute for the study of museums and exhibits; it might include among its immediate interests the location of relevant research that has already been done, making this research available, and coordinating and doing research. It is also recommended that we have an experimental museum for testing—I'm reading as fast as I can, we had a very verbal bunch of people.

What would you want to learn through research? We don't have too many items here; research is liberally interpreted. One, we would want a study of the relationship of the authentic object to the reproduction; what functions are served by the authentic object? Who gets what out of what exhibit? What functions are served, and for whom, by what kinds of reproductions? Two, how can we develop better reproductions technologically, with higher fidelity, more cheaply, etc.? Three, as some museums are nearing saturation, what can be done for them? Four, collections are often underutilized: how can they be better utilized? Five, how does subjective evaluation by reasonable individuals compare with scientific testing of the results of exhibits? Six, if you have to close part of the year for economic reasons, what days and months of the year are best—in other words, who visits when? Seven, what new technical devices can be used for the museum? Eight, can a single visit to a museum produce a measurable effect? Nine, what is the optimum number of museums: should we have a few big ones and move people to museums, or should we have one museum in every county seat? Ten, what is the need for film and TV that museums might produce; what are the functions they perform?

REPORT OF THE THIRD WORK GROUP (A. E. PARR)

When three groups have been given exactly the same questions to answer, it is inevitable that the reports will be somewhat redundant, particularly that of the third member to speak. It would, however, take more time to avoid redundancies than to commit them, so that if any of this is repetitive you will have to bear with me: I would need more of your time if I were not to repeat. I shall try to give my report as a sort of laundry list.

In regard to the first question, "What are the special advantages museums have to offer," we have the following list, all of which you will recognize, of course:

—that the pace and order is not forced, unless the member comes with a group which sets its own pace and order, but the museum does not force one;

—that there is an opportunity to observe things in the full third dimension, or all three dimensions, which most other media cannot offer;

—that more than one sense is involved in the experience (of course more than one sense is involved in the classroom or elsewhere, but this is by comparison with the symbolic message of the printed or spoken word);

—simultaneity: that is, things can be developed and presented so that, even though they happened at quite different times, there is an opportunity to compare simultaneously the messages they had been sending (reference was made to the psychological atmosphere peculiar to museums; I don't know whether that is good or bad);

—that the museums provide reinforcement of knowledge and retention and memory, and help create a new awareness of the things which can be sensually perceived in the environment;

—then, in number six, we have relevant relationships of actual source materials; by that, I believe the group meant materials which might be separated in space, as distinct from separated in time, placed side by side so as to permit a visitor to make comparisons science might have taken centuries to learn, because science found these things in very different places, and so on;

—elasticity of uses, which means that the museums' exhibits are available both to individuals and to masses, and to all ages and both sexes, to anybody at all; and to this I might add that the information is *more* available, because information given in a symbolic form is only available to those with a sufficiently developed knowledge of how to read, and I do not mean simply literacy; when you see the actual object, you can see something in it regardless of the level of your previous training;

—eight; the scholarly and technical potential of the museum;

—nine, the uniqueness and authenticity of the objects which the museums have to offer:

—and ten, a combination of all the foregoing.

"Are the museums capable of an expanded role in organized formal education?" the answer, quite simply, from my group is: yes, in two categories, fiscal expansion and expansion of activities.

Question three: "If so, what are the principal arguments for or against it?" I should say that up to part five we were able to stick to the series of the questions fairly well, but at five we broke down and there was a general free-for-all from about five to seven. But up to five we managed to march in an orderly manner, or fairly orderly.)

We started, then, with the arguments against:

—that overcrowding and haste may actually impede the learning process in a museum (we are now talking about overcrowding within existing premises; certain collections can actually be made accessible only to one or a few people at a time, if they are going to get anything out of them; there we must protect the individual's right of contemplation and intensive study, not only just the scholar's; there are many members of the public—"lay" is perhaps not exactly the right word—who do not have the necessary knowledge behind them, so naturally they will not get into the research collections, but nevertheless we have to protect their opportunities to contemplate in the exhibition halls);

—that certain types of museums cannot branch out, or cannot receive an increase (historical houses are a typical case; if a living room was built for a Christmas party of a maximum of twenty-four people, you can't let five hundred in);

—that over–use of the museum will introduce additional wear and tear, obviously;

—and then, an item that perhaps is more important, the danger of loss of independence, depending on the way in which the expansion is being sponsored and supported (that is, of course, a practical matter one has to watch);

—the group also saw a danger, strictly as a dog on a leash, in the expanding of present new developments in the school curriculum; we felt that the museums should expand by their own standards, rather than by those set by any other institution, though of course in full harmony and cooperation with other institutions (this is the same matter of defending the museum's independence as an educational institution in its own right).

And now we have some that are *for*, also:

—the expansion would serve a larger segment of the population;

—to help improve curricular changes already taking place, or contemplated in the future;

—to meet the demands of increased leisure time and increased population;

—and to take advantage of increasingly available funds.

That, I think, sums up the group's feelings under point three.

"If the role were accepted, what would the broad, social consequences be?"

—the museums would contribute to raise the general level of education, and to increase awareness of the world around us, and so on;

—it would help to stimulate what Rachel Carson has described as the "sense of wonder";

—it would increase the individual's perceptive powers;

—it would encourage the individuality of persons in a period when so much of the environment tends toward a "de-individualization," if that is a legitimate word;

—it would help the public broaden the comprehension of its own environment, of the separate individual's past, present, and future;

—it would provide emotional and spiritual enrichment; here there was general approval of something a Mexican architect told me of his view of an art museum as a place of communal devotion to beauty, rather than merely an educational place conveying specific information;

—the museum's impact on other cultural institutions, both in their structure and interrelationships, would be a beneficial one if the museum's role were expanded;

—museums could help to encourage individual creativity;

—and here is one I am not so convinced of, number nine (still in answer to question four), the museum's influence on political attitudes could be beneficial.

Then we go from five to seven, five beginning with how much an expanded role could be fulfilled in a specific instance. Now there is a ham or Hamlet in each of us, at least in my work group this was the case, so that we spent a lot of time conducting a mock investigation of a mock museum, and it was impossible to break that up for a while; I was not entirely sure that it was a productive way of going about it, but apparently it was great fun.[2]

But on five to seven combined we arrived at several fairly definite recommendations:

—There should be established a source of funds—or it should be identified for museums, if it already exists—to provide the means of arranging local conferences, to advise small museums, or communities considering the establishment of a museum, both as to what the museum can do and what the needs of the community are.

—There should be definite identification of the possible source to which communities or small museums can turn, without having to write every Tom, Dick, or Harry asking, "Where do we go?"

—There ought to be established regional museum centers, in which scholarly collections, circulating collections, and other materials might be deposited, and which might serve as an information center for smaller museums that have to supply more information than they can afford to keep available, and which would also serve as a center for the distribution of educational exhibits, and so on. Comparisons were made here with library exchanges, main libraries and branch libraries, and museums should be encouraged to lend or donate objects to regional centers, and to provide professional help; it might be desirable to urge the establishment of regional professional museum-consultants (comparisons were made with county agents, such as the Department of Agriculture has) whose entire time would be devoted to helping the museums in the region, or those they might want to see established.

—And, one further point, there should be local conferences which might address themselves to questions one through seven as set out here.

Among the further recommendations:

—a national profile survey of the people who attend museums, and of those who do not (included should be a study of the accessibility of museums, and the geographical distribution of opportunities attendance), and of their motivation (this differs somewhat from what was suggested before; I think our feeling was that as a small tail attached to a big dog we might not get so much as we would if we went all out and asked for a special survey);

—research on formal and informal uses of existing museum collections and programs;

—proposals for more efficient and new uses of already existing museum programs, including extension in depth, the problem of maintaining a professional staff of teachers, and so on;

—invention and establishment of new types of museums (here we got a very fine proposal, I think from Mrs. Sherburne, for "a drop-in museum for drop-outs," which is just about the best slogan I have heard in a long time, and which contains a very good suggestion);[3]

—a general study and analysis of types and effectiveness of non-verbal learning;

—seven, increased programs for educational use of the museums, by familiarizing future school teachers, in the course of their own education, with museums and their use, and making certain that they get proper credit for this in their future careers (there is agreement about *that*);

—then, participation of students in the museum's work, by adding educational staff to the museum itself;

—and, one that could be very useful, an invitation to all museums to share with each other through the American Association of Museums, by reporting to the AAM both the successes and the failures among the new things they attempt to do. So far there have been a certain number of reported successes, while all the failures are hidden like skeletons in the closet, so we all go on repeating each other's mistakes and learning little from each other's successes; I think it is important that both be emphasized; the man who doesn't dare make a mistake is never going to do much good, either, so I don't think we should feel too reluctant about sharing with each other the boners we make, as well as the things we succeeded in doing; so this is a very strong recommendation; that through the AAM we find some method of sharing with each other, by universal exchange, our experiences, good or bad.

That is the end of the list and it became, as I said from the beginning, more like an itemized laundry list, because otherwise I would have been repeating even more of what had been said before.

POSTSCRIPT

The end of Dr. Parr's summation was not, as it happened, the formal end of the conference, for the opportunity had been left to Edgar Richardson to present his paper at the very last. Given the demanding mission of writing a conference summation before the conference in question had taken place, Mr. Richardson had responded by producing a document which might well have summed up an imaginary conference—the one many of us may have wished at times that we were actually attending. Generously he had revised his text somewhat for actual delivery, but the reader will be able to get the sense and pleasure of it from the text as printed elsewhere in this volume (page 11). The chairman, at the close, invoked his prerogative of giving Mr. Richardson the last word, and does the same with equal satisfaction here.

1. Mr. Rath and Henry Allen Moe were subsequently good enough to send each member of the Conference a copy of the New York State Historical Association's *Selective Reference Guide to Historic Preservation,* a tangible illustration of the point Mr. Rath was making. (Ed.)

2. Dr. Parr is referring to an exercise in role playing spontaneously undertaken by members of his group, one of whom pretended to be the director of a small-town museum while others chimed in as superintendent of schools, editor of the local newspaper, etc. Regrettably the discussions of the work groups were not recorded, so that no transcript of this ingenious and imaginative performance survives. (Ed.)

3. Mrs. Sherburne's phrase caught on, and at least one informal discussion on the steps of the library, which included Messrs. Abbey and Butler, centered on the question of what a "drop-in museum for drop-outs" might contain; one suggestion was that a wrecked automobile be placed in it each week, visitors being invited to take away any parts they were able to remove. (Ed.)

Participants

David S. Abbey
Ontario Intitute for Studies in Education

Scarvia B. Anderson
Educational Testing Service

Stanley K. Bigman
National Colleges of Sciences and Arts

Stephan F. de Borhegyi
Milwaukee Public Museum

Frank Brown
Institute for Development of Educational Activities

J. Carter Brown
National Gallery of Art

Michael V. Butler
Cranbrook Institute of Science

Duncan Cameron
Janus Museum Consultants Limited

Peter Caws
Carnegie Corporation

Thomas M. Folds
Metropolitan Museum of Art

August Freundlich
University of Miami

Robert T. Hatt
Cranbrook Institute of Science

Bartlett H. Hayes, Jr.
Phillips Academy

James J. Heslin
The New-York Historical Society

Charles Keller
John Hay Fellows Program

Eric Larrabee (Editor)
State University of New York at Buffalo

Henry Allen Moe
New York State Historical Association

Frederick H. Mold
Fairbanks Museum and Planetarium

Helmuth J. Naumer
Fort Worth Children's Museum

Frank Oppenheimer
University of Colorado

Albert E. Parr
American Museum of Natural History

Joseph Allen Patterson
American Association of Museums

Douglas O. Pedersen
Whitney Museum of American Art

Courtland Randall
Oak Ridge Associated Universities

Frederick L. Rath, Jr.
New York State Historical Association

Edgar P. Richardson
Winterthur Museum

Hanna Rose
Brooklyn Museum

Edward Sherburne
Science Service

Mary Lela Sherburne
Educational Services, Inc.

Sue M. Thurman
Boston Institute of Contemporary Art

Hans Weltin
Lawrence Hall of Science
University of California

Stephen White
Carnegie Commission on Educational Television

Alma S. Wittlin
University of California

Ruth Zuelke
Birmingham (Michigan) Public Schools

Smithsonian Institution

S. Dillon Ripley

John Anglim
Charles Blitzer
Helen Bronheim
Keith Melder
Donald Squires
Frank Taylor

U. S. Office of Education

Kathryn Bloom
Richard Grove

National Endowment on the Arts

Observer: Mrs. Devon Meade, Acting Director of Visual Arts

Rockefeller Brothers Fund

Observer: Robert Armstrong

Chronological Bibliography Of Museum Visitor Surveys

STEPHAN F. DE BORHEGYI, *Director*
and IRENE A. HANSON, *Librarian*
Milwaukee Public Museum
1966

A revised and enlarged bibliography on audience surveys. As in the 1963 and 1964 mimeographed editions, the 122 articles and books listed are in chronological order to show the progressive growth of interest in this subject. In addition, 19 titles on methods of research and related information have been appended to the list. An asterisk (*) indicates studies and articles related to the Milwaukee Public Museum.

1897 FECHNER, G. T.
Vorschule der Aesthetik. Leipzig, Breitkopf und Hartel.

1928 ROBINSON, EDWARD S.
"The Behavior of the Museum Visitor" (Washington, D. C., Publications of the American Association of Museums, n.s., no. 5).

1929 BLOOMBERG, M.
"An Experiment in Museum Instruction" (Washington, D. C., Publications of the American Association of Museums, n.s., no.8).

1930 "Pennsylvania Museum Classifies Its Visitors," *Museum News*, 7:15, Feb. 1, pp. 7–8.

REA, PAUL MARSHALL
"How Many Visitors Should Museums Have?" *Museum News*, 8:1, May 1, pp. 9–12.

ROBINSON, E. S.
"Psychological Problems of the Science Museum," *Museum News*, 8:5, pp. 9–11.

1931 Robinson, E. S.
"Psychological Studies of the Public Museum," *School and Society,* 33:839, pp. 121–125.

1933 Goldberg, Nita
"Experiments in Museum Teaching," *Museum News,* 10:15, pp. 6–8.

Melton, A. W.
"Some Behavioral Characteristics of Museum Visitors," *Psychological Bulletin,* 30, pp. 720–721.

1934 Powell, Louis H.
"Evaluating Public Interest in Museum Rooms," *Museum News,* 11:15, p. 7.

1935 Melton, A. W.
"Problems on Installation in Museums of Arts" (Washington, D. C., Publications of the American Association of Museums, n.s., no. 14).

1936 Melton, A. W.
"Distribution of Attention in Galleries in a Museum of Science and Industry," *Museum News,* 14:3, pp. 5, 6–8.

Melton, A. W., Feldman, Nita Goldberg, and Mason, C. W.
"Experimental Studies of the Education of Children in a Museum of Science" (Washington, D. C., Publications of the American Association of Museums, n.s., no. 15).

1938 Porter, M. C.
"Behaviour of the Average Visitor in the Peabody Museum of Natural History, Yale University" (Washington, D. C., Publications of the American Association of Museums, n.s., no. 16).

Powell, Louis H.
"A Study of Seasonal Attendance at a Midwestern Museum of Science," *Museum News,* 16:3, June 1, pp. 7–8.

1939 Coleman, Laurence Vail
"Public Relations: Attendance," In *The Museum in America: a Critical Study,* Washington, American Association of Museums, vol. 2, pp. 297–301.

1940 Cummings, Carlos E.
"East is East and West is West: Some Observations on the World's Fairs of 1939 by One Whose Main Interest Is In Museums," Buffalo, Buffalo Museum of Science.

KEARNS, WILLIAM E.
"Studies of Visitor Behavior at the Peabody Museum of Natural History, Yale University," *Museum News*, 17:14, Jan. 15, pp. 5–8.

1941 BENNETT, GEORGE K.
"The Museum Technique Applied to Market Research," *Journal of Consulting Psychology*, vol. 5.

DERRYBERRY, MAYHEW
"Exhibits," *American Journal of Public Health*, 31, pp. 257–263.

1942 YOSHIOKA, JOSEPH G.
"A Direction–orientation Study with Visitors at the New York World's Fair," *Journal of Psychology*, 27, pp. 3–33.

1943 CALVER, HOMER N., DERRYBERRY, MAYHEW, and MENSH, IVAN N.
"Use of Ratings in the Evaluation of Exhibits," *American Journal of Public Health*, 33, pp. 709–714.

1946 NIELSON, L. C.
"A Technique for Studying the Behavior of Museum Visitors," *Journal of Educational Psychology*, vol. 37.

1949 COWEE, HOWARD M.
The Pilot Study of Display. National Association of Display Industries, Visual Merchandising Research Series, Report No. 1, New York, Prentice-Hall, Inc.

WITTLIN, ALMA S.
The Museum: Its History and Its Tasks in Education, London, Routledge and Kegan Paul, Ltd., (See especially Appendix to Chapter 2, pp. 235–260, figs. 9a–9j).

1950 COWEE, HOWARD M.
The Traffic-readership and Sales Study of Display. National Association of Display Industries, Visual Merchandising Research Series, Report No. 2, New York, Prentice-Hall.

1952 MONZON, A.
"Bases para Incrementar el Publico que Visita el Museo Nacional de Antropologia," *Anales del Instituto Nacional de Antropologia e Historia* (Mexico), vol. 6, part 2, no. 35.

1953* NIEHOFF, ARTHUR
"Characteristics of the Audience Reaction in the Milwaukee Public Museum," *Midwest Museums Quarterly*, 13:1, pp. 19–24.

SPORER, W.
"Presentation of Exhibit Techniques and Methods to Determine Their Effectiveness," *Midwest Museums Quarterly,* 13:1, pp. 16–18.

1955 BIGMAN, STANLEY K.
"Art Exhibit Audiences: Selected Findings on: Who Comes? Why? With What Effects?" Washington, Bureau of Social Science Research (mimeographed).

EWERS, JOHN
"Problems and Procedures in Modernizing Ethnological Exhibits," *American Anthropologist,* 57:1, pp. 1–12.

RAINEY, FROELICH
"The New Museum," *University Museum Bulletin* (Philadelphia), 19:3.

U. S. Information Agency
"Special Report (SR–4): The U. S. Exhibit and the 1955 Djakarta Fair, Dec. 15, 1955," Washington, D. C.

1956 BIGMAN, STANLEY K.
"Art Exhibit Audiences," *Museologist* (Rochester), no. 59, pp. 2–18, and no. 60, pp. 2–6.

BROOKS, J. A. and VERNON, P. E.
"A Study of Children's Interests and Comprehension at a Science Museum," *British Journal of Psychology,* 47:3, August, pp. 175–182.

Bureau of Social Science Research, Inc.
"The Japanese House: a Study of Its Visitors and Their Reactions," Washington. (Prepared for the Japan Society.)

* NIEHOFF, ARTHUR
"The Physical Needs of the Visitor," *Lore* (Milwaukee Public Museum quarterly), 6:4, pp. 155–157.

U.S. Information Agency

Survey and Research Studies, Program and Media Series, Washington, D. C.

PMS-3. The Impact of the U.S. Trade Fair Program: An Analysis of Visitor Reaction in the Far East, South Asia, Europe, and Latin America. 4/25/56.

PMS-4. Visitor Reaction of the U.S. Exhibit at the Ceylon Trade Fair. 5/21/56

PMS-6. Visitor Reaction to the U.S. Exhibit at the Paris Trade Fair. 7/27/56
PMS-10. The Impact of the U.S. Trade Fair Program: An Analysis of the Visitor Reactions in Kabul, Afghanistan. 12/30/56
PMS-11. Opinion Leader's Evaluation of the U.S. Exhibit at the Salonika Trade Fair. 12/30/56
PMS-12. The Impact of the U.S. Trade Fair Program at the Izmir International Fair. 4/8/57
PMS-13. The Impact of the U.S. Capitalism Exhibit at the Bogota Trade Fair. 3/18/57
PMS-15. Turkish Trade Fair Audience Reaction to Questions on American Aid and Related Matters. 5/17/57
PMS-16. The Impact of the U.S. Exhibit at the Bangkok International Trade Fair. 6/7/57
PMS-19. The Impact of the U.S. Industrial Exhibit at the Tokyo International Fair. 9/12/57
PMS-29. Visitor Reaction to the U.S. versus Major Competing Exhibits at the Brussels International Fair. 7/58
PMS-34. Highlights of the USIA Research on the Presidential Trade Fair Program. 11/58
PMS-35. Visitor Reaction to the U.S. versus Major Competing Exhibits at the 1958 Zagreb Trade Fair. 12/58
Special Memo. A Note on Reactions of Brussels Fair Visitors to Modern Art in the U.S. Pavilion. 2/59
PMS-38. Follow-up Study of Visitor Reaction to the U.S. versus Major Competing Exhibits at the Brussels International Fair. 6/59
PMS-40. Audience Reaction to the U.S. Rural Development Exhibit at Lahore. 9/60
PMS-46. The Impact of the USIS Exhibit "Youth USA" at the 1960 Berlin Industrial Fair. 4/61
PMS-61. Reactions of Visitors to the U.S. Small Industries Exhibition at Accra. 4/62
PMS-62. Reactions of Indian Visitors to the USIS Exhibit "Student Life in America." 5/62

VAN DER HOEK, G. J.
"Bezoekers Bekeken," *Mededilingen Gemeentemuseum van den Haag* (The Hague), 2:2. (English summary: Visitor Characteristics.)

1957 Bureau of Social Science Research, Inc.
"The Japanese Art Exhibit: A Study of Its Impact in Three Cities," *Clearing House for Western Museums Newsletter,* no. 211, September, pp. 1074–1080.

FRESE, H. H.
"The Living Museum," *Museum,* 10:4, p. 184.

GLUCK, J. F.
"Museale Ausstellungsprobleme und die Tibet-Ausstellung des Linden-Museums," *Baessler Archiv,* n.s., Bd. 5 (XXX Band), Heft, 2, pp. 161–191.

GOINS, ALVIN, and GRIFFENHAGEN, GEORGE
"Psychological Studies of Museum Visitors and Exhibits at the U.S. National Museum," *Museologist,* no. 64, pp. 1–6.

REED, V. D.
Report and Recommendations on Research Methods Used to Determine the Impact and Reactions to U.S. Official Exhibits in International Trade Fairs, OITP, Washington, D. C.

REIMANN, IRVING G.
"Post-mortem on a Museum Questionnaire, *Museologist,* no. 63, June, pp. 1–6.

1958 BORHEGYI, STEPHAN F. DE (ed.)
"The Modern Museum and the Community" (papers presented at the 5th International Congress of Anthropological and Ethnological Sciences, Philadelphia, September 1–9, 1956), Norman, Okla. *Clearing House for Western Museums Special Publication* No. 1. (A collection of articles by museum specialists; some apply to visitor surveys.)

GOINS, A. E., and GRIFFENHAGEN, GEORGE
"The Effect of Location, and a Combination of Color, Lighting, and Artistic Design on Exhibit Appeal," *Museologist,* no. 67, pp. 6–10.

GROVE, RICHARD, and MILLS, GEORGE
"The Exhibition as a Medium of Communication," *Clearing House for Western Museums Newsletter,* n.s., nos. 5–6, pp. 52–57.

* NIEHOFF, ARTHUR
"Evening Exhibit Hours for Museums," *Museologist,* no. 69, December, pp. 2–5.

REEKIE, GORDON
"Toward Well-being for Museum Visitors," *Curator,* 1:1, pp. 92–94.

WITTLIN, ALMA S.
"Exhibitions in an Age of Revolutionary Evolution," *Clearing House for Western Museums Newsletter,* n.s., nos. 5–6, pp. 44–48.

WRIGHT, G.
"Some Criteria for Evaluating Displays in Museums of Science and Industry," *Midwest Museums Quarterly,* 18:3, pp. 62–71.

1959 ABBEY, D. S., and CAMERON, DUNCAN F.
"The Museum Visitor: 1—Survey Design," *Royal Ontario Museum, Reports from Information Services,* no. 1.

* NIEHOFF, ARTHUR
"Audience Reaction in the Milwaukee Public Museum: the Winter Visitors," *Midwest Museums Quarterly,* 19:2, pp. 36–45.

WHITE, R. K.
"Soviet Reactions to Our Moscow Exhibit: Voting Machines and Comment Books, *Public Opinion Quarterly,* 23, pp. 461–470.

WITHEY, S. B.
"Public Opinions About Science and Scientists," *Public Opinion Quarterly,* 23:3, pp. 382–388.

1960 ABBEY, D. S., and CAMERON, DUNCAN F.
"The Museum Visitor: 2—Survey Results," *Royal Ontario Museum, Reports from Information Services,* no. 2.

* BORHEGYI, STEPHAN F. DE, and DODSON, ELBA A.
"A Bibliography of Museums and Museum Work," *Publications in Museology* (Milwaukee Public Museum) no. 1, section I-J, pp. 16–17. (Lists articles on museum visitors.)

CAMERON, DUNCAN F., and ABBEY, D. S.
"Investigating a Museum Audience," *Museologist,* no. 77, December, pp. 2–7.

"Visits versus Visitors: an Analysis," *Museum News,* 39:3, November, pp. 34–35.

DAIFUKU, HIROSHI
"The Museum and the Visitor." In *The Organization of Museums: Practical Advice* (Museums and Monuments Series 9) Paris, UNESCO, pp. 73–80.

FRESE, H. H.
"Anthropology and the Public: the Role of Museums." In *Mededelingen van Het Rijksmuseum voor Volkenkunde,* no. 14, Leiden, E. J. Brill. (See especially Chapter 3, "The Museum and the Public," pp. 73–97.)

ROBINSON, PAUL VIRGIL
"An Experimental Study of Exhibit Arrangement and Viewing Method to Determine Their Effect upon Learning of Factual Material." (Doctoral dissertation located at the University of Southern California.)

Survey Research Center, University of Michigan
Report of an Audience Evaluation Study of the "Atoms of Work" Mobile Exhibit of the United States Atomic Energy Commission. Ann Arbor.

1961 ABBEY, D. S., and CAMERON, DUNCAN F.
"The Museum Visitor: 3—Supplementary Studies, *Royal Ontario Museum, Reports from Information Services,* no. 3.

ABBEY, D. S., and CAMERON, DUNCAN F.
"Notes on Audience Research at the Royal Ontario Museum," *Museologist,* no. 80, pp. 11–16.

BIGMAN, STANLEY K.
"Implications of Studies of Visitors to Exhibits and Displays for Planning of an Exhibit, and for Visitor Research, at the New York World's Fair, 1964." (Mimeographed monograph prepared for International Business Machines Corporation. *Restricted.*)

* BORHEGYI, STEPHAN F. DE, DODSON, ELBA A., and HANSON, IRENE A.
"Supplementary Bibliography of Museums and Museum Work," *Publications in Museology* (Milwaukee Public Museum) no. 2, section I-J, pp. 22–23. (Lists articles on museum visitors.)

CAMERON, DUNCAN F., and ABBEY, D. S.
"Museum Audience Research," *Museum News,* 40:2, pp. 34–38.

* MACBRIAR, WALLACE N., JR.
"The Museum's New Office of Information Service," *Lore* (Milwaukee Public Museum quarterly), 12:1, pp. 37–39.

Office of International Trade Fairs
Services Report. Washington, D. C., U.S. Dept. of Commerce.

1962 CAMERON, DUNCAN F., and ABBEY, D. S.
"Museum Audience Research: The Effect of an Admission Fee," *Museum News,* 41:3, November, pp. 25–28.

GUSTAFSON, JOEL F.
"To Charge or Not to Charge," *Museum News,* 40:6, pp. 16–20.

LOTTER, V., and BOTHA, E.
"Preliminary Survey of the Visiting Population of the South African Museum, Cape Town," *South African Museums Association Bulletin* (SAMAB), 7:14, pp. 340–350.

MORRIS, RUDOLPH
"Leisure Time and the Museum," *Museum News*, 41:4, pp. 17–21.

PARR, ALBERT E.
"Guests or Customers?" *Museum News*, 40:9, pp. 16–19.

"Some Basic Problems of Visual Education by Means of Exhibits," *Curator*, 5:1, pp. 36–44.

REESE, DAVID, and MOORE, EMMA
"The Art Museum and the Public School: An Experiment," *Museum News*, 40:6, pp. 30–33.

WEISS, ROBERT S., and BOUTOURLINE, SERGE, JR.
"Fairs, Pavilions, Exhibits, and Their Audiences," 197 pp. plus appendix (mimeographed). (Obtainable from Dr. Robert S. Weiss, Brandeis University.)

1963* BORHEGYI, STEPHAN F. DE
"The Museum As a Cultural Centre in the Development of the Community," (Fifth UNESCO Regional Seminar, Mexico City, 17 September-14 October, 1962), Paris, UNESCO.

* El Museo Como Centro Cultural de la Comunidad. (Spanish version of above, published by UNESCO.)

* "Museum Exhibits: How to Plan and Evaluate Them," *Midwest Museums Quarterly*, 23:2, pp. 4–8.

* "Space Problems and Solutions," *Museum News*, 42:3, pp. 18–22.

* "Visual Communication in the Science Museum," *Curator*, 6:1, pp. 45–57.

FINE, P. A.
"The Role of Design in Educational Exhibits," *Curator*, 6:1, pp. 37–44.

MARSHALL, W. E.
"A Viewpoint," *Midwest Museums Quarterly*, 23:1, pp. 9–11.

STITES, RAYMOND S.
"Leisure Time and the Museum: A Reply," *Museum News*, 41:6, pp. 29–33.

TAYLOR, JAMES B.
"Science on Display: A Study of the United States Science Exhibit, Seattle World's Fair, 1962." Seattle, Institute for Sociological Research, University of Washington, 184 pp. plus 16 additional appendices in separate bindings (mimeographed).

VOWLES, VALERIE
"The Uganda Museum, Kampala: The Public," *Museum,* 16:3, pp. 149–162.

WEISS, ROBERT S., and BOUTOURLINE, SERGE, JR.
"The Communication Value of Exhibits," *Museum News,* 42:3, pp. 23–27.

1964* BORHEGYI, STEPHAN F. DE
"Chronological Bibliography of Museum Visitor Surveys," *Museum News,* 42:6, pp. 39–41.

* COOLEY, WILLIAM, and PIPER, TERRENCE
"Study of the West African Art Exhibit of the Milwaukee Public Museum and Its Visitors." (Mimeographed study located in the library of the Milwaukee Public Museum.)

* MACBRIAR, WALLACE N., JR.
"Testing Your Audience," *Museum News,* 42:8, pp. 15–17.

* MOCHON, MARION JOHNSON
"Visitor Testing in the Museum." (Paper read at the Central States Anthropological Society annual meeting in Milwaukee, Wis.)

PARR, ALBERT E.
"Remarks on Layout, Display and Response to Design," *Curator,* 7:2, pp. 131–142.

"Test and Criticism," *Museum News,* 43:2, pp. 36–38.

1965* ABLER, THOMAS S.
"Traffic Pattern and Exhibit Design: A Study of Learning in the Museum." (M.A. thesis located at the University of Wisconsin, Milwaukee, and at the Milwaukee Public Museum.)

* BORHEGYI, STEPHAN F. DE
"Test Your Knowledge," *Midwest Museums Quarterly,* 25:4, pp. 10–11.

"Testing of Audience Reaction to Museum Exhibits," *Curator,* 8:1, pp. 86–93.

Exhibit Surveys
"Measuring Exhibit Performance," Middletown, N. J.

Germer, Ernst
"Besuchertest im Museum für Völkerkunde zu Leipzig," *Jahrbuch des Museums für Völkerkunde,* Bd. 21, pp. 111–143.

* Parsons, Lee A.
"Systematic Testing of Display Techniques for an Anthropological Exhibit," *Curator,* 8:2, pp. 167–189.

* Parsons, Lee A., and Borhegyi, Stephan F. de
"The Milwaukee Public Museum: Display of Collection," *Museum,* 17:1, pp. 18–25 (Eng.); pp. 26–32(Fr.).

Shettel, Harris H., and Reilly, Pamela C.
"An Evaluation of Existing Criteria for Judging the Quality of Science Exhibits," Pittsburgh, American Institute for Research in the Behavioral Sciences. (U.S. Dept. of Commerce, TID-22703.)

Smits, Edward J.
"A Suburban Museum Looks at Its Visitors," *Museum News,* 42:9, pp. 30–34.

1966 White, Harvey
"The Design, Development and Testing of a Response Box: A New Component for Science Museum Exhibits." (Progress Report under a grant from U.S. Office of Education, Contract No. OE 6–10–056, May 16, 1966.)

APPENDIX TO BIBLIOGRAPHY

List of works related to testing and behavior reaction, arranged by authors in alphabetical order.

1960 Asch, Solomon E., Hay, John, and Diamond, Rhea M.
"Perceptual Organization in Serial Rote-learning," *American Journal of Psychology,* vol. 73, pp. 177–198.

1964 Battig, William F., Brown, Sam C., and Schild, Mary E.
"Serial Position and Sequential Associations in Serial Learning," *Journal of Experimental Psychology,* vol. 67, pp. 449–457.

1955 Bernays, Edward L. (ed.)
The Engineering of Consent. Norman, University of Oklahoma Press.

1963 Bose, A. B.
"The Pattern of Communication in an Exhibit," *Indian Journal of Social Research,* vol. 4, pp. 23–30.

1942 Derryberry, Mayhew
"Psychological Work in Public Health," *Journal of Consulting Psychology,* vol. 6.

1963 Ebenholtz, Sheldon M.
"Position Mediated Transfer Between Serial Learning and a Spatial Discrimination Task," *Journal of Experimental Psychology,* vol. 65, pp. 603–608.

"Serial Learning: Position Learning and Sequential Associations," *Journal of Experimental Psychology,* vol. 66, pp. 353–362.

1948 Flesch, Rudolf
"A New Readability Yardstick," *Journal of Applied Psychology,* vol. 32, pp. 221–233.

1954 Fosdick, John T.
"Exhibitors Can Be Given Audience Buying Patterns," *Sales Meetings Magazine,* October 1, 1954.

1956 "Now It Can Be Proven: Industrial Show Visitors Buy What They See," *Sales Meetings Magazine,* October 5, 1956.

1964 Glazer, R., and Reynolds J. H. (eds.)
"Teaching Machines and Programmed Learning: II. Data and Directions," Washington, D. C., National Education Association.

1964 Grossack, Martin M.
Understanding Consumer Behavior, Boston, Christopher Publishing House.

1960 Hoel, Paul G.
Elementary Statistics, New York, John Wiley.

1958 Holland, J. G.
"Human Vigilance," *Science,* vol. 128, pp. 61–67.

1949 Knutson, Andie
"Evaluating APHA Exhibits," *American Journal of Public Health,* vol. 39.

1962 Margulies, S., and Eigen, L. D.
Applied Programmed Instruction, New York, John Wiley.

1955 Schultz, Rudolph W.
"Generalization of Serial Position in Rote Serial Learning," *Journal of Experimental Psychology,* 49:4, pp. 267–272.

1965 Skinner, B. F.
"The Experimental Analysis of Behavior," *American Scientist,* vol. 45, pp. 343–371.

1954 "The Science of Learning and the Art of Teaching," *Harvard Education Review,* vol. 24, pp. 86–97.
"Teaching Machines," *Science,* vol. 128, pp. 969–977.

1960 Sweeney, J. J.
"The Museum In a Mass Society," *Daedalus,* vol. 89.

1959 Zelditch, Morris, Jr.
A Basic Course in Sociological Statistics. New York, Holt.

1968* Borhegyi, Stephan F. de, and Hanson, Irene A.
"The Museum Visitor: Selected Essays and Surveys of Visitor Reaction to Exhibits in the Milwaukee Public Museum," *Publications in Museology* (Milwaukee Public Museum) no. 3.

References

Annual Report, 1964–1965, Brooklyn Institute of Arts and Sciences.

The Antiquarian Bookman, July 25, 1966, p. 379.

Art Instructor in the Public Schools, National Education Association *Research Bulletin,* October 1963, pp. 90-93.

Carnegie Quarterly, 14:2, 1966, pp. 1–4. (General discussion of the National Assessment Project.)

Commager, Henry S., *The American Mind,* New Haven, Yale University Press, 1950.

Curator, 5:30, 1963, pp. 236–244.

"Early American Decorative Arts as Social Documents," *Mississippi Valley Historical Review,* 5:45, September 1958, p. 276.

"Education and American History, Commission on the Role of Education in American History," New York, The Fund for the Advancement of Education, 1965, p. 9.

Encyclopaedia Britannica, 11th ed.

"Field Trips with a Difference," Cleveland Health Museum.

"Handbook for Self-guided Tours," Chicago, The Museum of Science and Industry.

Jordan, Joye E., "The History Museum: Poor Relation?" *Museum News,* November 1964, pp. 17–19.

Kadushin, Charles, "Shakespeare and Sociology," *The Columbia University Forum,* Spring 1966.

Kamenitsa, Maxine Elliott, *Planning, Teaching, and Evaluating a Preschool Science Program for Children's Museums,* Denton, Texas, Texas Woman's University, August 1958. (Thesis for M.A. degree.)

Kramer, Hilton, "Art: Fete at Cleveland," *The New York Times,* June 14, 1966.

Kraus, Michael, *The Writing of American History,* Norman, Okla., University of Oklahoma Press, 1953.

"Making the Most of Your Museum Visit . . . ," The Metropolitan Museum of Art Junior Museum, distributed by the Board of Education of the City of New York.

Marrou, Henri I., *A History of Education in Antiquity,* New York, Sheed and Ward, 1956.

Museum News, 40:2, October 1961, p. 19.

——— 40:7, March 1962, p. 16.

——— 42:2, October 1964, p. 18.

Munsterberg, Hugo, *The Principles of Art Education,* New York, The Prang Educational Company, 1904.

The New York Times, July 6, 1966.

Reimann, Irving G., "Preparation for Professional Museum Careers," *Curator,* 3:3, 1960, pp. 279–285.

Report of the Commission on the Humanities (American Council of Learned Societies, Council of Graduate Schools in the U. S., United Chapters of Phi Beta Kappa), 1964.

——— Supplement to the Report of the Commission on the Humanities, 1964.

"Selective Reference Guide to Historic Preservation," New York State Historical Association.

Selltiz, Claire; Jahoda, Marie; Deutsch, Martin; and Cook, S. W., *Research Methods in Social Relations,* New York, Holt, Rinehart, and Winston, 1959.

"Study of Tourists' Interests in New York State, 1965," n.p., Albany, N. Y., 1966.

"Summer 1966 Science Workshops," Philadelphia, The Franklin Institute.

"Symposium: The Institutions of Art," *Arts in Society,* 3, 1965, p. 317.

Webb, E. J.; Campbell, D. T.; Schwartz, R. D.; and Sechrest, Lee, *Unobtrusive Measures: Nonreactive Research in the Social Sciences,* Chicago, Rand McNally, 1966.

Whitehead, Alfred North, *The Aims of Education,* London, Williams and Norgate, Ltd., 1950.

——— *Science and the Modern World,* New York, Mentor Books, 1956. (The book was based on lectures held in 1925.)

Wittlin, Alma S., *The Museum: Its History and Its Tasks in Education,* London, Routledge and Kegan Paul, Ltd., 1949.

"The World We Live In, 1966/1967, a program for the City of New York City Schools." New York, Department of Education, The American Museum of Natural History.

Designed by Crimilda Pontes

Printed in Linotype Granjon by The William Byrd Press, Inc.

Bound by L. H. Jenkins, Inc., of Richmond, Virginia